Praise for

Enterprise JavaBeans™

Enterprise JavaBeans™

Developing Component-Based Distributed Applications

Tom Valesky

Foreword by Mala Chandra, Director, Enterprise Java, Sun Microsystems, Inc.

Tom Valesky applies years of experience developing enterprise applications and a solid understanding of Enterprise JavaBeans technology to create a book filled with practical advice. Any developer interested in creating applications with Enterprise JavaBeans will find valuable information here, ranging from general design approaches to specific implementation details.

JIM INSCORE

TECHNICAL PUBLICATIONS AND INFORMATION DESIGN MANAGER, SUN MICROSYSTEMS

Those who prefer to learn by example will find this gentle introduction to Sun's Enterprise JavaBeans specification a welcome addition to their technical libraries. The casual and unassuming style makes EJB accessible to those just getting started, yet the book also provides the serious developer with real-world examples and coverage of advanced topics.

LIANE ACKER

SENIOR SOFTWARE ENGINEER, IBM

om Valesky has packed this excellent book with two things: hard core examples laden with code and understandable expert advice based on real experience. This book is like a GPS device for your boat; as the second wave of EJB sweeps over the enterprise, knowing where you are and where you're going will pay off handsomely. Buy it.

GARY MCGRAW, PHD
VICE PRESIDENT, RELIABLE SOFTWARE TECHNOLOGIES
COAUTHOR OF *SECURING JAVA: GETTING DOWN TO
BUSINESS WITH MOBILE CODE* AND *JAVA SECURITY:
HOSTILE APPLETS, HOLES, AND ANTIDOTES*

his book does an excellent job of placing EJB into the context of middleware and application servers. Even if the readers have little or no experience with multitier application development, they will have a good feel for it—and for EJB—after reading this book.

ETHAN HENRY
JAVA EVANGELIST, KL GROUP

his is a very easy-to-read tutorial loaded with very illustrative examples. *Enterprise JavaBeans*™ provides invaluable information for readers ranging from novices to experts. Tom Valesky does a superb job of addressing the reader in a friendly, informal style. A must buy for serious Java developers.

AJIT SAGAR
MEMBER OF TECHNOLOGICAL STAFF
I2 TECHNOLOGIES

ENTERPRISE JAVABEANS™

ENTERPRISE JAVABEANS™

Developing Component-Based Distributed Applications

Tom Valesky

ADDISON–WESLEY

An Imprint of Addison Wesley Longman, Inc.

Reading, Massachusetts • Harlow, England • Menlo Park, California
Berkeley, California • Don Mills, Ontario • Sydney
Bonn • Amsterdam • Tokyo • Mexico City

The publisher offers discounts on this book when ordered in quantity for special sales. For more information, please contact:

AWL Direct Sales
Addison Wesley Longman, Inc.
One Jacob Way
Reading, Massachusetts 01867
(781) 944-3700

Visit A-W on the Web: http://www.awl.com/cseng/

Library of Congress Cataloging-in-Publication Data

Valesky, Thomas B.
    Enterprise JavaBeans : developing component-based distributed applications / Tom Valesky.
        p.   cm.
    Includes bibliographical references.
    ISBN 0-201-60446-9
    1. JavaBeans.   2. Java (Computer program language)   3. Application software—Development.   4. Electronic data processing—Distributed processing.   I. Title.
    QA76.73.J38 V35 1999
    005.13′3—dc21

                                                              99–13379
                                                              CIP

Text printed on recycled and acid-free paper.

ISBN 0201604469

4 5 6 7 8 9   MA   02 01 00 99

4th Printing November 1999

To programmers everywhere. Hope this helps.

CONTENTS

FOREWORD

If industry buzz alone was a measure of success, then even before we went public with the first Enterprise JavaBeans (EJB) specification, the technology was a hit. The range of industry partners who joined us early on to define the EJB architecture gave us a clear indication that we were onto something significant. This initial support let us base our architecture on expertise and experience from throughout the industry, a collaboration for inclusion rather than exclusion. As a result, we knew that EJB technology stood a good chance of becoming the industry standard for enterprise application components.

But no technology is viable over the long term on buzz alone. So, a year after releasing the first specification, we're pleased to see the early promises of EJB technology being fulfilled. Today, a critical mass of enterprise computing vendors—developers of application servers, transaction process monitors, object request brokers, database management systems, and others—are rolling out robust, powerful implementations of the EJB technology. The era of "Write Once, Run Anywhere" server-side components is here.

To understand the momentum of EJB technology, a little background is in order. During the early 1990s, traditional enterprise information system providers began responding to customer needs by shifting from the two-tier, client-server application model to more flexible three-tier and multitier application models. The new models separated business logic from system services and the user interface, placing it in a middle tier between the two. The evolution of new middleware services—transaction monitors, message-oriented middleware, object request brokers, and others—gave additional impetus to this new architecture. And the growing use of the internet and intranets for enterprise applications contributed to a greater emphasis on lightweight, easy to deploy clients.

Multitier design dramatically simplifies developing, deploying, and maintaining enterprise applications. It enables developers to focus on the specifics of programming their business logic, relying on various backend services to provide the infrastructure, and providing client-side applications (both stand-alone and within Web browsers) for user interaction. Once developed, business logic can be deployed on servers appropriate to existing needs of an organization. However, despite these clear benefits, the model limits developers' ability to build applications from standardized components, to deploy a single application on a wide variety of platforms, or to readily scale applications to meet changing business conditions.

Within Java software, several development efforts pointed us toward what would become the EJB technology. First, the Java servlets technology showed that developers were eager to create CGI-like behaviors that could run on any Web server that supported the Java platform. Second, the JDBC technology gave us a model for marrying the "Write Once, Run Anywhere" features of the Java programming language to existing database management systems. Finally, the JavaBeans component architecture demonstrated the usefulness of encapsulating complete sets of behavior into easily configurable, readily reusable components on the client side. The convergence of these three concepts—server-side behaviors written in the Java language, connectors to enable access to existing enterprise systems, and modular, easy to deploy components—led us and our industry partners to the EJB standard.

Today, both within Sun Microsystems and throughout the industry, the momentum of the EJB technology is building. Large and small partners have released a variety of EJB products, or announced plans to do so. The variety of these offerings includes EJB servers, development and deployment tools, standardized EJB components, and complete component-based applications. In addition, Sun Microsystems has announced a roadmap for rolling out the Java 2 Enterprise Edition—a unified architecture for supporting the EJB components, along with reference implementations and compatibility tests to help developers achieve the ideal of "Write Once, Run Anywhere" in the server environment.

During the early days of EJB technology, much of our effort focused on infrastructure developers. Sun has issued specifications, white papers, FAQs, and other documents to help ensure a robust architecture. However, as the adoption of EJB technology grows and our partners introduce products based on the EJB architecture, interest among component and application developers is growing as well. Thus the need for a book like this, an introduction to EJB technology for the growing EJB developer audience.

This book is the first devoted exclusively to helping front-line developers implement application components with EJB technology. In it, you'll find guidelines on many of the issues that developers face in getting started in developing EJB components. It's a simple, step by step introduction to using the EJB technology, explaining both its background and how to use it to develop real-world applications. This book presents a sequence of easy-to-follow discussions, complete code examples, troubleshooting techniques, and even application design guidelines. All of these are written from the point of view of a hands-on developer with years of experience in writing and deploying enterprise applications.

Component-based, multitier applications are the future of enterprise computing. And EJB developers lead the way in realizing the benefits of these components: portability, scalability to a wide range of enterprise servers, simplified development, deployment, and maintenance. This book will equip the aspiring developer to understand the issues and reap the rewards of creating EJB components.

—Mala Chandra
Director, Enterprise Java
Sun Microsystems, Inc.

PREFACE

This book discusses Enterprise JavaBeans (EJB). It assumes that you have basic knowledge of Java, but does not assume detailed knowledge of distributed computing. The primary goal of this book is to provide a relatively short and easy-to-read document that will get you up to speed quickly on how to develop EJB. Its secondary goal is to serve as a good companion text for a short course on EJB development.

Chapter 1 provides an overview of EJB—that is, what it is and where it fits into the world of distributed computing. If you're looking for technical details, you won't find them in this chapter. Nevertheless, this discussion provides some background that you can use to convince your manager that EJB is a good thing.

Chapter 2 offers an overview of the EJB architecture. It describes the various components that make up an EJB system and covers the major classes and interfaces used in the development of an EJB bean.

Chapter 3 is the first chapter that contains coding examples. It presents a "hello, world!" EJB system. The "hello world" example was chosen for two reasons. First, in coming to terms with a new technology, a simple example is useful in helping you to figure out the core components of the system. Second, the main intent in this chapter is to highlight the steps you need to perform to write and deploy an EJB bean; in this case, a simpler bean provides fewer distractions from this discussion.

Two types of EJB beans exist: Session beans and Entity beans. Chapter 4 covers Session beans. It discusses the differences between stateful and stateless beans, and provides examples of each.

Chapter 5 discusses Entity beans. It describes the differences between bean-managed and container-managed entity beans, providing an example of each.

In Chapter 6, the issue is writing client programs that use EJB beans. It includes quite a few examples, including those demonstrating

- How to obtain and use handles to beans
- How to call a bean from a servlet
- How to call a bean from another bean
- How to call a bean from an applet
- How to use client-side transaction management
- How to obtain and examine EJB metadata

Chapter 7 focuses on the process of packaging and deploying EJB beans. It includes a detailed discussion of deployment descriptors and the values they contain. It also examines access control lists and shows how to use them to set up permissions on an EJB server. In addition, Chapter 7 includes an example that shows how a bean can retrieve and test a client's identity.

Chapter 8 contains a set of tips for constructing distributed systems—or any other type of system, for that matter. The goal of this chapter is to provide you with some concrete rules of thumb that you can use in your own development process and to help you avoid making a few common mistakes.

Chapter 9 includes a relatively nontrivial example program (a time management system) and a sort of "implementation diary" in which the author describes the process used to create the example. This process involves assessing the options available, analyzing the tradeoffs among them, and making the final choices.

In Chapter 10—the "wrap-up" chapter—currently available EJB servers are discussed. Currently, relatively few implementations are available, so we also discuss EJB servers that are not available as of this writing, but should be out soon. This chapter concludes with a discussion of the future of the EJB specification; fortune-telling is a risky business, so the predictions generally stick to issues that are certain to be included in future versions of the EJB standard.

As noted earlier, the goal of this book is to provide you with a quick but thorough introduction to EJB—quick, so you can start using EJB soon, and thorough, so that you won't be flummoxed by real-world situations because only a few canned examples were involved. If you have any comments or suggestions for improvement, please send me an e-mail at tvalesky@patriot.net.

It is a fact of life that the EJB specification and its associated documents will undergo some evolution over the next few years. To accommodate these changes, we've made an online supplement to this book available at the URL http://www.awl.com/cseng/titles/0-201-60446-9/. This supplement will track changes and new developments in the specification, include new examples that demonstrate new capabilities for EJB, and generally keep you up-to-date with what's going on in the EJB world. Be sure to stop by.

A note on Java versions is in order here. The examples in this book were developed in JDK 1.1, and the accompanying WebLogic software should be run under JDK 1.1 Throughout this book, notations have been made where things will change under Java 2 (formerly known as JDK 1.2). For late-breaking news, refer to his book's companion Web site.

A note about the formatting of the code examples: In the source code in this book, all actual new lines begin with a line number. In some cases, the lines were too long to be displayed correctly and have wrapped around to a new line. So, if you see a line in one of the examples like line 15 here:

```
15  System.out.println("this is a very very very
    long line");
16  System.out.println("this is shorter");
```

rest assured that all is well with the actual code.

Acknowledgments

Thanks to the WebLogic folks, especially Bob Pasker and Sriram Srinivasan. Their support has been first-rate.

Thanks to Jonathan K. Weedon of Inprise Corporation for the CORBA client example.

Thanks to the folks on the EJB-INTEREST list, for many happy hours of conversation about EJB, and for serving as a sounding board for many of my ideas.

Thanks to the team at EJBHOME for developing a freeware EJB implementation. The word will spread faster if the price of entry is not into five figures.

Thanks to the reviewers of this manuscript, James D. Frentress, Liane Acker, Gary McGraw, Ajit Sagar, J. Patrick Ravenal, Ethan Henry, and Jim Inscore, all of whom helped clarify and refine the manuscript.

Thanks to my teachers.

Thanks to Russ Marshall and the gang at BLS, for giving me my first programming job at a time when I had few qualifications other than enthusiasm, and for showing me the value of good requirements and thorough testing.

Thanks to the folks at Javasoft, for changing the world.

Thanks to David Kodama and Dana Gardner, my long-suffering editors at Advisor Publications, for keeping me honest.

Thanks to the staff at Addison Wesley Longman, especially Elizabeth Spainhour, Mary O'Brien, and Maureen Willard.

Thanks to Mom and Dad for putting me through college. Top o' the world, Ma!

Tom Valesky

CHAPTER 1

The Big Picture

Introduction

This book focuses on the development of **Enterprise JavaBeans (EJBs).** EJBs are write-once, run-anywhere, middle-tier components. To make sense of Enterprise JavaBeans, it is helpful to have an understanding of the context in which they arose. This first chapter gives a bit of historical background on the various forces in the industry that led to Enterprise JavaBeans and describes some of the problems that they were designed to solve. Along the way, it highlights some of the key concepts that are used in Enterprise JavaBeans. Toward the end of the chapter, we explain how EJB fits into the big picture.

The earliest model of interactive electronic computing to be widely adopted in the business world was the mainframe/terminal model (Figure 1.1). In this model of computing, all data and programs reside on a single machine. The user interacts with this machine through a terminal. The terminal has little intelligence; it knows only how to receive screens, respond to keystrokes, and send the data back to the host.

Transaction Processors

As the number of users of mainframe applications increased, it became necessary to develop a scheme for handling many concurrent client requests in an efficient manner. To fill this need, the transaction processor was invented. The transaction processor was designed to solve several business needs. First, it allowed several statements to be executed together as one logical unit, thereby guaranteeing that either all statements would be executed successfully or none would be executed at all. As an example of an application for which it would

Figure 1.1   The mainframe/terminal model of computing

be important to guarantee that multiple statements are executed as one unit, consider the "transfer funds" operation found on automated teller machines. Imagine that a bank's customer decides to transfer $200.00 from his savings account to his checking account to cover the purchase of a new graphics card. Typically, this operation, which appears to the customer as a single atomic transaction, would consist of at least two separate operations: one to remove the $200.00 from the savings account and one to add it to the checking account. Now consider what could happen if the system were to go down before the transaction had been completed. Potentially, the $200.00 could have been debited from the savings account without being credited to the checking account. This possibility is obviously a bad thing; the bank will certainly get a very irate call from the customer, and the customer might find another bank.

A transaction processor guards against this type of inconsistency by not committing a database update to the database until all of the changes are ready. A typical transaction processor provides an application programming interface (API) to the application program that consists of at least three calls: **"begin,"** **"commit,"** and **"rollback."** The "begin" call notifies the transaction processor that a transaction has begun; this transaction remains in effect until the program calls either "commit" or "rollback." If the program calls "commit," the transaction processor makes the actual updates to the database. If the program calls "rollback," it undoes whatever intermediate processing has been performed to this point; the net result is that the database returns to the state it was in before the transaction began.

Typically, this type of change management would be carried out via a logging mechanism. When a program begins a transaction, all subsequent database operations are written to the log file. When a transaction is committed, an entry is added to the log file indicating this fact, and the operations in the log file are actually performed in the database. If a rollback occurs, the intermediate entries would typically be removed from the log file. Note that this log file mechanism allows the system to protect a transaction's integrity even in the case of a system failure. If, when the transaction processor restarts, it finds a "begin" entry in the log without a corresponding "commit" entry, it simply ignores the entries. The bank customer in the previous example can therefore rest easy knowing that his money is safe.

A program that wishes to have guarantees of transactional integrity would implement all of its database accesses via the transaction processor. Because the transaction processor has full knowledge of the program's database activities, it can ensure that either all of the program's required changes occur together or none occurs at all.

In addition to providing guarantees of transaction integrity, a transaction processor manages the execution of programs and the sharing of resources. Instead of supporting one running instance of a program for each user, a transaction processor can maintain a pool of running instances and hand them out as needed in response to user requests. Resource pooling allows a system to support many more concurrent users than would be possible if it had to provide a duplicate set of resources for each user.

ACID Properties of Transactions

Transactions are characterized by four properties: atomicity, consistency, isolation, and durability. The acronym "ACID" is used to refer to these properties as a group. All transaction processors must provide these properties.

Atomicity.   This property states that all actions that are part of a transaction will execute as one logical unit; either all will complete successfully or the transaction will be undone.

Consistency.   This property states that the underlying database will always be in a reasonable state. It guarantees that, if a transaction fails in mid-operation, the database will not be left in a partially modified state; any changes to the database must be undone.

Isolation.   This property states that, until a transaction has been committed, its state is not visible from outside itself.

Durability.   This property states that, once the transaction has been completed, the changes are stored permanently.

OLTP Versus OLAP

Another interesting concept that developed during the mainframe era was the distinction between **online transaction processing** (OLTP) systems and other systems [these "other systems" have been referred to by several different names, such as **decision support systems** (DSS), **enterprise information systems** (EIS), and, lately, **online analytical processing** (OLAP) systems]. OLTP and DSS/EIS/OLAP systems provide different types of services and have different needs.

An OLTP system has the following characteristics:

- An OLTP system updates data in a database.
- Response time is critical for OLTP systems.
- An OLTP system typically handles a large volume of transactions.

A DSS/EIS/OLAP system has the following characteristics:

- It is used to review information; generally it does not involve database updates.
- Response time is not as critical as for an OLTP system; it may involve long-running queries.
- This type of system typically generates a smaller number of requests; because it provides data for review, user "think time" tends to be longer.

Enterprise JavaBeans are aimed squarely at the OLTP world. Although EJB can be used to implement DSS/EIS/OLAP systems, its main goal is to provide OLTP capabilities.

Two-Tier, Client-Server Architecture

In the 1980s, personal computers (PCs) became popular. PCs were attractive to businesses because they were relatively inexpensive, didn't require costly mainframe computing time, and gave their users a new sense of freedom and empowerment. A PC user could bring a set of data into a spreadsheet and manipulate it for hours without placing any requirements on the mainframe system. At first, most PCs were used as stand-alone units, but over time networking became more common. Eventually, many organizations began to build new systems on the PC instead of on the mainframe. Around this time, dedicated database management systems (DBMSs) began to appear. The combination of the database server and the PC client is commonly referred to as a "two-tier" architecture or a client-server architecture (Figure 1.2). (Actually, the term "client-server" can refer to *any* architecture involving a client and a server, but the term is most often used to describe the PC client–database server model).

In a two-tier system, transaction integrity is usually guaranteed by the database management system itself, rather than by an external transaction processor. Typically, the database vendor will provide "begin," "commit," and "rollback" functions to the user, either as part of the text of the database query or as part of the database's client API library. The client can then use these functions to group database updates into transactions.

Figure 1.2 Two-tier, client-server architecture

In the two-tier, client-server model, the application runs on the client machine and issues queries to the database server. Typically, the client contains both **presentation logic** (that is, the code needed to build and run the user interface) and **business rules** (the logic that governs how data are manipulated). As an example of a business rule, consider the following pseudocode:

```
pay = hours_worked * pay_rate
```

This pseudocode represents a simple business rule for determining the pay of a given employee. In a two-tiered environment, the application logic would follow this pattern:

1. Prompt the user for `pay_rate`, `hours_worked`, and an employee number (although the employee number is not directly involved in the calculation, it will be important when we update the database).
2. Calculate the pay for the employee.
3. Generate a Structured Query Language (SQL) statement to update the database. Such a statement would look something like the following:

```
Update payroll
set pay = <calculated pay>
where employee_id = <employee ID input by user>
```

4. Execute the SQL statement against the database.

Now the program is written and distributed to the data-entry personnel, the data are entered, and everyone is happy. Well, not quite. A problem exists with the business rule used to calculate pay: It doesn't account for overtime hours. As such, it violates the Fair Labor Standards Act and must be changed. Upon reviewing the business logic, the analysts decide that a better business rule would be

```
public double calculatePay(double hoursWorked, double payRate)
{
```

```
double pay;
if (hoursWorked <= 40)
{
pay = hoursWorked * payRate;
}
else
{
pay = 40.0 * payRate;
double overtimeRate = payRate * 1.5;
double overtimeHours = hoursWorked - 40.0;
pay += (overtimeRate * overtimeHours);
}
return pay;
}
```

The program is rewritten and distributed again, and, for a time, everyone is happy. Then someone in management notices that those employees who are exempt from the Fair Labor Standards Act (a category that, sadly, includes most programmers) are still being paid at the overtime rate when they should receive the same rate for all hours worked. When the analysts rework the business rule again, they come up with the following:

```
public double calculatePay(double hoursWorked, double payRate)
{
boolean isExempt;
//use a database query to see if the employee is
//exempt or nonexempt, storing the result in the
//isExempt variable double pay;
if (isExempt)
{
pay = hoursWorked * payRate;
return pay;
}
if (hoursWorked <= 40)
{
pay = hoursWorked * payRate;
}
else
{
pay = 40.0 * payRate;
double overtimeRate = payRate * 1.5;
double overtimeHours = hoursWorked - 40.0;
pay += (overtimeRate * overtimeHours);
}
return pay;
}
```

Once again, the client program must be changed and redistributed. At some point, it becomes obvious that, even though the user interface has remained the same, changes in business rules have caused the client program to be modified, tested, and distributed several times. Ideally, we should be able to separate the business rules from the user interface logic, so that we could update the rules without modifying the client itself. This separation of business rules from implementation logic is the driving force behind the three-tier architecture.

Three-Tier Architecture

In the three-tier approach (depicted in Figure 1.3), as in the two-tier approach, the database is the ultimate repository of information and the client remains responsible for providing the user-interface logic. The business rules, however, are separated into a middle tier. Instead of updating the database directly, the client makes a call to the middle tier, which then updates the database. Continuing with our pay-calculation example, a three-tier approach to the problem would consist of a client that presents the same user interface as the two-tier model. Instead of performing the pay calculation and database update itself, the client simply calls a function called update_pay() on a middle-tier object. It passes the update_pay() routine the user-supplied parameters hours_worked, pay_rate, and employee_id. The update_pay() routine then executes the business logic for determining the employee's pay and updates the database accordingly.

We haven't said much about the type of program that lives in the middle tier. In fact, the three-tier architecture can be implemented using a wide variety of approaches, including the following:

- Sockets
- RPCs
- CORBA

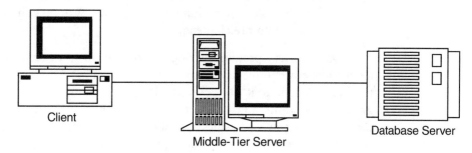

Figure 1.3 The three-tier architecture

- RMI
- OLE/DCOM
- Message queues

Sockets

Sockets are the lingua franca of the Internet. Most of the other approaches mentioned in the list above are built on top of sockets. Also, many standard Internet services, such as Simple Mail Transfer Protocol (SMTP) mail, Hypertext Transfer Protocol (HTTP, the protocol that Web browsers and servers use to communicate), and File Tranfser Protocol (FTP), are built on top of sockets.

Sockets act as an interface to networking services but hide the complexity of packet-level network programming. A client program specifies which socket to open on a remote machine through a combination of the machine's IP address and a port number. A **port number** is an unsigned integer that represents a particular application or service. The combination of IP address (which specifies a unique machine) and port number (which specifies a particular service on that machine) allows a programmer to access a particular service on any machine on the Internet.

Because sockets are relatively low-level technology, they tend to be the fastest method for communicating between applications. Why not use sockets for all of your distributed computing needs? The main reason is complexity.

- The socket client and server must have an agreed-upon protocol for conversation. If you're writing an SMTP client, for example, this protocol is standard. If you're not using a standard protocol, you must develop your own protocol.
- The server side of the socket equation must be able to handle many concurrent connections from various users. Writing concurrent code is a difficult task, as is writing network code. Writing concurrent network code is even more challenging.

Virtually every programmer possesses an element of bravado that says, "I can handle any complexity that you can throw at me." Sometimes this claim is true, and sometimes it isn't. Nevertheless, every hour, day, or week that a programmer spends on a task is costing someone money. Remember, your client is paying you to solve a business problem; typically, the client is uninterested in the technical details of your solution. He or she wants something that solves the problems at hand, and preferably yesterday.

RPCs

One of the earliest approaches to making sockets easier to use relied on the **remote procedure call** (**RPC**). RPCs are a thin layer on top of sockets that allow you to call a remote procedure as if it were any other procedure in your program. By calling an RPC in your client, you actually call a routine called a "stub." The stub takes your arguments and transfers them to the remote machine, which has an application listening on a port. When a procedure call comes in over the port, the server-side RPC component takes the data from the network, transforms it back into the types that were passed in by the client, and calls the server-side routine with these arguments. When the routine finishes, the process is repeated in reverse to handle any return value. The stubs are typically generated by a compiler that uses an **interface definition language** (IDL) to describe the procedure, its arguments, and its return types. (This IDL is not the same IDL as that used in CORBA; in fact, "IDL" is a generic term used for interface definition languages).

CORBA

As object-oriented computing grew in popularity, the need arose for a mechanism similar to RPC that could go beyond simple procedure calls and actually understand objects. The result was **Common Object Request Broker Architecture** (**CORBA**). In an oversimplification, CORBA can be envisioned as an object-oriented RPC mechanism. CORBA also uses an IDL to specify the argument types and return types of functions, but the CORBA IDL includes semantics for describing objects, unlike the stub IDL. A CORBA developer writes an IDL description of the objects that will be visible remotely, then runs this IDL through a compiler. The IDL compiler generates stubs and skeletons. A **skeleton** is the server-side analog to a **stub**; it reassembles the data that come in over the network into something recognizable, calls the server-side method, and sends its return value back to the client. The process in which the stub takes its parameters and transforms them into a format suitable for network transmission is called **marshalling**. The reverse process, whereby data from the network are transformed back into "normal" data types, is called **unmarshalling**. Enterprise JavaBeans includes a CORBA mapping that allows CORBA clients to use EJB objects.

The CORBA architecture (depicted in Figure 1.4) also includes an **object request broker** (**ORB**). The ORB is the component that allows clients to communicate with server objects and services. To gain access to a server service, the client makes a call to the ORB, specifying the desired service. The ORB locates this server service and returns a reference to it to the client.

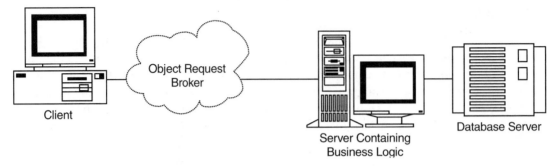

Figure 1.4   The CORBA Architecture

One very important facet of CORBA is that it allows objects written in one language on one platform to be called by objects written in a different language on a different platform. For example, a C++ client running on Microsoft Windows can use CORBA to invoke methods written in COBOL running on a mainframe. Enterprise JavaBeans includes a CORBA mapping, enabling any CORBA client on any platform to call EJBs (as long as the EJB server supports the CORBA mapping).

Why not use a pure CORBA approach instead of adding EJB to the mix? Again, the problem relates to complexity. Writing CORBA clients is generally a straightforward task, but writing CORBA server objects can prove more difficult. A typical CORBA server object is multithreaded; the programmer must explicitly ensure that the various threads do not interfere with one another. EJB allows you to keep the CORBA client, but vastly simplifies writing the server-side component. Note that CORBA clients can be used to access EJB objects in some implementations of EJB; in such a case, you can use CORBA clients, but still enjoy the simplicity of EJB on the middle tier.

RMI

Remote Method Invocation (RMI) is basically a Java-only version of CORBA. Because RMI is specific to Java, it's a bit simpler to use than CORBA. Instead of writing IDL to describe your objects, you run a program called **rmic** on your Java .class files; rmic then generates stub and skeleton classes directly from your .class files. Also, because RMI understands Java types, you don't have to write IDL to describe your objects; the RMI compiler can handle this automatically. Thus RMI greatly facilitates the creation of clients. Writing the server-side components of an RMI system, however, remains a fairly complex endeavor. EJB allows you to make client-side RMI calls to EJB objects, thus eliminating the need for complex server-side programming. (That's the second time we've mentioned this point, though without explaining what's so great about EJB for server-side programming. Don't worry, your questions will be answered soon.)

OLE/DCOM

Microsoft offers yet another approach to distributed computing based on the company's **Object Linking and Embedding (OLE)** architecture. This approach has been dubbed the Distributed Component Object Model (DCOM), Distributed interNetworking Architecture (DNA), and several other names. This book won't discuss DCOM in detail, because at this time it doesn't appear that DCOM will have many links to Enterprise JavaBeans. Strictly speaking, the EJB specification does not necessarily preclude someone from implementing a DCOM-to-EJB bridge or from using DCOM to communicate with EJB servers. Nevertheless, the current distributed computing world is basically split into two factions, with DCOM on one side and everything else on the other. Microsoft has voiced a strong commitment to the OLE/DCOM object model, and has expressed no interest in either RMI or CORBA. At this time, it appears that, if you're interested mainly in using DCOM, EJB is probably not for you.

Message Queues

All of the approaches to communication discussed so far have one thing in common: They're synchronous. That is, when a program makes a call to a remote program, it waits for that call to return before it proceeds.

A synchronous call is similar to a telephone call:

- Someone must be there to answer it.
- If no one picks up, the call fails (let's ignore answering machines for now).
- Both parties remain occupied for the duration of the call.

In many ways, e-mail is preferable to telephones:

- You can check your e-mail when you're not busy with something else, so you're not interrupted if you're deep in thought.
- You can send an e-mail to someone without worrying if they're available at that particular moment and still feel reasonably comfortable that they'll get it.
- You can send e-mail to many people at once, rather than telephoning each one individually.

The folks who developed message queuing must have liked e-mail as well. **Message queues** serve the same purpose for programs as e-mail does for you:

- It allows a server to process requests in a queue, rather than having to service each incoming request immediately.
- It allows a client to send a request to a server that's currently busy; the request goes into a message queue and remains there until the server can get to it.
- A message can be sent to several interested parties at once.

Although the EJB 1.0 specification does not mention message queuing, Javasoft does have a specification for message queuing called **Java Message Service (JMS)**. Its documentation mentions that JMS will be integrated with EJB in some future release of the EJB specification, so it will be possible to use message queues from EJB objects. In fact, you can already send JMS messages from an EJB bean (assuming that you have installed a JMS implementation or are using an EJB server that provides JMS functionality). The tricky part is receiving JMS messages sent to EJB beans. Eventually, the EJB specification will need to address the process by which an EJB server receives a JMS message, activates the appropriate bean, and delivers the message.

We have now reached the end of our short list of items that can be termed "middleware." This list is by no means complete, but merely hits the high points. We haven't finished with the three-tier model, however, as we haven't mentioned distributed transaction processing yet.

Distributed Transaction Processing

The need for transaction processing still exists in the multitier world (recently, it's become more common to use the term "multitier" in preference to "three-tier," in recognition of the fact that more than three levels might be involved in a given conversation). Transactions are a bit trickier in the context of a distributed system than they are for a monolithic host or a single database server, for several reasons:

- A distributed transaction is likely to involve several participants, rather than just a single client or a single server.
- The system must still guarantee the ACID properties of transactions.
- The systems involved might be running on different platforms, or even using different languages.

The usual approach used to manage transactions in a distributed environment is called two-phase commit. In two-phase commit, a transaction coordinator governs the actions of several transaction processors. In the first phase, the transaction coordinator tells each transaction processor to prepare the transaction. "Preparing the transaction" generally involves writing the desired updates to a transaction log file. Each transaction processor attempts to prepare its portion of the transaction, responding to the transaction coordinator with a "vote commit" if it succeeds, or a "vote rollback" if it fails. If the transaction coordinator receives even one vote for rollback, it must inform all of the other participants to roll back their transactions. If the transaction coordinator receives only votes for commit, it adds an entry to its own log indicating that the transaction should be committed and notifies each participant that it should commit the transaction. Each participant then writes its changes to permanent storage and reports back to the transaction coordinator that it has finished. When the transaction coordinator receives this notification from all participants, it clears its own log.

Another aspect of transactions is that they can be nested or flat. If **nested,** a second transaction can begin, execute, and complete inside another transaction. If **flat,** only one transaction executes at any given time.

EJB's Role

The reason that we began our discourse on the history of computing is because EJB can be best understood if it's discussed in the context of things that have come before. It is difficult to write an all-encompassing definition of EJB, as it tends to be long, buzzword-ridden, and deadly dull. Instead, we'll start by describing some of the facets of EJB.

1. EJB specifies an execution environment.

Chapter 2 discusses the architecture of EJB in some detail, but for now it's sufficient to note that the EJB specification describes something called a "container." The container is responsible for providing services to Enterprise JavaBeans. An Enterprise JavaBean is a Java class that implements either the SessionBean or the EntityBean interface. (We'll discuss these interfaces in the next chapter; don't worry about them for now, other than to note their existence.) The container provides services such as support for transactions, support for persistence, and management of multiple instances of a given bean. The EJB specification clearly describes what types of services a bean can expect. As long as the bean conforms to the specification, it will run in any compliant EJB container, on any platform.

The container does not allow the bean to be accessed directly from the client; rather, the container provides a proxy object for each bean. This approach gives the container a high degree of freedom in managing the beans and insulates the beans themselves from the slings and arrows of the outside world.

2. EJB exists in the middle tier.

Enterprise JavaBeans, like other middle-tier components, are used to encapsulate business rules. A typical Enterprise JavaBean consists of **methods** that encapsulate business logic. A remote client can invoke these methods, which typically result in the updating of a database.

3. EJB supports transaction processing.

An EJB container must support transactions. At development time, the bean developer can specify what type of transaction support is required. When the bean is deployed, the container reads this information and provides the necessary support.

Possible types of transaction support include the following:

- Requiring that the client provide an open transaction context
- Requiring that the container start a new transaction when the bean is invoked
- Requiring that the bean be allowed to manage its own transaction

EJB's approach to transactions makes life very easy for the EJB developer. You can simply declare what sort of transaction support your bean requires and then depend on the container to provide it, without writing even a single line of code (other than the occasional exception handler).

4. EJB can maintain state.

To date, much of Internet software development has been done in common gateway interface (CGI) scripts. CGI scripts are handy because they work against a well-defined interface. As applications become more complex, however, a weakness of the CGI mechanism appears: A CGI application has no built-in mechanism to store state information. Each invocation of a CGI application is therefore a fresh start. If the developer would like to build an application with several screens that handles complex input, he or she must build some sort of state-preservation mechanism into the application.

Enterprise JavaBeans, on the other hand, can maintain state across several method invocations. The EJB container keeps track of any state information that a bean needs. You can also build stateless Enterprise JavaBeans, as will be discussed in Chapter 4. If you have an application that needs to maintain some state information, however, EJB can handle it automatically.

5. *EJB is simple.*

The EJB container has many responsibilities: It must support the concurrent execution of many beans, keep track of their state, provide them with transaction support, and so forth. Because the server has such a heavy burden to bear, this approach lifts the corresponding burden from the shoulders of the developer. As a result, the business of actually writing Enterprise JavaBeans is very straightforward. With EJB, you don't have to worry about writing multi-threaded code, because the container handles concurrent requests. Furthermore, because the bean is a middle-tier object, an EJB developer does not need to create any user interface logic. The EJB developer must write only the code necessary to implement the application's business rules and manage its data.

Although EJBs are straightforward to write, they can take advantage of advanced services as concurrency, persistence, and transaction support. EJB shifts the burden of implementing these services from the shoulders of the application developer to those of the container provider.

At this point, you may be wondering why EJB has generated such a stir. After all, transaction processing has been around for a long time, as have three-tier computing and distributed objects. The reason for all the hubbub is that EJB brings together several trends in computing:

- Transaction processing
- Persistent storage of objects
- Platform independence
- Multitiered architecture

EJB provides all of these features in a straightforward, portable, easy-to-use framework.

Another reason for the high level of interest in EJB is that the EJB specification was written in close consultation with a broad spectrum of vendors. This strategy was intended to ensure that the specification would not contain elements that would be difficult or impossible to implement. As a result, many vendors have embraced EJB.

Finally, the "write once, run anywhere" aspect of EJB should not be overlooked. Although different Java implementations will have different bugs, Java remains the hands-down choice in applications requiring portability. Because an EJB bean can run in any EJB container, the potential exists for a new market in business-logic middleware. Traditional vertical-market vendors of inventory, accounting, and other software programs can dramatically expand their potential market by implementing EJB versions of their software.

Before we get too carried away with the possibilities that EJB provides, let's inject a note of hard-nosed realism at this point. EJB is a new technology; at this writing, actual implementations of EJB are still scarce. Even after the release of the initial implementations, inconsistencies will undoubtedly appear among the different implementations. Don't expect that EJB will immediately deliver complete seamless compatibility and interoperability. The current version of EJB is nevertheless quite compelling as an application server platform, and it will only improve as time goes on.

Conclusion

In this chapter, we discussed a variety of mechanisms that have evolved to address business needs such as transaction processing and distributed communication. With this groundwork in place, we examined EJB's relationship to these various mechanisms. This discussion provides a framework for understanding EJB's place in the world and gives a sense of how EJB evolved. In Chapter 2, we turn to the details of EJB's architecture.

CHAPTER 2

EJB's Architecture

The preceding chapter offered a high-level overview of EJB's place in the world and the types of services it provides to applications. Chapter 3 will introduce our first coding examples. This chapter presents an overview of EJB's architecture. Our intention is that, by the time you begin coding your first EJB example, you'll have a solid grasp of how EJB is put together, what it does, and where it fits into the great scheme of things. The remainder of the book will focus on the details of building EJB applications.

Logical Architecture

An EJB system is logically a three-tier system. The three tiers are as follows:

- The client
- The EJB server
- The database (or other persistent store)

This structure is a "logical" architecture because the three tiers don't necessarily have to reside on three different machines. For example,

- The EJB server and the database might reside on the same machine. This case could arise if the EJB server includes built-in functionality for persistent storage.
- The client and the EJB server might reside on the same machine. This case occurs when an EJB bean makes a call to another EJB bean in the same container. The caller EJB bean is acting as a client in this instance.
- If you combine the two cases above, all three tiers might reside on a single machine.

Figure 2.1 shows a typical physical architecture for an EJB system. Most commonly, the client, the EJB server, and the database will reside on separate machines—though not necessarily. For example, if you're using an application server that supports servlets, you may put your servlet clients on the same physical box as your EJB objects. If you're using an application server that directly supports persistent data storage, you may not involve an external database at all.

EJB's role in each of these tiers is as follows:

- A program on the client side makes calls to remote EJBs. The client needs to know how to find the EJB server and how to interact with the objects that reside on the EJB server.
- The EJB components live in the middle tier. The EJB objects reside inside an **EJB container,** which in turn resides in an **EJB server.**
- The underlying database resides in the third tier. EJB beans can access the database themselves, typically via Java Database Connectivity (JDBC), or they can allow the container to handle their data storage needs for them.

Overview of EJB's Software Architecture

The diagram in Figure 2.2 presents a high-level view of the EJB architecture, showing the relationship between the various components. It illustrates several key features of the EJB architecture:

- The EJB bean exists within the container.
- The client never communicates directly with the EJB bean; rather, it talks to the bean through its **home interface** and its **remote interface,** both of which are provided by the container.

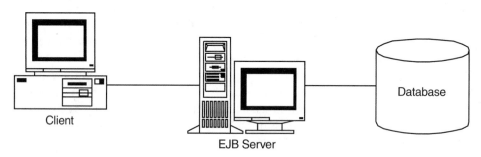

Figure 2.1 A typical physical architecture for an EJB system

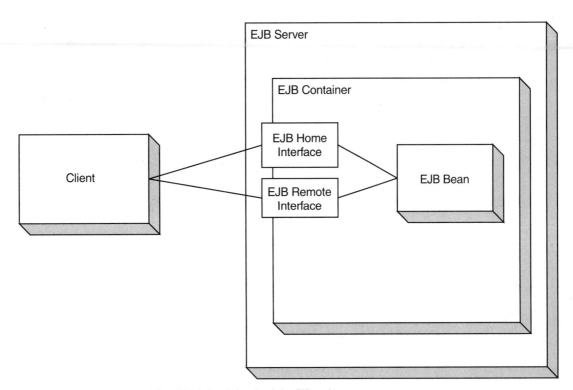

Figure 2.2 A high-level sketch of the EJB architecture

- The EJB server does not take part in the logical conversation between client and EJB bean. Actually, the server is performing a lot of work behind the scenes—remember, the server must handle requests for the container and feed the container incoming client requests. Even though the server is working hard, however, neither the bean nor the client directly accesses the server—all access is performed against the container.

EJB Servers

The EJB server is a "container container"—it contains the EJB container. This server is responsible for providing the container with lower-level services such as network connectivity. The 1.0 version of the EJB specification did not outline the exact interface between the EJB container and the EJB server. It notes (EJB specification, page 10) that, although the interface between servers and containers may be specified in the future version, the choice of interface between the server and the container is currently left up to the individual vendor. Your server vendor and your container vendor will likely be one and the same, at least until the server-container API is specified in a future release of the EJB specification.

The uncertainty inherent with this situation is somewhat unfortunate for prospective container authors. It is hoped that vendors will publish their interface standards to allow third parties to develop containers for their servers. At an abstract level, though, the relationship between the container and the server is such that the server will provide the container with low-level implementations of the services required by the container. This layered architecture is used in many areas in the computer field. Figure 2.3 draws an analogy between EJB, and both the TCP/IP and an operating system. As can be seen in this figure,

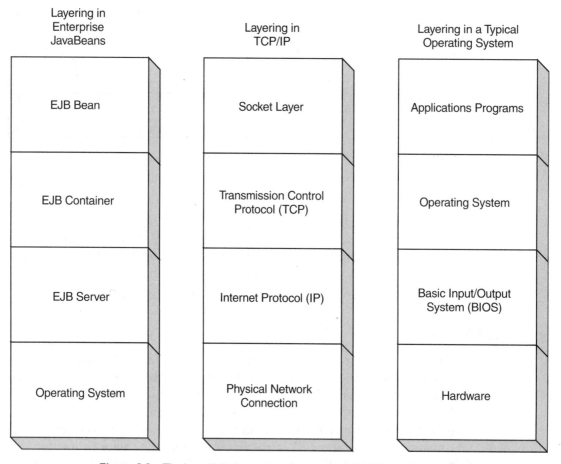

Figure 2.3 The layered division of services employed by EJB can also be found in other areas of computing

- In networking, the Internet Protocol (IP) layer provides services to the Transmission Control Protocol (TCP) layer, which in turn provides services to the socket layer.
- In operating systems, the Basic Input/Output System (BIOS) provides services to the operating system, which in turn provides services to the applications.
- In EJB, the server provides services to the container, which in turn provides services to the Bean.

EJB Containers

An EJB container is an environment in which Enterprise JavaBeans execute. Its primary role is to serve as a buffer between an EJB and the outside world. Clients do not directly connect to the EJB bean itself; rather, they connect to a representation of the bean provided by the container, which then forwards the client's requests to the bean. This scheme provides the container with a high degree of flexibility in servicing client requests; in many instances, the container can create a pool of Enterprise JavaBeans and use them as needed, rather than creating a new instance for each client connection. The container is also responsible for providing the beans with services, so that the bean can remain blissfully unaware of the underlying mechanisms used in implementing these services. These services are as follows:

- Support for transactions
- Support for management of multiple instances
- Support for persistence
- Support for security

Likewise, the container generally provides support for managing and monitoring EJBs as well as for version management.

Support for Transactions

Chapter 1 discussed the ACID (atomicity, consistency, isolation, and durability) properties of transactions. EJB containers provide the EJB beans with these properties.

If you have used transactions in another environment, you probably know that you must bracket your transaction with "begin" and "commit" calls; the "begin" notifies the transaction manager that a transaction has begun, and the "commit" orders the transaction manager to write the results to persistent storage. Although this approach to transaction management is possible in Enterprise JavaBeans, EJB also provides another approach, called

declarative transaction management. In declarative transaction management, the author of the bean can specify what type of transaction support the bean requires. When the bean is deployed, the container reads the **deployment descriptor** associated with that particular EJB bean and automatically provides the necessary transaction support. EJB provides six possible modes of transaction management:

- TX_NOT_SUPPORTED
- TX_BEAN_MANAGED
- TX_REQUIRED
- TX_SUPPORTS
- TX_REQUIRES_NEW
- TX_MANDATORY

TX_NOT_SUPPORTED means that the bean does not support any transactions, and can't be used from within a transaction. If the client attempts to use the bean from within a transaction, the client's transaction will remain suspended until the bean completes its operation; the client's transaction will then resume.

In **TX_BEAN_MANAGED,** the bean manages its own transaction. This option is the only type of transaction support in which the bean can directly manipulate the transaction.

For the **TX_REQUIRED** mode, if the client has a transaction open when it invokes the bean's method, the bean runs within the client's transaction context. Otherwise, the container starts a new transaction.

TX_SUPPORTS means that if the client has a transaction in progress when it invokes the bean's methods, the client's transaction is used. Otherwise, no new transaction is created.

If you choose **TX_REQUIRES_NEW**, the bean always starts a new transaction (even if a transaction is already in progress). If a transaction is under way, the container temporarily suspends it until the bean's transaction finishes.

For **TX_MANDATORY**, the bean requires that the client have a transaction open before the client attempts to use the bean. If no transaction is available, an error occurs. (This mode differs from TX_REQUIRED in that, in the latter, the container will create a new transaction if none exists.)

Keep in mind that EJB transactions are not nested. That is, if a bean has TX_REQUIRES_NEW as a transaction attribute, receives a call with an active transaction context, and suspends the transaction, the suspended transaction will be completely oblivious to the new transaction. Furthermore, after the new transaction has committed, it remains in that state even if the previously suspended transaction fails and is rolled back.

Support for Management of Multiple Instances

EJB classes are written as if they were simple single-threaded classes being accessed by only one client. This is true for some beans (in particular, stateless Session beans); however, other types of beans may be used concurrently by multiple clients. The EJB container must ensure that each client's requests are serviced in a timely manner. To accomplish this goal, the server may perform several tasks behind the scenes:

- Instance passivation
- Instance pooling
- Database connection pooling
- Precached instances
- Optimized method invocations

Instance passivation is the temporary swapping of an EJB bean out to storage. If a container needs resources, it may choose to temporarily swap out a bean. Both Session and Entity beans can be passivated. For Session beans, **passivation** is strictly performed as a convenience for the EJB container, to allow it to free up space. For Entity beans, the mechanism used to passivate the bean is also used to synchronize its state with the underlying data store.

Instance pooling means that the container shares instances of EJB beans among multiple clients. This task is typically undertaken for purposes of efficiency; it allows the EJB container to instantiate fewer copies of a given bean to service requests. Instance pooling is not possible in all cases; because a stateful Session bean tracks conversational state in its instance variables, the container must provide one Session bean per client.

Database connection pooling is a strategy commonly employed in middleware applications. In this approach, when a component wishes to access a database, it does not create a new database connection; instead, it simply grabs a connection from a pool of available connections. Database connection pooling is beneficial for two main reasons:

- It avoids the overhead of establishing a new database connection. In EJBs, the duration of a database connection will typically be relatively brief, but database accesses will occur frequently. In such a situation, the overhead of connecting to a database becomes a significant portion of the overall work that must be performed. Database connection pooling allows EJBs to avoid this overhead.
- Maintaining an open database connection consumes resources on the database. This overhead is not significant for a small number of users,

but can become substantial as the number of concurrent connections grows. Some databases have built-in upper limits on the number of simultaneous connections available, either because the product has its own limitations or because only a certain number of concurrent licenses have been purchased for the database. Connection pooling allows a system manager to provide an application with the resources it needs, without creating unnecessary overhead on the database.

Precached instances may be used when an Enterprise JavaBean needs to load some state information from a database when it is created. To speed up the loading process, it is possible to keep a cache of EJB state information in some readily accessible place (either in memory or in a highly indexed database table) to accelerate the initial creation of EJBs.

Optimized method invocations are employed to combat overhead costs associated with remote invocation. Whether the client of an EJB is a remote client or another EJB in the same container, the APIs used to gain access to it are always the same. A typical EJB interaction is as follows:

- Use a naming service to locate the EJB's home interface.
- Make a call on the EJB's home interface to gain access to its remote interface.
- Make calls to the business methods against the remote interface.

If two EJBs exist in the same container, using a full-blown remote protocol for communication adds needless overhead. A container may instead detect that both beans live in the same container and then short-circuit the remote protocol so as to allow one bean to invoke **methods** on the other with only local calls (of course, this invocation would be done through a proxy object; the fact that two beans live in the same container doesn't entitle them to break the rules). Because remote invocation adds significant overhead to a method call, this type of optimization can speed things up dramatically. Container providers that implement this approach must be careful that their implementation does not produce side effects that would cause EJBs invoked locally to exhibit different behavior from EJBs invoked remotely; the only difference should be an increase in speed.

The EJB specification details the approach that a container provider should use for instance passivation; it does not require any of the other optimizations mentioned here (although it notes that instance pooling is a good idea). Nevertheless, a container vendor might easily provide these types of optimizations to a bean.

One optimization you probably won't see is cached writes of transactional information. Because EJB transactions tend to be relatively brief and occur in high numbers, it would be nice if you could simply cache the database updates that the transactions perform and handle them all in a batch at a later time. This approach would definitely speed things up, but it would also violate the durability portion of the ACID properties of transactions. If a database engine uses caching to buffer transactional updates and a power outage or other serious problem occurs, the updates would be lost.

Support for Persistence

EJB containers also provide support for persistence to beans. Actually, support for persistent EJBs (Entity beans) is not mandatory in the 1.x version of the EJB specification, but it will become mandatory in the 2.0 version. Indeed, most EJB vendors already support Entity beans even if they are not yet required to do so. Persistence means that the state of an object is saved to some sort of persistent storage (typically a file or a database), allowing the object to be read in and used at some later time, instead of being recreated each time. In olden times, you had to implement an object's persistence yourself, typically by implementing database calls to save and restore its state. In certain types of EJBs (such as Entity EJBs with container-managed persistence), you can simply specify the fields that should be persistent, and the container will then take responsibility for saving and restoring these fields.

The container bears a lot of responsibilities in the EJB architecture—one of the architecture's great benefits. Every additional requirement for the container developer is one less requirement for the EJB developer. The shifting of responsibility for transaction management, concurrency, security, and persistence to the container means that the bean developer can concentrate on the business rules of his or her application, while still reaping the benefits that these services provide. It also means that, rather than having to write your own code to handle these complex issues, you can take advantage of tested and debugged code written by the vendor's expert programmers. You can therefore make immediate use of these advanced services without having to become an expert in issues like network programming and concurrency.

Support for Security

The main mechanism used in EJB security is the **access control list (ACL)**. An ACL is a list of persons or groups that are allowed to access particular pieces of functionality. A deployer can specify ACLs for a bean as a whole, as well as for any of the bean's methods. Only those users who are included in the ACL will be able to access the ACL-protected beans.

Enterprise Beans

Now that we've covered the container and the server, it's time to talk about the beans themselves. Figure 2.4 illustrates the various types of EJBs and their relationships to one another. Take a look at it now; it probably won't make too much sense at this point, but we'll refer back to it frequently.

Before delving too deeply into the hierarchy depicted in Figure 2.4, let's talk about home and remote interfaces. In addition to the implementation of the EJB object itself, an EJB bean provider must supply a home interface and a remote interface for the bean. It's noteworthy that the EJB developer must pro-

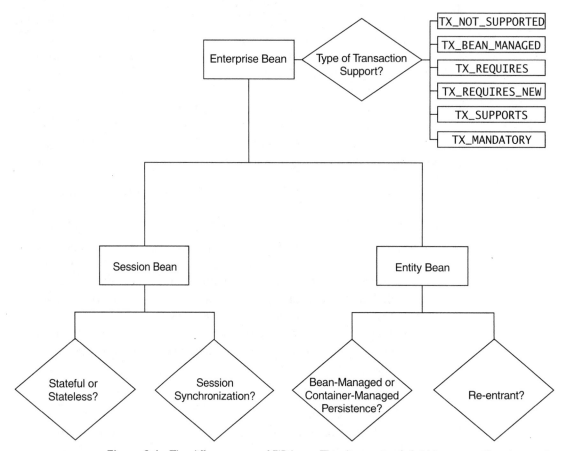

Figure 2.4   The different types of EJB beans. This diagram is a hybrid between a flowchart and an inheritance diagram. Rectangular boxes represent classes (Session beans and Entity beans inherit from a common ancestor, the Enterprise bean class). Diamond-shaped boxes represent options for a particular class. For example, the "Stateful or Stateless?" box under the "Session Bean" box indicates that Session beans can be either stateful or stateless.

vide only home and remote interfaces, rather than full implementations. The container is responsible for generating the implementations of these interfaces.

The EJBHome Interface

All home interfaces must extend the **EJBHome** interface.

```
public interface javax.ejb.EJBHome
    extends java.rmi.Remote
{
public abstract EJBMetaData getEJBMetaData();
    public abstract void remove (Handle handle);
    public abstract void remove (Object primaryKey);
}
```

The home interface serves as the initial point of contact for a client. When the client uses a **naming service** to look up an EJB bean, the naming service returns a reference to an object that implements the bean's home interface. The home interface requires the implementation of three methods:

```
getEJBMetaData()
```

This call returns a reference to an object that implements the EJBMetaData interface.

```
public interface javax.ejb.EJBMetaData
{
    public abstract EJBHome getEJBHome();
    public abstract Class getHomeInterfaceClass();
    public abstract Class getPrimaryKeyClass();
    public abstract Class getRemoteInterfaceClass();
    public abstract boolean isSession();
}
```

Builder tools can use the information in the EJBMetaData class to generate wrapper classes to invoke methods on the bean.

```
remove(Handle handle)
```

This method removes an EJB object using a Handle, which is a serializable reference to a particular bean.

```
remove (Object primaryKey)
```

This method removes an EJB object by its primary key. (Only an Entity bean can have a primary key).

Interestingly enough, the EJBHome interface does not provide any methods by which a client can create new beans or look up existing ones. Instead, the EJB bean developer must write the method signatures for these tasks in their own interfaces. The particular methods supplied differ for Session and Entity beans, as discussed later.

A client uses a naming service [in particular, **Java Naming and Directory Interface (JNDI)**] to look up an EJB, getting a reference to an object that implements its home interface in response. The client then calls a method on the home interface (we'll discuss this method momentarily) to get a reference to the bean's remote interface.

The EJBObject Interface

All remote interfaces extend the **EJBObject** interface:

```
public interface javax.ejb.EJBObject
    extends java.rmi.Remote
{
    public abstract EJBHome getEJBHome();
    public abstract Handle getHandle();
    public abstract Object getPrimaryKey();
    public abstract boolean isIdentical(EJBObject obj);
    public abstract void remove();
}
```

getEJBHome()

This method returns a reference to an object implementing the EJB object's home interface.

getHandle()

This method returns a **handle,** which is a serializable reference to the object. The Handle interface specifies one method, getEJBObject(), which can be used to recreate a remote reference from the handle.

getPrimaryKey()

This method returns the primary key used by the EJB object. Although it exists on the interfaces for both Session and Entity beans, it really makes sense to use this method only on an Entity bean; Session beans do not expose a primary key to the outside world, and indeed need not have a primary key at all. A future version of the EJB specification will specify that the getPrimaryKey() implementation on a Session bean's home interface should throw an exception.

isIdentical()

This method provides a way to test whether two EJB object references refer to an identical object. It is mainly useful for Entity beans (because Session beans don't advertise their identities). Two Entity beans that are from the same home interface and have the same primary key are considered identical. The two references in this method do not necessarily point to the same object in memory (containers are free to create multiple instances of Entity beans), but all of these instances are considered to have the same identity.

```
remove()
```

This method allows the caller to remove the remote EJB object.

To create a remote interface for your EJB bean, you simply create an interface that inherits from EJBObject and add the method signatures of your own methods. Interestingly, your EJB object does not have to implement its remote interface; in fact, it's recommended that you not do so. Instead, the container generates a proxy object that interacts with remote clients and passes their method calls to the bean. If you don't implement a remote interface in your bean, you ensure that remote clients will always have to go through the container's proxy object to reach your EJB implementation.

Let's press on and begin our trip through the EJB hierarchy.

The EnterpriseBean Interface

At the top level of the diagram in Figure 2.4 is the "Enterprise Bean" box. The top-level type in the EJB class hierarchy is the **EnterpriseBean** interface.

```
public interface javax.ejb.EnterpriseBean
    extends java.io.Serializable
{
}
```

This interface doesn't really do much. It merely serves as a common point of ancestry for the Session and Entity beans, and requires that its subinterfaces be serializable.

The transaction attributes logically belong with the Enterprise Bean interface, even though they're not associated directly with it. Either a Session or an Entity bean can be assigned any of the six available transaction attributes.

Underneath the "Enterprise Bean" box, the world bifurcates into the **SessionBean** and **EntityBean** interfaces. We'll take a depth-first approach in navigating this tree—we'll first descend on the "Session Bean" branch, then return to the "Enterprise Bean" box and descend on the "Entity Bean" branch.

Session Beans

As their name implies, **Session beans** are generally tied to the lifetime of a given client session. They are relatively short-lived; stateful Session objects are created in response to a single client's request, communicate exclusively with a single client, and die when the client no longer needs them. Thus a Session bean would typically be used to provide a service to a particular client. A Session bean is required to implement the `javax.ejb.SessionBean` interface:

```
public interface javax.ejb.SessionBean
    extends javax.ejb.EnterpriseBean
{
    public abstract void ejbActivate();
    public abstract void ejbPassivate();
    public abstract void ejbRemove();
    public abstract void setSessionContext(SessionContext ctx);
}
```

All of the methods declared in this interface are **callback** methods; that is, they are invoked by the container to notify the Session EJB that some event has occurred.

ejbPassivate()

The container calls the `ejbPassivate()` method on your EJB class immediately before the container swaps your object out to "semi-persistent" storage. The storage is "semi-persistent" because Session EJBs do not carry the same sort of guarantee of long life as Entity EJBs do. If the EJB container crashes or restarts, the Session beans that existed before the crash or restart are destroyed. Session beans also have an associated timeout value; after the timeout expires, they are destroyed. If none of these events happens, however, the Session bean can be swapped back in at some later time.

The `ejbPassivate()` call warns the session EJB that passivation is ready to occur, enabling it to perform any necessary cleanup beforehand. For example, if a Session EJB has a file open and it receives a call to `ejbPassivate()`, it should close the file and save any information needed to reopen the file in its internal variables.

Passivation of Session beans is accomplished via standard Java serialization or by some vendor-implemented method that provides the same semantics as standard Java serialization. For example, a particular vendor implementation may carry out all of its passivation to a relational database instead of to a file. This approach is perfectly acceptable, as long as the passivation process behaves the same way as standard serialization does.

ejbActivate()

The `ejbActivate()` method is essentially the inverse of the `ejbPassivate()` call; that is, it is called by the container after a Session bean's state has been restored from "semi-persistent" storage, but before it becomes available to the outside world. A bean can use the `ejbActivate()` call to restore any resources that it closed before being passivated; for example, if the bean had to close a file, it can reopen the file in `ejbActivate()`.

ejbRemove

This callback method is invoked by the container as a result of a client calling the **remove**() method of a bean's home or remote interface. The client's invocation of the `remove()` method notifies the container that this particular Session bean instance should be destroyed. In turn, before the container destroys the instance, it invokes the instance's `ejbRemove()` method. The bean therefore has one final chance to close any open resources and perform any last-minute processing before it is destroyed or sent back to the pool.

setSessionContext(SessionContext ctx)

This method is called at the very beginning of a Session bean's life. The container passes the Session bean an object that implements the SessionContext interface. The bean stores this object in an object variable, and can then use the SessionContext to interact with container-provided services such as security and transaction management.

The EJBContext Interface

The SessionContext interface inherits from the **EJBContext** interface. The EJBContext interface is the parent interface of both the SessionContext and EntityContext interfaces.

```
public interface javax.ejb.EJBContext
{
    public abstract Identity getCallerIdentity();
    public abstract EJBHome getEJBHome();
    public abstract Properties getEnvironment();
    public abstract boolean getRollbackOnly();
    public abstract UserTransaction getUserTransaction();
    public abstract boolean isCallerInRole(Identity role);
    public abstract void setRollbackOnly();
}
```

getCallerIdentity()

This method is used to get a `java.security.Identity` object that represents the identity of the client. It can be used in concert with `isCallerInRole()` to allow the EJB object to perform authorization checks before performing an operation. A few important notes about this method follow:

- In Java 2, the use of the `java.security.Identity` object is deprecated, which means that this method will be changed in a future release of the EJB specification. Sun Microsystems intends to preserve the `java.security.Identity` version for backward compatibility, however.

- The EJB specification does not indicate how the client's identity should be propagated to the EJB container; implementation of this mechanism is left to the vendor. A future version of the EJB specification will provide for a uniform client-side authentication API.

- Although EJB objects may perform on-the-fly examination of user identity through this method, a more typical approach to authorization will be to set up ACLs on the EJB container to control access to objects and methods. Using this mechanism, access can be controlled at fine granularity.

getEJBHome()

A bean can invoke this method to get a reference to its own home interface (as discussed earlier in this chapter). It can use this interface to create or find other instances of itself, or to do several other things.

getEnvironment()

This call returns the EJB's environment properties. When a bean is packaged, a list of environment properties can be included. These properties can be adjusted at deployment time (for example, a bean might require a database connection string as one of its environment properties; the deployer will set this string to point to a database that exists in the deployment environment). A bean can then use `getEnvironment()` to get a list of these properties.

getRollbackOnly()

EJB supports distributed transactions. If any of the players in a distributed transaction cannot continue for some reason, it can mark the transaction as "rollback only." A "rollback only" transaction can never complete; it must be rolled back. A bean can use `getRollbackOnly()` to check the status of a transaction before attempting to participate in it. If the transaction is marked as "rollback only," the bean can simply opt out of the transaction.

getUserTransaction()

Earlier, we discussed the TX_BEAN_MANAGED transaction type. In this type of transaction, the bean is responsible for beginning, committing, and possibly rolling back its own transactions. If a bean has a transaction attribute of TX_BEAN_MANAGED, it can use `getUserTransaction()` to gain access to the transaction. This method returns an object of type `javax.jts.UserTransaction`.

The UserTransaction Interface

```
public interface javax.jts.UserTransaction
{
    public final static int STATUS_ACTIVE;
    public final static int STATUS_COMMITTED;
    public final static int STATUS_COMMITTING;
    public final static int STATUS_MARKED_ROLLBACK;
    public final static int STATUS_NO_TRANSACTION;
    public final static int STATUS_PREPARING;
    public final static int STATUS_PREPARED;
    public final static int STATUS_ROLLEDBACK;
    public final static int STATUS_ROLLING_BACK;
    public final static int STATUS_UNKNOWN;
    public abstract void begin();
    public abstract void commit();
    public abstract int getStatus();
    public abstract void rollback();
    public abstract void setRollbackOnly();
    public abstract void setTransactionTimeout(int seconds);

}
```

The **User Transaction** interface provides the classic "begin," "commit," and "rollback" operations, as well as the `getStatus()` operation, which allows the caller to see the status of the transaction. The status returned will correspond to one of the public final static int declarations in the class. This interface also allows the caller to set a transaction timeout, enabling the caller to set some upper bound on the execution time of the transaction.

The name of the package in which the UserTransaction interface resides has been changed from `javax.jts` to `javax.transaction`. This change is not reflected in the 1.0 version of the EJB specification, but will be incorporated into future versions. Please check the online supplement to this book (the Preface gives instructions for accessing this supplement) for the most up-to-date information.

isCallerInRole()

This Boolean method can be used to test whether the caller has assumed a given role. An EJB developer might specify several different roles that can be played by the users of the class. For example, a transaction processing system might include many data entry operators and a few managers that have some level of expanded permissions. An EJB developer could model this system by providing two roles; a "user" role with a normal set of permissions, and a "manager" role with expanded permissions.

```
setRollbackOnly()
```

Calling this method sets the current transaction to "rollback only." We discussed the implications of this action earlier.

The SessionContext Interface

Before our discussion of the EJBContext and UserTransaction interfaces, we were examining the `setSessionContext()` method of the SessionBean interface. Although we discussed the EJBContext interface in some detail, we didn't consider the SessionContext interface itself. Without further ado, here it is:

```
public interface javax.ejb.SessionContext
    extends javax.ejb.EJBContext
{
    public abstract EJBObject getEJBObject();
}
```

Because the EJBContext interface provides such a rich set of functionality, the SessionContext interface can get by with only one additional method, `getEJBObject()`, which returns a reference to an `EJBObject`. This remote reference to an object implements the bean's remote interface, and can be used if the bean wants to pass a reference to itself to some other entity.

At this point, a discussion of the relationship between a Session bean's home and remote interfaces is in order. The requirements for a Session bean's remote interface are straightforward; it must inherit from the EJBObject interface, and it must provide method signatures that correspond to the signatures of your business methods. The EJB container is responsible for creating objects that implement your remote interface; these objects act as proxies, forwarding the business method calls on to your object.

A Session bean's home interface, in addition to inheriting from the EJBHome interface, must provide one or more "create" methods. "Create" methods are invoked by clients to create new instances of a particular EJB object. A create method can take any arguments that are acceptable to RMI, but its return type must match your EJB object's remote interface. When a client invokes a `create()` method on your bean's home interface, the container creates an object of the appropriate type, calls its `setSessionContext()` method, and then calls a method in your EJB class called **ejbCreate()**. As a developer, you are responsible for implementing one `ejbCreate()` method in your class for each `create()` method that you declare in your home interface. The rules for an `ejbCreate()` method in Session beans are as follows:

- The method must have a void return type. The container will pass the remote interface back to the client.

- The number and type of arguments to the `ejbCreate()` method must exactly match the number and type of arguments in the corresponding `create()` method declared in your home interface.

The following steps are therefore involved in the creation of a new Session bean:

- The client calls a `create()` method in the bean's home interface.
- The container sets aside storage for the object and instantiates it.
- The container calls the object's `setSessionContext()` method.
- The container calls the `ejbCreate()` method whose signature matches the `create()` method invoked by the client.

Session Bean Summary

To summarize, each Session EJB must provide three classes:

- The EJB class itself
- The home interface
- The remote interface

The EJB class must provide the following items:

- An implementation of the SessionBean interface
- Implementations of your business methods
- Implementations of your `ejbCreate()` methods

The home interface must provide the following functions:

- Inherit from the EJBHome interface
- Provide method signatures for the various `create()` methods

The remote interface must provide the following functions:

- Inherit from the EJBObject interface
- Provide method signatures corresponding to your business methods

The role of the `ejbCreate()` method is roughly analogous to that of a constructor in an ordinary Java program. It initializes the state of a class with any necessary argument variables.

Stateful and Stateless Session Beans

Now that we've discussed the general roles and responsibilities of Session beans, we can descend further into the hierarchy shown in Figure 2.4 and talk about **stateful** and **stateless** Session beans. A stateless Session bean is one that doesn't keep track of any information from one method call to another—

essentially, a bean with no instance variables. Any two instances of a stateless bean are equivalent. As an example, consider a hypothetical object that provides a set of methods to calculate sales tax depending on the locality. When the object's calculateSalesTax() method is invoked with a dollar amount and a locality as arguments, the object looks up the tax rate for the locality in a database table, multiplies the argument dollar amount by the tax rate, and returns a value representing the amount of tax to be paid. Calling this method has no effect on the internal state of the object. A container can easily handle a stateless Session bean, because instances of a stateless bean can be created and destroyed at will, without worrying about their state at the time of their destruction.

A stateful Session bean, is a bean that changes state during a conversation—that is, a bean that has instance variables. The classic example of a stateful bean is a "shopping cart" bean, which allows a customer to select several items for purchase during the course of a session. The shopping cart bean keeps track of the items that have been added, and, when the customer is ready, allows the customer to purchase the items. The life cycle of a stateful bean is more complex (for the container) than the life cycle of a stateless bean because, if the container wishes to swap out a stateful bean for some reason, it must save the bean's state to persistent storage. Later, when the client makes a request to the bean, the server must read the bean's state out of the persistent storage and restore it.

We have defined stateful and stateless beans in terms of instance variables, ignoring static variables. According to the EJB specification, EJB objects are not allowed to have static variables (unless they're declared as final, in which case they're not really variables at all).

The SessionSynchronization Interface

We have almost finished with Session beans. Nevertheless, one final distinction can be made: A Session bean may or may not implement the **Session-Synchronization** interface.

```
public interface javax.ejb.SessionSynchronization
{
    public abstract void afterBegin();
    public abstract void afterCompletion(boolean committed);
    public abstract void beforeCompletion();
}
```

A Session bean can implement the SessionSynchronization interface if it wishes to be notified by the container about the state of any transaction in which it may be involved. Even if a Session bean does not manage its own transactions via the UserTransaction interface, it may still implement the

SessionSynchronization interface. All of the methods in the Session-Synchronization interface are callbacks.

`afterBegin()`

This method notifies the bean that a transaction has begun.

`beforeCompletion()`

This method indicates that a transaction is nearly complete. If the bean wishes to roll back the transaction for some reason, it can call the `setRollbackOnly()` method of the SessionContext interface to do so.

`afterCompletion()`

The container calls this method after a transaction has been completed. Its Boolean argument will be set to true if the transaction was committed successfully, and false if the transaction was rolled back.

You might choose to implement this interface because the state of instance variables in a Session bean is not transactional. That is, if the instance variables in a Session bean are modified during the course of a transaction and the transaction is then rolled back, the instance variables will not be automatically reset to their original state prior to the transaction. To reset your instance variables, you must implement the SessionSynchronization interface and use the `afterCompletion()` callback to read your state variables back out of the database.

Note that a stateless Session bean cannot implement the Session-Synchronization interface. Because it has no state, there's no point in trying to synchronize its state with the database.

We have now reached the end of our traversal of the "Session Bean" branch of the hierarchy tree. Let's ascend to the "Entity Bean" branch and see what it holds.

Entity Beans

Entity beans are long-lived; they exist across client sessions, are shared by multiple clients, and remain alive even after a restart of the server or other failure. Typically, an Entity EJB object represents a set of data in persistent storage. Just as a Session bean must implement the SessionBean interface, so an Entity bean must implement the **EntityBean** interface.

The EJB 1.0 specification does not require support for Entity objects. Although this book discusses them, and it appears that most vendors will support them, you should be aware that an EJB 1.0-compliant environment is not required to provide this support.

The EntityBean Interface

```
public interface javax.ejb.EntityBean
{
    public abstract void ejbActivate();
    public abstract void ejbLoad();
    public abstract void ejbPassivate();
    public abstract void ejbRemove();
    public abstract void ejbStore();
    public abstract void setEntityContext(EntityContext ctx);
    public abstract void unsetEntityContext();
}
```

ejbActivate() and ejbPassivate()

These methods are analogous to the methods of the same name in the SessionBean interface. They are called before an Entity object is swapped out (ejbPassivate()) and after it is swapped back in (ejbActivate()).

ejbLoad() and ejbStore()

These operations allow the Entity bean to synchronize its state with an underlying database. Their meaning is slightly different for bean-managed versus container-managed persistence. We'll defer detailed discussion of them for the moment.

setEntityContext() and unsetEntityContext()

setEntityContext() is similar in function to setSessionContext(). It passes an object that inherits from EJBContext() to the EJB instance.

```
public interface javax.ejb.EntityContext
    extends javax.ejb.EJBContext
{
    public abstract EJBObject getEJBObject();
    public abstract Object getPrimaryKey();
}
```

The getEJBObject() method in this interface is analogous to the method of the same name in the SessionContext interface. The getPrimaryKey() method returns the **primary key** for this object. In the context of entity EJBs, a primary key is an object of some user-defined type (strictly speaking, you can use any type that implements the java.io.Serializable interface) that can be used to look up a reference to a particular Entity EJB.

Because Entity EJBs can exist across many client invocations, the Entity-Bean interface includes an unsetEntityContext() method that allows the bean to discard its previous context when it is destroyed.

For both Session and Entity beans, the setXXXContext() method is invoked only once, at the bean's creation. You may wonder how the context variable remains valid for a stateless Session bean or Entity bean that may be invoked by many clients over its lifetime. Typically, SessionContext or EntityContext variables will be implemented so that they actively interrogate the container for current information when their methods are called (rather than the container simply assigning them some initial values and then ignoring them). Thus, when you invoke getCallerIdentity() on a context, the context in turn interrogates the container for the identity of the current caller.

ejbRemove()

Even though Entity EJBs are long-lived, a client can still remove them. The container invokes the ejbRemove() method when a client has called the remove() method of the bean's home interface; the bean then has one last chance to put its affairs in order before being destroyed.

In addition to implementing the methods required by the EntityBean interface, the Entity EJB developer must implement the **ejbFindByPrimaryKey()** method. (Actually, the developer is required to implement this method only if using bean-managed persistence; in container-managed persistence, the container will generate it for you. Bean-managed persistence and container-managed persistence will be discussed shortly.) The container invokes this method when a client invokes the findByPrimaryKey() method on an EJB's home interface with a particular primary key; the method should return a single object that is represented by the primary key. (Note that other finder methods can potentially return collections of objects, but findByPrimaryKey() should always return a single reference.) This key is passed to the container, which uses it to look up the object and return a reference to its remote interface to the client.

Entity EJBs may also implement ejbCreate() methods to allow clients to create new Entity EJBs, though this approach is not required. Instead, an Entity EJB implementer may choose to have the Entity EJBs represent objects already in a particular database and to not allow the creation of new ones. If you choose to implement ejbCreate() methods, you must also implement corresponding ejbPostCreate() methods, which have the same number and type of arguments as their corresponding ejbCreate() methods, but are invoked only after the successful creation of the object.

An Entity bean's remote interface does not differ significantly from that of a Session bean. It must inherit from the EJBObject interface, and must provide method signatures for any business methods that the client should be able to invoke.

An Entity bean's home interface, like the Session bean's home interface, inherits from the EJBHome interface. You must also provide method signatures for any create() methods you've implemented, the findByPrimaryKey() finder method, and any other finder methods you've implemented.

Entity Bean Summary

To summarize, each Entity EJB must provide three classes:

- The EJB class itself
- The home interface
- The remote interface

The EJB class must provide the following items:

- An implementation of the EntityBean interface
- Implementations of your business methods
- Implementations of your `ejbCreate()` methods, if any
- A corresponding `ejbPostCreate()` method for each `ejbCreate()` method implemented
- An implementation of `ejbFindByPrimaryKey()` (for bean-managed persistence only)
- Any other finder methods implemented

The home interface must provide the following functions:

- Inherit from the EJBHome interface
- Provide method signatures for any `create()` methods
- Provide a method signature for the `findByPrimaryKey()` method
- Provide method signatures for any other "finder" methods

The remote interface must provide the following functions:

- Inherit from the EJBObject interface
- Provide method signatures corresponding to your business methods

Bean-Managed and Container-Managed Persistence

Entity beans are intrinsically tied to an underlying database representation. The internal state of an active Entity EJB should always be synchronized with its underlying data after a transaction concludes (there will be a period during the transaction when the state variables have been modified, but the database has not yet been updated). The EJB specification permits two approaches to maintaining this synchronization:

- Bean-managed persistence
- Container-managed persistence

In **bean-managed persistence,** the author of the bean must write any necessary database calls to send the object out to persistent storage and read it back in again. To implement bean-managed persistence, you would place your database calls in the ejbLoad() and ejbStore() routines. The container calls ejbLoad() to notify the object that it should load its state in from a database; in ejbLoad(), you would place calls to read your state from the database. Similarly, ejbStore() notifies the object that it should write its state out to the database; you would place a call in ejbStore() to write your data out to a database.

In **container-managed persistence,** you don't have to do anything to synchronize with the database. In your Entity bean's deployment descriptor (discussed shortly), you specify which fields that the container should manage; you must also make the container-managed fields public in your EJB implementation class. At runtime, the container will invoke ejbLoad() (after it has already loaded your state) and ejbStore() (after it has stored your data), but you need not provide any implementations to these methods (but you must provide at least empty methods in order to compile).

If container-managed persistence is so straightforward, why would anyone use bean-managed persistence? Typically, this option is preferred if your Entity beans actually represent aggregations of data in several underlying tables, or if you have other complex "data-massaging" to do between the state of the data in the object and its state in an underlying database.

Reentrant and Nonreentrant Entity Beans

By default, Entity EJBs are nonreentrant. That is, if a call is being processed and another call to the same object comes in with the same transaction context, the program will throw a RemoteException and the call will not be allowed. (This situation is *always* the case for Session EJBs.) It is possible to specify in a deployment descriptor that an Entity EJB is reentrant—that is, it will accept more than one call in the same transaction context. You might choose this approach so as to allow a remote object invoked by a client to perform callbacks to the client. If possible, you should avoid making your beans reentrant.

We have now wrapped up our whirlwind tour of the EJB classes. Several ancillary classes remain to be discussed (such as deployment descriptors), but that discussion will be deferred to later chapters. The purpose of the discussion here is simply to introduce the major players in EJB. Now let's pull back to a somewhat higher level and look at how everything works together.

A High-Level View of an EJB Conversation

In the EJB architecture, the client undertakes the following tasks:

- Finding the bean
- Getting access to a bean
- Calling the bean's methods
- Getting rid of the bean

Finding the Bean

The EJB specification mentions two ways in which a client can find a bean. The first way is by using the Java Naming and Directory Interface (JNDI); this Java API provides a uniform interface to naming and directory services. A **naming service** is a service that associates a symbolic name with an object. For instance, **Domain Name Service (DNS)** is a commonly used naming service that is used to translate symbolic machine names (such as "www.javasoft.com") into numeric IP addresses. Most likely, if you are using TCP/IP networking, a DNS in your environment handles this task for you. Before DNS, it was necessary to maintain a file (on UNIX systems, this file is called "/etc/hosts"; on Windows systems, it is called "hosts") containing a list of symbolic host names along with the numeric IP addresses that they should resolve to. This approach was problematic for several reasons:

- If your /etc/hosts file developed errors, you couldn't resolve symbolic names.
- Someone at your site had to maintain the /etc/hosts file as addresses changed and new machines were added.
- If a machine did not appear in the /etc/hosts file, you had to know its numeric IP address to connect to it.

Using the DNS approach allows you to avoid many of these annoyances. It works as follows:

1. A client makes a query to a DNS server.
2. If the DNS server knows how to resolve the address, it returns the address.
3. If the DNS server does not know how to resolve the address, it passes the query to another DNS server.
4. Once the server is able to resolve the name, it returns the address to the client. Typically, it also caches the result so that, if the request is made again, it can be handled immediately.

Where does JNDI fit in? JNDI provides a uniform interface to naming services. Thus, if a user wishes to look up a name in DNS and another name in another naming service, he or she can use the same interface for both calls. Behind the scenes, each name service provider provides a JNDI-compliant interface to its service, using JNDI's Service Provider Interface (SPI). The JNDI client uses the server's SPI to access its services.

A Java client can use JNDI to look up an EJB component. The JNDI call returns a reference to an object implementing the EJB component's "home" interface, which can then be used to gain access to the EJB object itself.

The other way to find an EJB component is to use CORBA's **Common Object Services (COS)** naming service. COS refers to a group of services, including naming, that is provided as part of the CorbaServices specification. In addition to using COS naming directly, you can make use of it via JNDI.

Getting Access to a Bean

The result of the naming lookup is a reference to an object implementing the EJB component's home interface. A client uses the home interface to look up existing EJB instances, or to create new ones. This lookup results in a reference to an object that implements the EJB object's remote interface. The client uses the remote interface to interact with your EJB objects on the server.

Calling the Bean's Methods

After the client has a reference to an object implementing the object's remote interface, it can then invoke the methods that the EJB object makes public in the remote interface.

Getting Rid of the Bean

Finally, when the client has finished with an EJB object, it can call the remove() method on the home interface or on the object's remote interface. In some cases, the client may leave the object in existence. More specifically, you would usually call remove() on a stateful Session bean when it is no longer needed, so that the container can discard it and use the space for other beans. You *can* invoke remove() on a stateless Session bean, but doing so generally has no effect; the server simply returns the instance to a pool. For Entity beans, invoking remove() signals that you would like to remove the underlying object from persistent storage. For example, if an Entity bean represents a customer and you invoke remove() on it, the customer's data will be deleted from the underlying database.

Clients can interact with Enterprise JavaBeans either through CORBA or through RMI. The following sections describe CORBA and RMI and discuss how clients can use them to connect to EJBs.

RMI Clients

Remote Method Invocation (RMI) has been included as part of the standard Java API distribution since the release of **Java Development Kit (JDK)** 1.1; it can be found in the java.rmi package. This API allows a Java program to find and use Java classes that reside on remote machines. RMI was intended to make the use of distributed objects within a Java program as simple and transparent as possible. An RMI client interacts with objects on a server through the server object's remote interface. To the client, the object represented by the remote interface appears to be an ordinary Java class. When a method of a remote class is invoked, however, the invocation is passed on to a class called a stub. This stub class handles the nitty-gritty details of invoking the remote object, such as converting any arguments to a format suitable for transfer over the network, sending the data, and receiving any responses. One very cool aspect of Enterprise JavaBeans is the fact that the EJB container automatically generates these stub classes; the EJB developer need only create a Java interface that contains the method signatures of those methods that the client will invoke, and the container does the rest. EJB, therefore, requires essentially no server-side RMI programming.

Typically, an EJB client that uses RMI will use the JNDI API to locate the home interface of the desired bean. The client will then invoke a `find()` or `create()` method contained in the bean's home interface; this call results in a reference to the bean's remote interface. Once you've retrieved a reference to the remote interface, you can then use it as if it were a normal class. The only difference is that you must include exception-handling code to catch the java.rmi.RemoteException exception. This exception will be thrown by the stub if any network problems occur during your conversation.

CORBA Clients

The EJB specification includes a mapping that allows you to use CORBA to communicate with EJB objects. In CORBA, the developer specifies the interface for an object in an IDL file, which defines the methods and variables that will be made available in a platform- and language-independent way. The IDL description is then run through a language-specific compiler, which generates the classes necessary to converse over the network. Thus, an application written in C++ running on a UNIX workstation can call methods of an application written in Java running on a Windows NT platform. An ORB makes the connection between applications possible. Applications register the objects they wish to be made available with an ORB's naming service, and other applications can then query the ORB's naming service to locate the objects and interact with them.

Using Enterprise JavaBeans via CORBA is very similar conceptually to using them via RMI. Instead of using JNDI to locate a bean's home interface, however, you use CORBA's COS naming service. Other than that, the same pattern is followed:

1. You use a naming service to find the bean's home interface.
2. You call one of the `find()` or `create()` methods of the bean's home interface to create a new bean or obtain a reference to an existing bean.
3. You use the bean in your application.

Building and Deploying EJBs

Writing the EJB

As noted earlier, each EJB must provide three required classes:

- The EJB implementation class
- The home interface
- The remote interface

Some additional files must be provided as well. For example, for each Enterprise JavaBean, you must provide a deployment descriptor. The deployment descriptor is a serialized instance of a Java class that contains information about how to deploy the bean. (Chapter 7 provides a detailed discussion of the deployment descriptor.) For now, you should know that deployment descriptors come in two flavors: SessionDescriptors, which apply to Session EJBs, and EntityDescriptors, which apply to Entity EJBs. A deployment descriptor contains information such as the following:

- The name of the EJB class
- The name of the EJB home interface
- The name of the EJB remote interface
- ACLs of entities authorized to use each class or method
- For Entity beans, a list of container-managed fields
- For Session beans, a value denoting whether the bean is stateful or stateless

In addition to the deployment descriptor, you may need to generate a .properties file containing any environment properties that your bean expects to see at runtime. (The deployment descriptor contains an area that can be used to store and serialize properties, but it's nice to provide a .properties file as well, as a convenience for the deployer.)

Finally, you need to create a manifest file. This file will be used in the creation of the ejb-jar file, which is the medium used to distribute EJBs. This manifest, which contains lists of all the files that you intend to package in your ejb-jar file, has the following format:

```
Name: <file name goes here>
Enterprise-Bean: <Boolean value>
```

You don't need to provide a full list of all files in your directories in the manifest file; the Java Archive (JAR) packager will add new entries automatically. For each EJB in your ejb-jar file, though, you should insert an entry in the manifest file.

Deploying the EJB

At this point, the task of the EJB developer is complete; the ejb-jar file is ready for deployment. At deployment time, the EJB container must read the ejb-jar file, creat implementations for the home and remote interfaces, read the deployment descriptor and ensure that the bean has what it wants, and add the bean's property settings to the environment so that they're available to the bean at runtime.

Connecting to the EJB

The last step is to access the bean from a client. As discussed earlier, the client can use either RMI or CORBA to connect to the EJB. In either case, the general pattern is the same: The client looks up the EJB's home interface using a naming service (either JNDI or COS), invokes a find() or create() method on the home interface to get a reference to an EJB object, and then uses the EJB object as if it were an ordinary object.

Roles in EJB

To this point, we have thrown around terms like "EJB developer" and "container provider" with abandon. The EJB specification gives a clear description of each of these roles and their associated responsibilities. Here we briefly describe these roles.

Enterprise Bean Provider

The Enterprise bean provider is the person or group that writes and packages EJBs. It might be a third-party vendor of EJB components, or it might be an information systems programmer who writes EJBs to implement his or her company's business logic. Because the container must provide transaction and network communication support, the enterprise bean provider does not need to be an expert at low-level systems programming, networking, or transaction processing. The bean provider needs to be concerned only with the business logic to be implemented.

The end result of the Enterprise bean provider's labor is an ejb-jar file, which contains the Enterprise bean, its supporting classes, and information that describes how to deploy the bean.

Deployer

The deployer takes an ejb-jar file and installs it into an EJB container. The deployer's task begins with the receipt of an ejb-jar file, and ends with the installation of the ejb-jar file in the container.

In the management information systems (MIS) world, this task would typically be handled by a systems administrator.

Application Assembler

An application assembler builds applications using EJB classes. For example, an MIS programmer might purchase a prepackaged set of EJBs that implement an accounting system. The programmer might then use tools to customize the beans. The application assembler might also need to provide a user-interface client program.

This role is roughly analogous to that of a systems integrator in the MIS world.

EJB Server Provider

An EJB server provider provides a server that can contain EJB containers. The EJB 1.0 specification does not describe the interface between the server and the container, so the EJB server provider and the EJB container provider will likely be one and the same for any given product.

The diagram in Figure 2.5 shows the relationships among the EJB server, the EJB container, and the EJB bean. The idea that you should take away from this diagram is that an EJB server contains and provides services to an EJB container, and an EJB container contains and provides services to an Enterprise JavaBean.

The role of the EJB server provider is similar to that of a database systems vendor. The server provider offers the container whatever services it needs to do its job. The server provider will typically have a great deal of expertise in areas such as concurrent programming, transaction processing, and network communications.

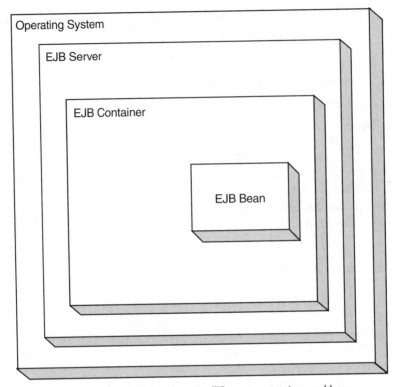

Figure 2.5   The relationships among the EJB server, container, and bean

EJB Container Provider

An EJB container is the world in which an EJB bean lives. The container services requests from the EJB, forwards requests from the client to the EJB, and interacts with the EJB server. The container provider must provide transaction support, security, and persistence to beans. It is also responsible for running the beans and for ensuring that the beans are protected from the outside world.

System Administrator

System administrators are responsible for the day-to-day operation of the EJB server. Their responsibilities include keeping security information up-to-date and monitoring the performance of the server.

The role of the system administrator will likely be undertaken by a company's current system administration staff.

This book focuses on Enterprise bean providers. The aim is to provide you with sufficient understanding to go forth and provide EJBs.

CHAPTER 3

Hello, EJB!

In this chapter, we'll build a very simple EJB system. When coming to grips with a new technology, a "hello world" example is usually invaluable in demonstrating the core of what needs to be done to use the technology. In this chapter, we'll create and use a very simple Enterprise JavaBean, highlighting the key points along the way. This simple example will also be used to illustrate the actual conversation between the client and the bean. Later chapters will simply include code snippets highlighting the important bits of what's going on; this chapter, however, goes through the examples line by line, explaining each minor point in excruciating detail. At this point, it's better to give too much detail than too little.

Requirements

The first step in any programming project is deciding what you want to do. More formally, this step is called "requirements analysis." On a large and complex project, requirements analysis can take several months, or even years, and employ several analysts. For this chapter, the requirements are few and straightforward:

- We want to build an example that illustrates the process of building, deploying, and using an Enterprise JavaBean.
- This example should be as simple as possible, allowing us to focus on the architectural aspects of the system, rather than on the complexities of the example itself.
- Following from these requirements, we want to build a simple client that calls a method on an Enterprise JavaBean.

- Because we want to study the process of passing arguments and return values, the method that the client calls should take an argument and return a value.

Design

Now that the requirements are set, we can proceed to the next step—designing the system. Because the requirements are so basic, we can specify the design simply. For the server-side object, we need one method that takes an argument and returns a result. At this point, we make a design decision to use a String for both the argument and the result. For this "hello world" example, we'll name the method sayHello(), and its method signature will be as follows:

```
public String sayHello(String s)
```

The design of the client can be expressed as follows:

1. Find the bean's home interface.
2. Get access to the bean.
3. Call the bean's sayHello() method with a string as argument and save the return value.
4. Display the return value to the user.

Because the bean doesn't have to remember anything between method calls from the client, we'll use a stateless Session bean. Stateless Session beans are the simplest sort of bean for a server to handle, because they don't require any sort of state management. A stateless Session bean has only one potential state of existence: either it's ready to receive method invocations or it doesn't exist at all (perhaps that's really two states). Because the server doesn't manage state, it can treat any instance of a stateless Session bean as being the same as any other instance, which means that it can use a pool of stateless Session beans to handle requests from clients. Typically, the number of active stateless Session beans in this pool will be much less than the number of clients (because a typical client will intersperse its remote calls with periods of inactivity).

Another reason for opting to use a Session bean (whether stateless or stateful) in this example is that Entity beans are not required as part of the EJB 1.0 specification. In fact, all the EJB implementations that the author has encountered to date have included support for Entity beans, but it is not outside the realm of possibility that some will not.

Implementation

We are now finished with design and ready to move on to implementation. Here's a quick overview of the plan:

1. Create the remote interface for the bean.
2. Create the bean's home interface.
3. Create the bean's implementation class.
4. Compile the remote interface, home interface, and implementation class.
5. Create a session descriptor.
6. Create a manifest.
7. Create an ejb-jar file.
8. Deploy the ejb-jar file.
9. Write a client.
10. Run the client.

Before we get too deeply into discussing the development process, you should make sure that your EJB server and development environment are set up. The process of setting up an EJB server will vary from vendor to vendor; consult the documentation included with your chosen EJB implementation for further instructions.

Now, on to the development process!

Step 1: Create the Remote Interface for the Bean

Listing 3.1   Code for the Remote Interface

```
1  package book.chap03.ex3.build;
2  import javax.ejb.*;
3  import java.rmi.*;
4
5  public interface Hello extends EJBObject
6  {
7      String sayHello(String s) throws RemoteException;
8  }
```

Listing 3.1 shows the code for the bean's remote interface. A remote interface is the interface with which the client interacts. The EJB container uses the remote interface for your bean to generate both the client-side stub and a server-side proxy object that passes client calls to your EJB object. In EJB, the client is never allowed to obtain a direct reference to your EJB implementation; access to the implementation is always brokered through the container.

Let's discuss the code line by line. The first line is a package declaration; it specifies that the `Hello` class will be part of the package
`book.chap03.ex3.build`. If you want to refer to this class directly in your client
program, without including the package, you would use the name
`book.chap03.ex3.build.Hello`. Packages are important because they prevent
name collisions. A name collision occurs when two objects in the same program
have the same name. In an environment such as EJB, where classes from many
different vendors may be installed on a single server, it's important to use packages. To illustrate, consider the following situation. You decide not to use packages. You include a class called `Account`. Because you have not used packages,
this class will reside in the default namespace. Now imagine that another developer builds another EJB, also deciding not to use packages. Coincidentally,
she also creates a class called `Account`. Now, when a program wishes to load a
class of type `Account`, it has two options and no way to choose between them.
It therefore picks the first occurrence of the class that it finds in the class path
and loads it. Thus one of the programs that uses the `Account` class will end up
with the wrong one; most likely, this situation will result in a runtime error
when the class tries to invoke a nonexistent method.

On the other hand, consider the situation if packages had been used.
You create a package called `com.mycompany.myproject`, and then create
your `Account` class within it. The other developer creates a package called
`com.hercompany.herproject`, and then creates an `Account` class within that
package. Because each of the `Account` classes resides in a different package,
both versions of `Account` can happily coexist without stepping on one another.
Indeed, a single program may even use both `Account` implementations, as long
as it refers to at least one of them by its full name (including the package specifier). If you've used JDBC, you may have encountered this situation with the
`Date` class. The JDBC package, `java.sql`, includes a class named `Date`. The
`java.util` class also includes a class named `Date`. You can't write the following code:

```
import java.sql.*;
import java.util.*;
public class Test
{
    public static void main(String[] argv)
    {
    long dateval = 123456;
    Date d = new Date(dateval);
    }
}
```

The preceding code does not specify which version of the `Date` class you
need. In contrast, the following code works well:

```
import java.sql.*;
import java.util.*;
public class Test
{
    public static void main(String[] argv)
    {
    long dateval = 123456;
    java.util.Date d1 = new java.util.Date(dateval);
    java.sql.Date d2 = new java.sql.Date(dateval);
    }
}
```

One further note about packages: To guarantee uniqueness of names, JavaSoft suggests that you use your Internet address as a prefix for the package. For example, if your company has registered the address "foobar.com," and you have a project called "account manager," you would put your classes into the package called com.foobar.accountmanager.

Typically, the series of names in a package (for example, book.chap03. ex3.build) maps to a series of directories in the file system of the machine that's running the program (for example, book\chap03\ex3\build). That is, if your CLASSPATH environment variable includes only the single directory c:\myclasses, and you attempt to run a program that declares itself as part of the package book.chap03.ex3.build, the **Java Virtual Machine (JVM)** will look for the program's classes in the directory c:\myclasses\book\ chap03\ex3\build; if it doesn't find the classes in this directory, it will report a ClassNotFoundException. This exception will occur even if you've placed the classes in the directory c:\myclasses, which is part of your class path. To ensure that the classes in your package are found, you should create an appropriate directory path under a directory that is contained in your CLASSPATH.

In line 2 of Listing 3.1, all classes in the package javax.ejb are imported. This package is prefixed with "javax" rather than with "java" because it is an extension to Java, and not a part of the core JDK packages. Other packages that use the "javax" prefix include the packages used in JNDI (javax.naming and javax.naming.directory) and the Java Transaction Service (javax.jts and later, javax.transaction). This prefix does not mean that these packages are not standardized; it simply means that they are not distributed as part of the core Java library.

In line 3, the classes in the java.rmi package are imported. Note that the java.rmi package is included as part of the standard JDK package. This package is imported because line 6 references the java.rmi.RemoteException.

Line 5 declares the public interface Hello as extending the javax.ejb. EJBObject interface. At deployment time, the container must generate a class that implements the Hello interface. The container-generated class passes method invocations to the EJB implementation class and allows the client to perform the following tasks:

- Get a reference to the bean's home interface (via the `getEJBHome()` method).
- Get a reference that can be saved and then restored at a later time (via the `getHandle()` method).
- Get rid of the object (via the `remove()` method).
- Test whether two remote objects are identical (via the `isIdentical()` method).

Line 7, supplies the **method signature** of our one business method. This method is straightforward; it takes a String as an argument and returns a String. All arguments and return types for EJB business methods follow the same rules that are required for RMI; that is, they must either be primitive types, be serializable, or be a remote reference. This situation occurs because the arguments and return values must be serialized so as to be passed over the wire from the client to the server.

Note that the business method throws a `java.rmi.RemoteException`. This exception can be thrown at any time if a network problem occurs on the connection between the client and the server. Because network outages can arise at any time, a client should be prepared to handle a RemoteException gracefully. All business methods must include the java.rmi.RemoteException exception in their "throws" clause. (You may choose to throw other exceptions in your business methods, but you *must* include the RemoteException.)

Remember, the implementation for the remote interface is created by the container; the EJB developer is required to supply only the interface.

Step 2: Create the Bean's Home Interface

The next step in building an EJB application is to create a home interface for your EJB implementation. The home interface is the client's initial point of contact with your EJB components. The client obtains a reference to an object implementing the home interface via JNDI (we'll see exactly how this process works when we discuss the construction of the client). After the client has obtained this reference, it can use a `create()` method to obtain a reference to an object that implements the remote interface discussed in step 1.

Listing 3.2   Code for the Home Interface

```
1   package book.chap03.ex3.build;
2   import javax.ejb.*;
3
4   public interface HelloHome extends EJBHome
5   {
6       public Hello create() throws java.rmi.RemoteException,
            javax.ejb.CreateException;
7   }
```

Line 1 declares that this class will be part of the package `book.chap03.ex3.build`. In line 2, we again import the classes in the javax.ejb package.

Line 4 declares the home interface `HelloHome` as extending the `EJBHome` interface. The `EJBHome` interface contains two types of method signatures:

- `remove()` methods, to allow a client to delete EJB instances.
- The `getEJBMetaData()` method, which returns an object that implements the `EJBMetaData` interface. The data structure returned contains information about the EJB implementation's home and remote interfaces, as well as other information. Higher-level development tools can use this method to discover necessary information about the bean through introspection.

In line 6, we declare our only `create()` method. The `create()` methods essentially replace constructors in EJB as the means of initializing an object, thereby allowing the container implementers to avoid the overhead of instantiating a new object each time a client requests a reference. The container can maintain a cache of already-instantiated objects and use the `create()` call to initialize the internal state of the object; this process is speedier than instantiating an object from scratch. You can specify as many different `create()` methods as you wish; if you're creating a stateless Session bean, however, you're allowed to have only one `create()` method that takes no arguments. Some particulars about `create()` methods follow:

- At least one `create()` method must be supplied in a Session bean's home interface. (For Entity beans, this requirement does not hold; Entity EJBs need not have `create()` methods. We'll see why in Chapter 5.)
- The `create()` method must be public, because it will be called from outside its package.
- The return type must be the type of the remote interface.
- The "throws" clause must include `java.rmi.RemoteException` and `javax.ejb.CreateException`.
- The "throws" clause may also include other application-specific exceptions.

The `javax.ejb.CreateException` notifies the client that a new EJB object could not be created. This exception may be thrown by the EJB object itself or by the container.

As with the remote interface, note that the EJB developer is not responsible for providing an implementation of the home interface. Instead, the EJB container generates the implementation class at deployment time.

Step 3: Create the Bean's Implementation Class

Now that we have created the home and remote interfaces, it's time to implement the EJB bean itself. The code appears in Listing 3.3.

Listing 3.3   Bean Implementation

```
1   package book.chap03.ex3.build;
2   import javax.ejb.*;
3
4   public class HelloBean implements SessionBean
5   {
6       SessionContext ctx;
7       public void ejbCreate()
8       {
9       }
10
11      public String sayHello(String s)
12      {
13          return "Hello there, " + s;
14      }
15
16      public void ejbRemove()
17      {
18      }
19      public void ejbPassivate()
20      {
21      }
22      public void ejbActivate()
23      {
24      }
25
26      public void setSessionContext(SessionContext ctx)
27      {
28          this.ctx = ctx;
29      }
30
31  }
```

Line 1 of Listing 3.3 declares that this class is part of the package book.chap03.ex3.build. In line 2, we import the classes in the javax.ejb interface.

Line 4 declares that the implementation, HelloBean, implements the SessionBean interface. The SessionBean interface contains the following method signatures:

- public abstract void ejbActivate();
- public abstract void ejbPassivate();
- public abstract void ejbRemove();
- public abstract void setSessionContext(SessionContext ctx);

Because we are using a Session bean, it implements the SessionBean interface. Entity beans (naturally) implement the EntityBean interface. We'll explain the function of each of these methods in due course. For now, note that, because we have declared these methods in the SessionBean interface, we must provide an implementation of them—even if that implementation is merely an empty method.

Line 6 declares a class variable to hold a reference to a SessionContext variable. The bean uses the SessionContext to interact with the container. At this point, you may say, "Hey! I thought that this bean was stateless; why does a stateless bean have a member variable?" In fact, the SessionContext is not a normal member variable. The life cycle of a stateless Session bean has two states: either the bean doesn't exist or it's ready to receive method calls. Each time you create a stateless Session bean, its setSessionContext() method is invoked. The only transition out of the "method ready" state for a stateless Session bean is for the container to destroy the bean. Thus, because the container always invokes setSessionContext() on the bean before it's added to the pool, the stateless Session bean is assured of always having a valid reference to a SessionContext.

At this point, another question may occur to you: "You said that the SessionContext variable is set only once, when the bean is created. In Chapter 2, you said that a stateless Session bean can be invoked by many different clients. So, if the SessionContext is set only once, how can the bean have current information in the SessionContext?" The reference that's passed in setSessionContext() is not simply a static object; rather, it's an interface that allows the EJB class to query its container for the current state. The container is responsible for making sure that when the bean calls getUserTransaction() on its SessionContext, the transaction that is returned applies to the current client.

Line 7 contains the declaration for our ejbCreate() method. This ejbCreate() method corresponds to the create() method declared in the home interface in step 2. When the container generates an implementation for the home interface, it calls a bean's ejbCreate() method for each corresponding create() method in the home interface. The EJB developer must write these ejbCreate() methods. Each ejbCreate() method must follow several rules:

- It must be declared as public.
- It must have a void return type. Even though the create() method returns an object that implements the remote interface, the actual creation of this object is the responsibility of the container.
- The number and type of arguments in an ejbCreate() method must mirror the number and type of arguments in the create() method.

- The ejbCreate() method is not required to throw any exceptions. The java.rmi.RemoteException and javax.ejb.CreateException in the "throws" clause of the create() method are required, because the container may throw these exceptions. The EJB developer can choose to throw these exceptions from an ejbCreate() method, but they are not required. It's also possible to throw arbitrary exceptions from within an ejbCreate() method. In such a case, they must also be declared in the "throws" clause of the corresponding create() method.

Even though our class has no variables that must be initialized within the ejbCreate() method, we must still provide an implementation of it. In fact, a stateless Session bean must have exactly one ejbCreate() method, and it must take no arguments.

Line 11 contains our lone business method. This method signature exactly matches the one declared in our remote interface back in step 1, except that it does not throw a java.rmi.RemoteException. An EJB class can have any number of business methods, as long as each business method has a corresponding declaration in the remote interface.

Line 16 contains an empty implementation of the ejbRemove() method. The container calls this method to notify the EJB instance that it will soon be removed. This strategy allows the instance to take care of any last-minute housekeeping (closing files, writing data, committing transactions) before it passes out of existence.

Line 19 contains an empty implementation of the ejbPassivate() method. The EJB container can swap out EJB instances to temporary storage if necessary. Before the container swaps a Session bean out to temporary storage, it invokes the bean's ejbPassivate() method. The bean then has an opportunity to free up any resources it may be using (for example, if it has an open socket connection, it must close the socket before being passivated).

Line 22 contains an empty implementation of the ejbActivate() method, which is also called by the container. The ejbActivate() method is the inverse of the ejbPassivate() method; the container calls it just after the Session bean has been read back in from temporary storage. This method gives the bean the opportunity to restore any connections that it may need before going back into service.

Line 24 implements the setSessionContext() method of the SessionBean interface. Remember that the SessionContext interface is a special case; it is the only object variable that a stateless Session bean will normally have. (A stateless bean could have other information stored in object variables; for example, a sales tax bean would need to keep a database reference to perform its lookups. The key thing to remember with stateless Session beans is that you should not store conversational state in your beans, because your client does not have a long-term relationship with any particular bean.)

Step 4: Compile the Remote Interface, Home Interface, and Implementation Class

This step is the easiest one so far. Just do javac*.java. If you get any ClassNotFoundExceptions, check your class path to ensure that it includes the javax.ejb package.

Step 5: Create a Session Descriptor

The SessionDescriptor class passes information about your bean to the eventual deployment environment. At development time, the bean developer creates an instance of the SessionDescriptor class, fills it in with information, and then serializes it. At deployment time, the deployer deserializes this instance and uses the information it contains to deploy the bean. Typically, the vendor of your EJB development environment will provide some type of tool for generating descriptors. You must set a few key values in the SessionDescriptor class for the HelloBean:

- Make sure you're creating a SessionDescriptor, and not an EntityDescriptor. Session and Entity beans each have their own descriptor.
- Set the BeanHomeName property to HelloHome. The JNDI naming service will then associate this name with your home interface. Clients will look this name up via JNDI and be presented with a reference to an object implementing your home interface. You can pick any name you like—you could name it "Fred" if you wanted to. The name you associate with your bean in JNDI need not map to a particular class name in your bean.
- Set the EnterpriseBeanClassName property to book.chap03.ex3.build. HelloBean.
- Set the HomeInterfaceClassName to book.chap03.ex3.build. HelloHome.
- Set the RemoteInterfaceClassName to book.chap03.ex3.build.Hello.
- Set the StateManagementType property to STATELESS_SESSION.

As noted earlier, your EJB development environment will likely supply some sort of tool to generate a serialized deployment descriptor. BEA Web-

Xpress's WebLogic product, for example, supplies the class `weblogic.ejb.utils.DDCreator`. This class can be run from the command line

```
java weblogic.ejb.utils.DDCreator <file name>
```

where `<file name>` is the name of the file containing the information that your `SessionDescriptor` or `EntityDescriptor` should contain. The easiest way to create a new descriptor file is to start with an old one and modify it to suit your needs. If you're using WebLogic, you can say

```
java weblogic.ejb.utils.DDCreator -example
```

The DDCreator utility will then spit out a sample file in the proper format. Taking this file as a starting point, simply adjust the various properties until they reflect your desired attributes, and then run the DDCreator utility on the file to create a serialized deployment descriptor that contains the appropriate information.

If your development environment does not include a tool that can be used to generate deployment descriptors, you can create your own descriptors by writing a Java program to fill in the values of a `SessionDescriptor` class and then serialize the class. Listing 3.4 is a brief example program that does just that:

Listing 3.4 Java Program to Provide Values for and Serialize a
SessionDescriptor Class

```
1    import javax.ejb.deployment.*;
2    import java.io.*;
3    import java.util.Properties;
4
5    public class DDWrite
6    {
7        public static void main (String argv[])
8        {
9            System.out.println("This program creates a
             serialized deployment descriptor");
10           SessionDescriptor sd = new SessionDescriptor();
11
12           //set bean class name
13           sd.setEnterpriseBeanClassName("book.chap03.
             ex3.build.Hello");
14
15           //set home interface name
16           sd.setHomeInterfaceClassName("book.chap03.ex3.
             build.HelloHome");
17
18           //set remote interface class name
19           sd.setRemoteInterfaceClassName("book.chap03.ex3.
             build.HelloRemote");
20
21           //set environment properties
```

```
22          Properties p = new Properties();
23          p.put("myprop1," "myval");
24          sd.setEnvironmentProperties(p);
25          //session-specific entries
26
27          //session timeout -- value in seconds (0 means use
            container-specific timeout)
28          sd.setSessionTimeout(0);
29
30          //state management type -- stateless or stateful
31          sd.setStateManagementType(SessionDescriptor.
            STATELESS_SESSION);
32
33          try
34          {
35          FileOutputStream fos = new FileOutputStream
            ("foo.ser");
36          ObjectOutputStream oos = new ObjectOutputStream
            (fos);
37          oos.writeObject(sd);
38          oos.close();
39          }
40          catch (IOException ioe)
41          {
42              System.out.println("Error writing serialized
                deployment descriptor: " + ioe);
43          }
44
45      }
46  }
```

NOTE: This is just an example; to use it, you'll need to change the information in this class to correspond to your bean.

In line 10, the program creates a new instance of the `SessionDescriptor` class. In lines 12–18, the program sets the name of the bean's class and the names of its home and remote interfaces. At deployment time, the vendor's tools can use `Class.forName()` to load instances of these classes, and can then use introspection on these classes to determine their method names.

Lines 21–24 create a `java.util.Properties` object, and set the property `myprop1` to the value `myval`. The EJB container must make these properties available to your beans at runtime and should also allow you to edit them during the deployment process. Properties are a useful mechanism for encapsulating any outside references that your bean may require at runtime. For example, if your bean must obtain a reference to another bean, it will need to use JNDI (or CORBA COS naming, but let's stick to JNDI for the moment). To get a JNDI InitialContext, you must tell JNDI where to obtain an initial context. You accomplish this task by setting the environment property `java.naming.factory.initial` to point to a suitable InitialContextFactory. (A factory is a class whose sole purpose is to create and return instances of another class. The factory idiom is often used in the JDK specification; for example, `java.rmi.server.RMISocketFactory` is used to create RMI sockets, and the Swing package includes several factory classes for the creation of graphical objects.) Setting the `java.naming.factory.initial` property allows you to avoid hard-coding a reference to the initial context factory, which allows for more flexibility in deployment.

Line 28 sets the timeout value for the session bean to 0, thereby instructing the container to use its default value for timeouts. Line 31 instructs the container that this bean is a stateless Session bean. The container must be told whether the bean is stateless or stateful, because the life cycles of stateless and stateful beans differ. Session bean life cycles are examined in detail in Chapter 4; for now, it's sufficient to say that a stateless bean has a much simpler life cycle than a stateful bean. If the container wants to swap out a stateful bean, it must first serialize the bean to some type of persistent store, so that the bean can be reinitialized when it is needed again. On the other hand, if the container needs to discard a stateless Session bean, it can simply get rid of it.

Lines 33–43 create the serialized deployment descriptor. Line 35 opens a file output stream to a file named foo.ser—this file will contain the serialized deployment descriptor. Line 36 wraps the `FileOutputStream` object with an `ObjectOutputStream` object. Line 37 invokes the `ObjectOutputStream`'s `writeObject()` method, which performs the actual serialization. Line 38 closes the file, and the program then exits.

After running this program, you should find a file named foo.ser on your disk. This file should contain a serialized deployment descriptor.

Step 6: Create a Manifest

A manifest file is a text document that contains information about the contents of a jar file. Actually, the **jar** utility will automatically create a manifest file even if none exists. For an ejb-jar file, however, you must include a pair of lines similar to the following:

```
Name: book/chap03/ex3/build/HelloBeanDD.ser
Enterprise-Bean: True
```

These lines must be present for each EJB bean in the jar file. They notify the container that they represent an Enterprise JavaBean. Note that the `Name:` field includes the full package name of the file.

The information in your manifest will be added into the standard set of information created by the jar program. Don't be surprised if, after you create your ejb-jar file, the manifest file that it contains includes more information than you included in your manifest file.

Step 7: Create an ejb-jar File

Use the jar program that comes with the Java JDK to generate your ejb-jar file. The invocation looks much like the following line:

```
jar cmf book\chap03\ex3\build\manifest hello.jar book\chap03\
ex3\build
```

where
jar = The program name
cmf = The options (c = create; m = include manifest; f = file name)
book\chap03\ex3\build\manifest = The path from the current directory
                                 to the manifest
hello.jar = The name of the jar file to deploy
book\chap03\ex3\build = The directory to include in the jar file

The end result is an ejb-jar file suitable for deployment. At this point, you must switch roles—from being an EJB developer to being a deployer. It's time to deploy the bean.

Step 8: Deploy the ejb-jar File

The deployment process will vary slightly, depending on which EJB implementation you use. We'll use BEA WebXpress's WebLogic application server here, so we'll describe the steps taken to deploy a bean in WebLogic. For specific instructions on how to deploy a bean in a particular EJB implementation, consult your vendor's documentation. Typically, the vendor will provide some type of deployment tool that examines either the jar file itself or the serialized deployment descriptor contained therein, generates any additional classes required to run the bean (for example, implementations of the home and remote interfaces), and installs the bean in the server's class path.

In WebLogic, the tool used to deploy a bean is a Java class called weblogic.ejbc ("ejbc" stands for EJB compiler). This program takes the name of a serialized deployment descriptor as argument and performs the following steps:

- Creating additional classes, such as the implementation classes for the home and remote interfaces

- Moving your EJB classes to the appropriate directory in the WebLogic server's class path.

After running ejbc on your deployment descriptor, you must undertake one final step to deploy your beans in WebLogic. In the top-level directory in which you installed WebLogic (on the author's machine, this directory is c:\weblogic), you'll find a file called weblogic.properties. It contains information and directives that the WebLogic server reads when it is started up. Set the property weblogic.ejb.deploy to point to your deployed jar file. The weblogic.ejb.deploy property should already exist in the file, but it is initially commented out; simply do a text search for it, uncomment it (remove the "#" character at the beginning of the line) and add a reference to your ejb-jar file to it.

After you've modified the weblogic.ejb.deploy property to include a reference to your ejb-jar file, start the server (say t3server on the command line). The server should then load your EJB and make it ready for use.

Step 9: Write a Client

Now that the bean is in place on the server, it's time to write a client. EJB clients can be written using RMI or CORBA. For this example, we'll use the RMI approach in Listing 3.5. Both approaches will be described in detail in Chapter 6.

Listing 3.5 Client Written with the RMI Approach

```
1   import book.chap03.ex3.build.*;
2   import java.rmi.*;
3   import javax.naming.*;
4
5   public class HelloClient{
6
7   public static void main(String[] args) {
8
9   try
10  {
11  InitialContext ic = new InitialContext();
12  HelloHome home = (HelloHome) ic.lookup("HelloHome");
13  Hello hel = home.create();
14  String retval = hel.sayHello("Tom Valesky");
15  System.out.println("returned: " + retval);
16  hel.remove();
17  }
18  catch (java.rmi.RemoteException e)
19  {
20      System.out.println("remote exception occurred:" + e);
21  }
22  catch (javax.ejb.CreateException e)
23  {
```

```
24        System.out.println("create exception occurred:" + e);
25    }
26  catch (javax.ejb.RemoveException e)
27  {
28        System.out.println("remove exception occurred:" + e);
29    }
30  catch (javax.naming.NamingException e)
31  {
32        System.out.println("naming exception occurred:" + e);
33    }
34  }
35  }
```

In keeping with the tone of this example, we have written a very simple client. It has virtually no user interface; it simply invokes our business method, prints the results to standard output, and then exits. At first glance, it might seem that such a limited client has no use. In reality, this sort of simple client is very useful in the development process as a test:

- Because the client is simple, it can be put together quickly. As a result, you don't have to build the user interface portion of your system before doing any testing.
- You can build a suite of test cases that exercise your methods, and then run through all the test cases by running the client. For example, a suite of test cases for the program in this chapter might include a call to sayHello() with a null string as the argument, and a call to sayHello() with a really long string as the argument. A suite of test cases represents a valuable tool in ensuring that incremental changes in your bean's code do not break other features. Developing a suite of test cases is relatively simple in EJB; you simply implement calls to your various business methods, passing them the various arguments they require.
- In the event that problems emerge with the full-blown client, you can run the test client as a sanity check to isolate the problem as occurring on the server or the client.

Let's go through Listing 3.5 line by line. Line 1 is simply the package declaration. Line 2 imports the RMI classes. Line 3 imports the JNDI classes. This client uses JNDI to look up a reference to our EJB object's home interface, so we must include this package. In line 11, we create a class of type javax.naming.InitialContext(). The InitialContext class serves as the client's interface to JNDI; it can contain bindings to a variety of naming services (JNDI, CORBA COS, DNS, and so on). The InitialContext class provides the client with a single interface that can be used to link to any naming services in the client's environment that support JNDI. This statement can throw a `javax.naming.NamingException` if it cannot complete; this exception is caught in the catch block in lines 30–33.

Line 12 uses the `InitialContext` class to perform a lookup on the name `HelloHome` (the name of the home interface in this example). JNDI searches its namespace for an occurrence of this name and returns the object to which this name has been bound. In our case, the object is a generated object that implements the `HelloHome` interface.

One of the container's deployment-time tasks is to create a JNDI name that is bound to an implementation of the bean's home interface. The bean developer includes such a name in the deployment descriptor, but the deployer has the final say as to what the interface's JNDI name will be. Because the `InitialContext.lookup()` call returns an object of type `Object`, we must cast it into a variable that can hold a reference to our home interface before using it. The syntax is as follows:

```
HelloHome home = (HelloHome) ic.lookup("HelloHome");
```

According to the EJB specifications, the following syntax should be used:

```
HelloHome home =
javax.rmi.PortableRemoteObject.narrow(ic.lookup("HelloHome,"
HelloHome.class);
```

Unfortunately, at the time this book was written, the PortableRemote-Object syntax was not available. Thus a simple cast is used instead.

Line 13 invokes the `create()` method on the home interface to obtain a reference to an object that implements our bean's remote interface. The EJB container generates this object as part of the deployment process.

After invoking the `create()` method, we can then invoke any necessary business methods. In line 14, we invoke our sole business method, `sayHello()`, with the argument string `"Tom Valesky"`, and receive the return value of this method.

Now that we have finished the bean, we use the `remove()` method in line 16 to tell the container to discard it. Session beans will eventually go away on their own, either as a result of their timeout period expiring or as a result of a server crash or shutdown. Nevertheless, the best strategy is to invoke the `remove()` method of an object when you no longer need it; this approach allows the server to free up the Session bean and any of its associated resources.

Following the logic are a number of catch blocks to handle any exceptions that might be thrown in the process of looking up, creating, conversing with, and removing the remote bean. Lines 18–21 catch the `java.rmi.RemoteException`. Recall that this exception can be thrown at any time during a remote conversation; typically, it indicates that some sort of communication problem has occurred between your client and the server. Lines 22–25 catch the `javax.ejb.CreateException`. Either the bean or the container can throw this exception if a problem occurs during the creation of a bean. The `javax.ejb.RemoveException` handled in lines 26–30 is a similar exception; it can be thrown either by the bean or by the container if a problem occurs during the removal of a bean. Lines 30–33 handle the `javax.naming.NamingException`; this exception can be thrown during the creation of the JNDI `InitialContext` or during the lookup step.

Step 10: Run the Client

JNDI will need to know where it can find an `InitialContextFactory`. It finds this information in the environment property `java.naming.factory.initial`. In this example, we simply pass a value for this property as a command-line argument. Here's the invocation of the client:

```
java -Djava.naming.factory.initial=weblogic.jndi.
T3InitialContextFactory
HelloClient
```

Your client should run and print the following message:

```
returned: Hello there, Tom Valesky
```

Feel free to substitute your own name if you like.

Note that your client must be able to find the following classes in its class path:

- Your bean's home interface
- Your bean's remote interface
- The `javax.naming.InitialContext` class
- The stub classes generated by the deployment process to handle communication

You have several options for making these classes available to your client program:

- You can include them with your code and write an installer routine to set everything up on the client.
- In an intranet environment, you can establish the application and its associated classes on a shared file server and then make sure that the users include the file server's directories in their CLASSPATH.
- If you've written an applet, you can simply include the classes as part of the CODEBASE.

What's Really Going on Here?

To this point, we have discussed the communication between the client and the server at a fairly high level. Now let's move to a somewhat lower level and discuss what really happens when you call a method on a remote object. The diagram in Figure 3.1 shows the entities involved in an EJB conversation as well as the role that each entity plays.

1. In your client program, you invoke a remote method on a remote interface.

2. The method invocation goes to a client-side stub (a proxy object that implements the remote interface), which serializes the arguments and sends them over the wire. The process of serializing the arguments into a form suitable for transmission over the network is called **marshalling**. This marshalling process has several implications:

- Any variables that you pass as arguments to a remote object must obey the rules for RMI serialization. Additionally, any classes contained within those classes obey the same rules. Breaking these rules will cause an exception to be thrown.
- Because all argument classes and their contents must be serialized and sent over the wire, it's best to keep these classes as small and simple as possible. Serializing and passing a large object remotely can be an expensive process in terms of time and resources.

Objects are sent over the wire as a stream of bytes.

3. The arguments are received by a skeleton on the remote host, which deserializes the arguments and passes them to the EJBObject. The skeleton is the server-side counterpart of the stub; it is usually generated automatically during the deployment process. It receives the stream of bytes generated by the client-side stub and transforms them back into Java objects (a process called **unmarshalling**). The **EJBObject** here is the class that implements your remote interface; the container generates it as part of the deployment process. Acting as a proxy for client requests, the EJBObject interposes between the client and the EJB object. This approach allows the server to better manage incoming calls to the EJB object and gives the server a place to handle the automated transaction features of EJB.

4. The EJB object, in turn, calls the actual method on your bean. Your method then does any necessary processing and eventually returns.

5. When the method returns, the return value is passed to the EJBObject. When the EJBObject invokes the bean by a method call, it receives the return value as it would any normal return value.

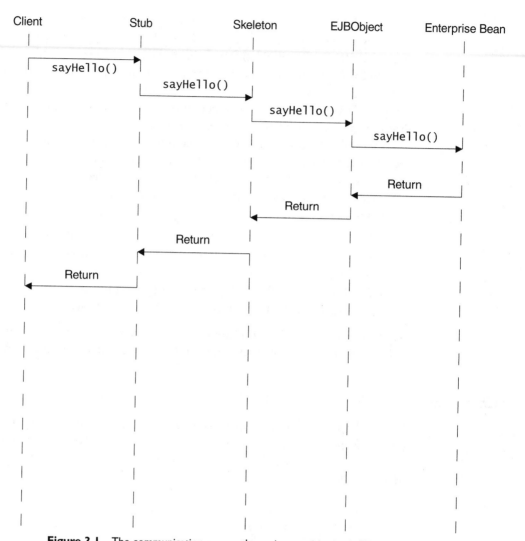

Figure 3.1 The communication among the various entities in an EJB system during the course of a method call. Note: The division between the stub and the skeleton is also the division between the client platform and the remote EJB platform.

6. The EJBObject passes the return value to the skeleton. Again, it receives the return value after the method has finished executing.

7. The skeleton serializes the return value and sends it over the wire to the stub.

8. The stub deserializes the return value (that is, converts it back to a Java object) and returns it to the calling routine.

Both RMI and CORBA use a similar process. In general, the stubs and skeletons are generated automatically. In RMI, you simply run a program called rmic (for "RMI compiler") on your Java classes to generate stubs and skeletons. In CORBA, you describe your interfaces in IDL and then use an IDL compiler to generate your stubs and skeletons automatically. Typically, if you're using a CORBA-based EJB implementation, your vendor will provide a tool to directly translate your EJB interfaces into IDL.

Tools like rmic usually do not maintain their generated .java files after they've generated the necessary .class files. If you would like to examine your stubs and skeletons, most tools include a "keepgenerated" option that tells the tool to leave the .java classes in place. It is not a good idea to modify these files for two reasons:

- The container will assume that the generated files will behave as they were generated to behave; if you modify this behavior, unforeseen side effects may result.
- Modifying these files will unnecessarily complicate your life; it's best to just allow the container to generate them automatically.

Nevertheless, if you're curious about how the serialization and invocation procedures are actually implemented, it's instructive to examine these files.

Conclusion

In this chapter, we've implemented a very basic EJB bean. More importantly, we've covered the implementation steps in great detail. Now that we've built a basic bean and understand how it works, we're ready to discuss Session beans in greater detail.

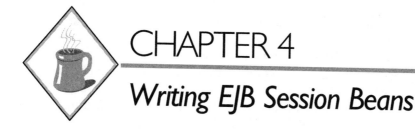

CHAPTER 4

Writing EJB Session Beans

This chapter will focus on Session beans. The EJB 1.0 specification requires support for Session beans; support for Entity beans will not be required until EJB 2.0. Therefore, you can be sure that any EJB container will implement Session beans. Apparently, few EJB containers will not implement support for Entity beans. Nevertheless, Session and Entity beans are useful for different circumstances, so it is best to have a good understanding of both.

When to Use Session Beans

In designing an EJB application, when should you use a Session bean? Typically, you would employ a Session bean in any situation where you might currently use an RPC mechanism such as RMI or CORBA. Session beans are intended to allow the application author to easily implement portions of application code in middleware and to simplify access to this code. Entity beans are essentially a transactional object persistence mechanism; if you don't need to save your object's state to persistent storage, you'd typically use Session beans.

Constraints on Session Beans

Enterprise JavaBeans in general must abide by a series of constraints. These constraints are listed in section 16.4 of the EJB specification. Some of these constraints are described below.

- Enterprise JavaBeans cannot start new threads or use thread synchronization primitives. At first, this restriction may seem onerous, but remember that the EJB container is responsible for creating and managing new bean instances. Even though EJB beans are not allowed to spawn threads themselves, the container can run multiple beans concurrently. In fact, the prohibition against usage of threads exists to prevent the bean from interfering with the container's management of its beans. In EJB, you can obtain multithreaded behavior without writing multithreaded code, which is famously hard to debug. This situation is a big win.

- Enterprise JavaBeans cannot directly access the underlying transaction manager. Again, this restriction arises because the container has the responsibility for managing transactions. One minor exception to this rule exists: a bean that declares its transaction management to be `TX_BEAN_MANAGED` is allowed to use a `javax.jts.UserTransaction` to manage the state of its own transaction.

- Similarly, a bean with any sort of transaction support enabled (that is, with a transaction attribute other than `TX_NOT_SUPPORTED`) cannot use the JDBC commit and rollback primitives. Again, this constraint exists because the container is responsible for issuing the commit and roll-back instructions for transaction-enabled beans. A bean with a transaction attribute of `TX_NOT_SUPPORTED`, however, can use JDBC commit or rollback, because no external transaction manager exists.

- Enterprise JavaBeans are not allowed to change their `java.security.Identity` at runtime. This identity is typically set up at deployment time by the system administrator; disallowing runtime changes to it is intended to prevent malicious beans from acquiring unintended privileges. The `java.security.Identity` class is deprecated in Java 2 and will likely be replaced in a future release of the spec. For more current information, refer to the online supplement for this book.

- Enterprise JavaBeans cannot have read/write static variables. That is, if you put a static variable into an EJB bean, it must be "static final."

In addition to these generic restrictions on Enterprise JavaBeans, the author of a Session bean must be aware of some other constraints. For example, Session beans can irrevocably disappear from the server in one of three cases:

- If the Session bean's timeout value (configured as part of the deployment process) expires
- If the server crashes and is restarted
- If the server is shut down and restarted

If any of these events occurs, any state information that was contained in your Session bean instance is irrevocably lost. Actually, this problem is not as bad as it sounds. First, the Session timeout value is configurable—you can set your timeout value to a long period, perhaps hours or even days. Second, server crashes and restarts should be fairly rare events. Finally, for cases where the state of a Session bean is fairly trivial in nature (for example, when the Session bean is used to handle a fill-in order form or survey), you might simply notify the user that a nonrecoverable error has occurred and ask the user to try again later. If that approach is unacceptable, two other options exist. First, you could cache a copy of the state of the Session bean in your client, and try to recreate a new bean in the event that the original bean dies. To accomplish this task, you must supply an appropriate `ejbCreate()` method that takes all the necessary parameters to restore state. A second option is to use a database on the server side to hold the state of the client's conversation. If the Session bean dies during a conversation, the client can reconnect and pass in a unique customer identifier into an `ejbCreate()` method. The bean can then use this unique identifier to query the database to retrieve whatever state information was saved prior to the failure of the Session bean.

A related issue of which you should be aware is the fact that a Session bean's state is not transactional. That is, if you begin a transaction, modify a Session bean's internal state, and then roll back the transaction, the rollback will not affect the Session bean's internal state. You must manually reset the Session bean's state to whatever it was before the transaction began.

A stateless Session bean cannot implement the SessionSynchronization interface. This interface is intended to provide a Session bean with hooks into the transaction process, thereby enabling it to synchronize its internal state with the database as the transaction progresses. Because stateless Session beans lack a conversational state and cannot hold a transaction across method invocations, it would be superfluous to implement this interface in a stateless Session bean.

A final constraint on Session beans is that they are not reentrant. That is, if one thread is currently using a Session bean, the container will throw a `java.rmi.RemoteException` in response to any other requests to connect to the Session bean.

Session Bean Life Cycle

Stateful Session beans and stateless Session beans have two very different life cycles. First, let's examine the life cycle of a stateless Session bean.

Figure 4.1 shows the life cycle of a stateless Session bean. As can be seen, the stateless Session bean has only two states:

- Nonexistence
- Method-ready state

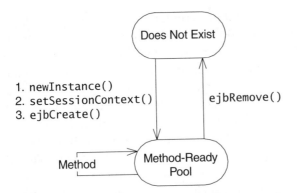

1. newInstance()
2. setSessionContext()
3. ejbCreate()

ejbRemove()

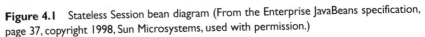

Figure 4.1 Stateless Session bean diagram (From the Enterprise JavaBeans specification, page 37, copyright 1998, Sun Microsystems, used with permission.)

When you create a stateless Session bean, the container calls the following methods on it:

- newInstance(), which allocates space for the bean and brings it into existence
- setSessionContext(), which gives the bean a SessionContext
- ejbCreate(), which allows the bean to perform any necessary initializations

The last two methods deserve some additional commentary. First, because stateless Session beans have no state, they can be reused by many clients in the course of their existence. So how can setSessionContext(), which is called only once, be valid for subsequent invocations? When several EJB implementers were asked this question, they indicated that the SessionContext that is passed in is not a stand-alone class containing static information; rather, it points to a dynamic object that the container updates each time a stateless Session bean's methods are invoked. Thus, even though your bean is stateless, you retain access to the useful methods of the SessionContext interface.

With respect to the ejbCreate() method, a stateless Session bean can have only one such method, and it must take no arguments. Remember that the ejbCreate() method is essentially analogous to a constructor for Enterprise JavaBeans; it initializes an instance's internal state variables. Because a stateless Session EJB has no client-specific state variables, it does not require any arguments.

Looking at the end of the life of a stateless Session bean, we see that the container invokes the ejbRemove() method of the bean before destroying it. You could potentially use the ejbCreate() and ejbRemove() methods to create and destroy any socket or database connections that your stateless bean might require. Otherwise, `ejbCreate()` and `ejbRemove()` can simply be methods with no implementations.

One interesting aspect of the life cycle of a stateless Session bean is that, even though a client invokes a `create()` method to gain access to a stateless Session bean and a `remove()` method to relinquish this access, these methods do not necessarily result in an actual instance being created or removed in the container. Typically, the container will maintain a pool of stateless Session beans. This pool will be large enough to ensure that any client that needs to invoke a method receives an instance on which to do so; because stateless Session beans can be shared, however, the number of stateless Session beans in existence at any point in time may be smaller than the number of clients. That is, if a client is not currently invoking a method, it does not remain associated with a particular Session bean, so the pool of available Session beans needs to be merely large enough to handle all clients that concurrently invoke methods. Typically, this number will be much smaller than the total number of clients in existence, which should potentially allow stateless Session EJBs to handle a larger number of clients than stateful Session beans, given the same resources. The system administrator will normally set the number of stateless Session beans in the instance pool, adjusting this number as necessary to provide the required level of service. A container might also manage the pool of instances itself, creating and removing instances as necessary to serve the current client load.

The life cycle of a stateful Session bean (depicted in Figure 4.2) is a bit more complex. At initial creation, the container invokes the same three methods that are invoked on a stateless Session bean:

- `newInstance()`, which allocates space for the bean and brings it into existence
- `setSessionContext()`, which gives the bean a `SessionContext`
- `ejbCreate()`, which allows the bean to perform any necessary initializations

The only difference in these method invocations is that a stateful Session bean can implement any of several `ejbCreate()` methods that take different sets of arguments. Only one of the available `ejbCreate()` methods will be invoked at creation time, however. Within the `ejbCreate()` method, you set the various class variables of your EJB bean; also, if your bean requires any special socket or database connections, you can initially establish them in the `ejbCreate()` method.

Once the `ejbCreate()` method executes, the bean enters the "method-ready" state. It remains in this state as long as only nontransactional methods are invoked on it (that is, if the bean or its method specifies a transaction

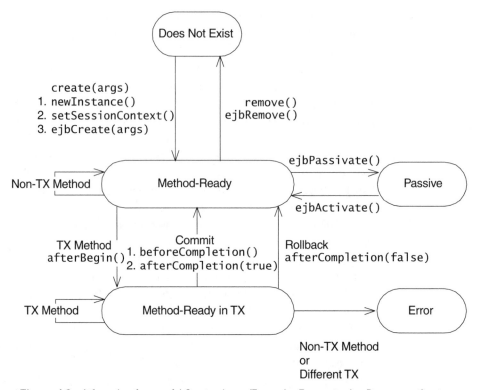

Figure 4.2 Life cycle of a stateful Session bean (From the Enterprise JavaBeans specification, page 29, copyright 1998, Sun Microsystems, used with permission.)

declarator of TX_NOT_SUPPORTED, or if it specifies TX_SUPPORTS and is invoked by a client that does not currently have an open transaction).

Three transitions out of this state are possible:

- The bean can enter a transaction.
- It can be passivated.
- It can be removed.

The bean enters a transaction if one of its transactional methods is invoked (a transactional method is a method with a transaction declarator of TX_BEAN_MANAGED, TX_REQUIRED, TX_REQUIRES_NEW, TX_MANDATORY, or, if the caller has a transaction in effect, TX_SUPPORTS). If the bean implements the SessionSynchronization interface, the container invokes its afterBegin() method to notify it that it is entering a transaction. The bean then moves to the "method-ready in transaction" state, where it remains until the transaction concludes. If the transaction was created specifically for the method invocation, the bean will exit the "method-ready in transaction" state immediately after the completion of the method. If the client supplied the transaction, or if the bean itself has created a transaction that will last across method invocations (possible with a TX_BEAN_MANAGED bean), the bean remains in this state until a commit or rollback occurs.

If a commit occurs while the bean is in the "method-ready in transaction" state, the beforeCompletion() method of the SessionSynchronization interface is invoked, and then the afterCompletion() method of the Session-Synchronization interface is invoked with a Boolean value of true as the argument. This sequence of invocations allows the bean to perform any database updates before the transaction commits, and provides it with definitive notification that the transaction has successfully committed. After these methods finish, the bean returns to the "method-ready" state.

If, on the other hand, a rollback occurs while the bean is in the "method-ready in transaction" state, beforeCompletion() is not invoked; rather, afterCompletion() is invoked with a Boolean argument of false. This sequence of events notifies the bean that the transaction has definitely been rolled back and allows it to reset its internal state to what it was prior to the transaction. As noted earlier, the bean's internal state can be reset either from an internal state cache initialized in the afterBegin() method or from an underlying database.

If a bean is in the "method-ready in transaction" state, you should not attempt to call the bean in a different transaction context or with no transaction. Calling a bean with a different transaction context could happen if a client has passed its transaction context to the bean (for example, if the bean has transaction attributes of TX_REQUIRED or TX_SUPPORTS), creates a second transaction, and then makes a call to the bean with the second transaction as the transaction context.

The second transition out of the "method-ready" state for the bean involves passivation. (A bean in the "method-ready in transaction" state cannot be passivated; only beans in the "method-ready" state are subject to passivation.) When a bean is passivated, the container invokes its ejbPassivate() method and then writes it out to some type of persistent storage; it also removes the bean from memory. If you have opened any database or socket connections in your ejbCreate() method, you should include code in the ejbPassivate() method to close these connections; a bean cannot maintain open database or socket connections when it is passivated. Later, when the bean is returned to active duty, the container invokes the bean's ejbActivate() method; you can reestablish any database or socket connections in this method.

The final transition out of the "method-ready" state is caused by the removal of the bean. Unlike stateless Session beans, stateful Session beans are actually removed by the container in response to a client's call to the remove() method on the bean's remote interface. Before removing the bean, the container calls the bean's ejbRemove() method, which gives it one last opportunity to write out database updates before it passes out of existence. Also, if the bean has any open socket or database connections, the ejbRemove() method should close these connections. After ejbRemove() has executed, the bean is destroyed and cannot be resurrected. (Of course, you can create another bean and pass arguments to its ejbCreate() method such that the internal state of the bean matches that of the bean that has been removed; even though the new bean is functionally identical to the old bean, it is in fact new.)

Transactions and EJB

Table 4.1 shows the various transaction specifiers, illustrating which transaction is in effect in various situations. The table includes two rows for each type of transaction support. The first row indicates what occurs if the client calls the bean without a transaction context; the second row indicates what happens if the client calls the bean with a transaction in effect. The following rules apply.

TX_NOT_SUPPORTED means that the bean should never be called within a transaction. If the client calls the bean without a transaction in effect, the bean method is invoked. If the client calls the bean while the client has a transaction

Table 4.1   Transactions

Transaction Attribute	Client's Transaction	Enterprise Bean's Transaction
TX_NOT_SUPPORTED	None	None
TX_NOT_SUPPORTED	T1	None
TX_REQUIRED	None	T2
TX_REQUIRED	T1	T1
TX_SUPPORTS	None	None
TX_SUPPORTS	T1	T1
TX_REQUIRES_NEW	None	T2
TX_REQUIRES_NEW	T1	T2
TX_MANDATORY	None	Error
TX_MANDATORY	T1	T1

T1 and T2 represent two different transactions.
From the Enterprise JavaBeans specification, page 102, copyright 1998, Sun Microsystems, used with permission.

in effect, the container suspends the client's transaction temporarily, invokes the bean method, and, after the method has finished executing, resumes the client's transaction.

TX_REQUIRED means that the bean's methods must always be invoked within a transaction. If the client does not currently have a transaction in effect, the container creates a new transaction, invokes the method within the transaction, and then terminates the transaction prior to returning to the client. If the client does have a transaction in effect, it serves as the transaction context for the bean's method invocation.

TX_SUPPORTS means that the bean can be invoked in a client-supplied transaction context. If the client does not supply a transaction context, it invokes the bean's method with no transaction context (as in TX_NOT_SUPPORTED). If the client supplies a transaction context, this context is used as the transaction context for the bean's method (as in TX_REQUIRED, when the client supplies a transaction context).

TX_REQUIRES_NEW means that the bean's method must always be invoked in a new transaction context. If the client has not supplied a transaction context, the EJB container creates a new one. If the client has supplied a transaction context, the container creates a new one anyway, suspending the client's transaction context until the bean's transaction has been completed.

TX_MANDATORY means that the client is required to supply a transaction context. If the client attempts to invoke a TX_MANDATORY bean without a transaction context, the container will throw a TransactionRequiredException to the client. If the client supplies a transaction context, the bean will use this context to invoke the method.

TX_BEAN_MANAGED is a bit of a special case. Table 4.2 displays four potential situations applying to it:

Table 4.2   TX_BEAN_MANAGED Transactions

Client's Transaction	Instance's Current Transaction	Transaction Used by Method
None	None	None
T1	None	None
None	T3	T3
T1	T3	T3

T1 and T3 represent different transactions.
From the Enterprise JavaBeans specification, page 103, copyright 1998, Sun Microsystems, used with permission.

- In the first case, neither the client nor the bean has a transaction context open. The bean's method is therefore invoked without a transaction context.
- In the second case, the client has a transaction context open, but the bean does not. The client's transaction is suspended, and the bean is invoked with no transaction context.
- In the third case, the client has no transaction context open, but the bean does. The bean's method is invoked in its own transaction context.
- In the fourth case, the client has a transaction context open, as does the bean. The client's transaction is suspended, the method is invoked in the bean's transaction context, and the client's transaction context is resumed after the method completes.

TX_BEAN_MANAGED transactions also differ depending on whether the Session bean is either stateful or stateless:

- A stateful bean can maintain an open transaction across method invocations. That is, it can open a transaction in one method, respond to several method invocations within that transaction, and then close the transaction in yet another method. In this situation, the container suspends the bean's transaction context after each invoked method completes, then resumes it when the next method is invoked.
- A stateless bean cannot maintain an open transaction across method invocations. Stateless Session beans can potentially be invoked by many different clients during the course of their life, so it would be erroneous to attempt to maintain an open transaction context across different method invocations. If a stateless bean uses transactions, each transaction must either commit or roll back before the method returns.

Stateful Session Bean Example

Enough talk—let's see some code. The first example in this chapter will implement a stateful Session bean for online shopping. Despite its familiarity, the online shopping example is truly valuable for demonstrating the functionality of a Session bean. Just to be different, though, we'll call our shopping receptacle a bag instead of a cart.

Requirements

Before delving into coding, we should nail down some requirements:

- It should provide the client with a way to retrieve a list of inventory items.
- It should allow the user to order items.
- It should allow the user to remove an item from the shopping bag.
- The system should remain relatively small and straightforward.
- It should interact with an underlying inventory database.
- The user should be able to order one or more of an item.
- The user should be able to query the system to obtain the current contents of the shopping bag.
- The user should not be allowed to place an order if the item is not currently in stock.
- The user should be able to set up the billing information in a database, so that he or she does not have to enter it each time.

Design

From these requirements, some of the necessary methods are readily apparent:

- A getInventory() method should query the inventory database and present a list of available products. To simplify matters, part of this list will consist of a unique identifier that we can use later to look up or order items.
- An orderItem() method will take an item identifier code as its argument. Because orders for one customer shouldn't end up as part of another customer's order, we'll need a unique identifier for each customer.
- A removeItem() method will remove a particular item from the shopping bag.
- A getBagContents() method will return a listing of all items currently in the shopping bag.
- A createCustomer() method will enter a new customer into the database. This method will return an account number for the customer.
- A finalizeOrder() method will execute the order once the customer is satisfied with the shopping bag's contents.

From the above, it is apparent that we'll need several database tables. An INVENTORY table will contain one row for each available product. For each product, the table will hold:

- A string that describes the product
- A unique code that identifies the product
- A field that contains the quantity of the product currently in stock
- The price for one unit of the product

The following data definition language is used to create the INVENTORY table:

```
create table INVENTORY (
ITEMCODE VARCHAR(5) ,
ITEMDESC VARCHAR(64) ,
QUANTITY SMALLINT ,
PRICE DOUBLE PRECISION );
```

In this definition,

- ITEMCODE is a unique code for each product in the inventory database.
- ITEMDESC is the textual description of the item. This field will be used in a future client program to display user-friendly descriptions of the items.
- QUANTITY contains the number of items in stock.
- PRICE contains the price per item.

This table's primary key is ITEMCODE.

A CUSTOMERS table contains the following items:

- A unique identifier for each customer
- The customer's name
- The customer's address

The data definition language used for the CUSTOMERS table follows:

```
create table CUSTOMERS (
CUST_ID SMALLINT ,
CUST_NAME VARCHAR(64) ,
CUST_ADDR VARCHAR(64) );
```

In this definition,

- CUST_ID is a unique identifier for each customer.
- CUST_NAME is a field that can contain the customer's name.
- CUST_ADDR is a field that can contain the customer's address.

In this example, CUST_NAME and CUST_ADDR are really just placeholders to demonstrate the association between the customer ID and whatever data you'd like to store about the customer. For a production database, for example, you'd probably separate the CUST_NAME field into first name, last name, and middle initial, and the CUST_ADDR field into street address, possibly apartment number, city, state, and ZIP code.

The CUSTOMERS table's primary key is CUST_ID, which the system generates for each new customer. Customers who have previously used the online shopping system can access it again by passing in their customer ID.

An ORDERS table contains the following items:

- The customer's ID code from the CUSTOMERS table
- The product's ID from the INVENTORY table
- The quantity of the item ordered

The data definition language for the ORDERS table follows:

```
create table ORDERS (
CUST_ID SMALLINT ,
ITEMCODE VARCHAR(5) ,
QUANTITY SMALLINT );
```

The ORDERS table uses the foreign key CUST_ID from the CUSTOMERS table and the foreign key ITEMCODE from the INVENTORY table to form a composite key.

To keep our tables nicely normalized, we won't include any field in the ORDERS table that indicates the cost. Upon creation of the bill, we can find the price of the item via a lookup on the INVENTORY table.

Implementation

The first implementation step is to create the home and remote interfaces. Let's look at the home interface first.

The Home Interface

Appendix A provides the full source code for the home interface. Additionally, all source code for the examples in this book can be found on the accompanying CD-ROM.

The home interface for the bag bean provides method signatures for two different create() methods that can be used by the client. The first,

```
public Bag create(int custID) throws RemoteException,
CreateException;
```

is used for customers who have used the system previously and received a customer ID. The second,

```
public Bag create(String custname, String custaddr) throws
RemoteException, CreateException;
```

is used for brand-new customers; the implementation behind this method must allocate a new customer ID and populate the CUSTOMERS table with the information that has been passed to this create() method. Note that both of these methods are declared as throwing both RemoteException and CreateException. Even if your own code does not throw these exceptions, the container itself may throw them during the course of object creation, so you must declare your create() methods as throwing them.

The Remote Interface

Several methods are required as part of the remote interface. For example the getInventory() method returns an array of InventoryItem classes representing all the items in inventory at the present time. (In the real world, you probably wouldn't want to return a listing of your entire inventory to a client; more likely, several methods would return different elements of the inventory.) The InventoryItem class is a simple data structure with no real behavior. Note, however, that it implements both the java.io.Serializable interface and the java.lang.Cloneable interface. The java.io.Serializable interface allows it to transmit via RMI from the server to the client. The Cloneable interface allows you to clone an entry in the inventory list and attach it to the list of items in the user's shopping bag. We could have placed a reference to the inventory item itself in the shopping bag instead, but then any changes to the entry in the shopping bag would also modify the inventory line, which is not correct behavior. Cloning the inventory object creates a new object that can be modified without also changing the original object.

The addItem() method adds a given quantity of a particular item to the user's shopping bag. In addition to the usual RemoteException, this method throws the ItemNotFoundException. We created the ItemNotFoundException to handle situations where the inventory does not include a requested item or where the client attempts to remove an item that is not already in the shopping bag. This method demonstrates how your own methods can throw arbitrary user-defined exceptions as well as the core exceptions like RemoteException.

The removeItem() method is essentially the inverse of the addItem() method. It removes a given quantity of a particular item from the user's shopping bag.

The getBagContents() method allows the client to check the current contents of the shopping bag.

The client calls the finalizeOrder() method when the customer finishes browsing and modifying the contents of the bag. This method actually submits the order.

The getCustID() method returns the customer ID of the current customer. It is especially useful after a client has added a new customer. In this case, the client can use getCustID() to discover which ID has been assigned to the customer.

The remote interface is now complete. Let's direct our attention to the implementation class itself.

The Bean Implementation

Appendix A provides the full source code for the implementation class. Some of the high points are discussed here.

This bean includes some commented-out code that accesses a WebLogic-specific logging routine. These lines illustrate a typical mechanism for writing to a server log. In writing a server-side application, you generally do not have access to standard output, dialog boxes, or any of the other usual methods for interacting with the user. Thus, when something unusual happens and your application must notify someone, it typically writes an entry to a log. The commented-out code in this example allows you to write messages to WebLogic's own log file. You could also create your own log file. If you decide to use a similar approach, you must add logic to properly manage the connection in the event that the bean becomes passivated, and to remove the connection if the bean is removed.

The ejbCreate() methods are responsible for obtaining initial database connections and initializing the instance variables. One of them invokes a createCustomer() method, which will insert a new customer record into the CUSTOMERS table. The other accepts an existing customer ID as its argument and initializes the instance variables by looking up the customer ID in the database.

The following snippet of code loads the JDBC driver. In this code, the line numbers correspond to the line numbers in Appendix A, making it easier for you to locate the code in context.

```
   public void init() throws CreateException
74 {
75      Properties props = ctx.getEnvironment();
76      databaseURL = (String) props.get("bagBean.databaseURL");
77      JDBCDriverName = (String) props.get("bagBean.
        JDBCDriverName");
78      //load the JDBC driver
79      try
80      {
81      Class.forName(JDBCDriverName).newInstance();
82      }
83      catch(Exception e)
```

```
84       {
85         throw new CreateException("Could not load JDBC driver");
86       }
87  }
```

Line 75 calls the getEnvironment() method of the SessionContext, which returns an object of type Properties that contains the bean's runtime properties. The bean's deployment descriptor includes two properties:

- bagBean.databaseURL, which contains a JDBC uniform resource locator (URL) that can be used to look up the database that the application will use
- bagBean.JDBCDriverName, which contains a string that gives the full class name of the JDBC driver to use

These properties are read into class variables in lines 76 and 77, respectively. Lines 79–86, use the value of the bagBean.JDBCDriverName environment property to load the appropriate JDBC driver, throwing a CreateException if the program cannot load the driver. This approach allows us to avoid hard-coding the name of a JDBC driver into the bean. Using properties permits the configuration of the actual JDBC driver at deployment time without recompilation of the source code.

The findItem() method looks through the array of InventoryItem objects that are cached by the Session bean. This cache represents the inventory of available items. If the item is not found in the inventory, this method throws an ItemNotFoundException. (In an actual production system, you would not use this approach for a frequently changed table like an inventory database; caching can be useful for data such as sales tax tables and the like, which are changed only rarely).

The ejbActivate(), ejbPassivate(), and ejbRemove() methods manage the JDBC connection that we established in the ejbCreate() method. If the bean becomes passivated at some point during its lifetime, ejbPassivate() is called before passivation occurs. This bean's implementation of ejbPassivate() will close the database connection. Remember that resources such as open sockets and open database connections cannot be serialized when a bean is passivated; they must be closed in ejbPassivate() and reopened in ejb-Activate(). Not coincidentally, our implementation of ejbActivate() reopens the connection to the database. Finally, when the client no longer needs the bean and calls ejbRemove(), the implementation of ejbRemove() closes the database connection permanently.

If you're worried about the overhead of closing and reestablishing a connection in ejbActivate() and ejbPassivate(), you shouldn't fret. Typically, Session beans will be swapped out only if the server is running low on resources and needs to swap other beans in. In that event, the beans chosen to be swapped out typically comprise the beans used least recently. Passivation and activation resemble the paging that occurs in operating systems; if you encounter a situation where there is a constant stream of activation and passivation, you can probably solve the problem by the simple expedient of adding more system memory.

The bean's `addItem()` method uses a hash table called `bag()` to hold the contents of the shopping bag (for a stateless bean, we would keep this information somewhere else—either on the client or on the server). This method uses the `java.util.Hashtable`'s `containsKey()` method to discern whether the item is currently contained in the bag hash table. If it is, the method simply calls the `java.util.Hashtable`'s `get()` method to obtain a reference to the underlying `InventoryItem` object, then increments the quantity field of the `InventoryItem` object by the argument quantity. If item does not appear in the bag, the `addItem()` method uses the `findItem()` method to obtain a reference to the `InventoryItem` object in the master inventory list. Recall that, if the requested item code is not found in the inventory list, `findItem()` will throw an ItemNotFoundException; you must therefore declare the `addItem()` method as throwing this exception. The exception could also be handled locally within the method, but it's best in this situation to throw the exception back to the client. Assuming that the inventory list contains the item, the item is cloned in line 186, then assigned the argument quantity as its own quantity value and inserted into the bag. Why did we clone it? Because the bag should not contain references back to the inventory list; in such a case, modifying the quantity field of an item in the bag would cause the master inventory list to contain the same quantity value for the item. This approach is not correct behavior.

The `removeItem()` method allows the client not only to remove an item completely from the bag, but also to remove only a certain number of a particular item from a bag. For example, if the customer wanted 2 units of some item, but inadvertently ordered 22, the program could call removeItem() with the item's code and 20 as arguments to remove 20 of the items from the shopping bag. The `remove()` method first checks whether the shopping bag contains an instance of the item to be removed. If the item does not appear, the method throws an ItemNotFoundException. If the item is found in the inventory, the `removeItem()` method obtains a reference to it from the bag hash table. Next, the `removeItem()` method checks whether the requested quantity to remove is greater than or equal to the quantity already ordered. If so, it simply removes the item from the bag hash table, using the `java.util.Hashtable` class's `remove()` method. If the quantity to be removed is less than the quantity in the bag, the method decrements the quantity field by the argument quantity.

The getBagContents() method is straightforward. First, it calls the size() method of the java.util.Hashtable class to obtain the size of the hash table (that is, the number of elements that the hash table contains). Next, it uses the size to construct an array of InventoryItem objects. Then it calls the hash table's keys() method, which returns an enumeration of all keys in the hash table, and iterates through this list of keys to obtain each object in the hash table. Once built, the array is returned to the client.

```
228  public int createCustomer(String name, String address)
229  {
230      //given a name and address, create a customer
231      //in the database, and return the customer identifier
232      try
233      {
234          String query = "insert into customers (cust_id,
             cust_name, cust_addr) values ((select max(cust_id)
             from customers) + 1, '" +name + "', '" + address +
             "')";
235          Statement stmt = c.createStatement();
236          int count = stmt.executeUpdate(query);
237          stmt.close();
238          stmt = c.createStatement();
239          query = "select max(cust_id) from customers";
240          ResultSet rs = stmt.executeQuery(query);
241          rs.next();
242          int custid = rs.getInt(1);
243          rs.close();
244          stmt.close();
245          return custid;
246      }
247      catch (SQLException e)
248      {
249          log("SQLException in createCustomer: " + e);
250          return 0;
251      }
252  }
```

The createCustomer() method is called by the ejbCreate() method. Line 234 contains the SQL used to create the customer entry. Note that a subquery selects the maximum customer ID in the table and adds 1 to it. Because the value of CUST_ID is not interesting in itself, except that it serves as a key to the CUSTOMERS table, you could potentially use an autoincrement field (a field where the database itself assigns a new value upon insertion of a new row). Not all databases support this functionality, however. Because our goal is to be as generic as possible, we chose to implement our own mechanism.

After the new customer row is inserted, a second query selects the maximum value from the CUST_ID field of the CUSTOMERS table. Because we are using the TRANSACTION_SERIALIZABLE isolation level (discussed in the "Aside" that follows), and because we have just inserted a value that was 1 larger than the previous maximum, the value returned is the one we just inserted as the new customer ID. The new customer ID is then returned, to be used in the calling ejbCreate() routine to set the class variable custID. This approach will not necessarily hold up if a lower isolation level is used.

ASIDE: Transaction Isolation Levels

Transaction isolation levels allow you to specify how much or how little of other transactions your application will see during the course of its own transaction execution. An inverse relationship exists between higher levels of isolation and the level of concurrency. That is, an application that requires a high degree of isolation must maintain more locks for a longer period of time than an application for which a lower degree of isolation is acceptable.

Two programs attempting to simultaneously access a database can have essentially three types of problem interactions:

Problem 1: Transaction A modifies a row; transaction B reads it; transaction A does a rollback and the row disappears. This situation is called a "dirty read."

Problem 2: Transaction A reads a row; transaction B modifies the row; transaction A reads the row again and sees a different value. This case is called a "nonrepeatable read."

Problem 3: Transaction A selects a set of rows that satisfy a given search condition; Transaction B inserts rows that satisfy the same condition. If transaction A executes the same query again, it will receive additional data. This situation is called a "phantom read."

Four levels of transaction isolation are possible:

- TRANSACTION_READ_UNCOMMITTED, which permits dirty reads, nonrepeatable reads, and phantom reads
- TRANSACTION_READ_COMMITTED, which permits only nonrepeatable reads and phantom reads
- TRANSACTION_REPEATABLE_READ, which permits only phantom reads
- TRANSACTION_SERIALIZABLE, which does not permit any of these situations to occur

The `finalizeOrder()` method is invoked after the customer has finished browsing the inventory and modifying the shopping bag; invoking this method places the actual order. This routine uses a JDBC prepared statement. Other portions of this example have not used prepared statements because they're mainly useful when you must perform the same query repeatedly. Typically, calling `prepareStatement()` creates a temporary stored procedure containing your SQL query and compiles it on the server. Because your query is compiled only once, subsequent invocations of the procedure should proceed more rapidly than if you simply passed a raw SQL query each time. In JDBC PreparedStatements, question marks inserted into the text of the query string indicate parameters that will be passed in when the procedure is actually invoked. You can modify actual values for these parameters for each row without recompiling the entire SQL statement.

There's something else that this procedure should do: It should update the `INVENTORY` table to reflect the ordering of various quantities of items. Implementation of this functionality is left as an exercise to the reader.

The Client

This example implements a very simple, low-tech client that simply exercises the various methods of the `BagBean` class. This client is very straightforward indeed, as a perusal of the full text in Appendix A, will reveal. The basic flow is the same as that employed in the client from Chapter 3; indeed, most of the clients in this book have a similar look and feel. On line 55 of the program, the bean's `remove()` method is called. The bean is then removed by the server and can no longer be used. Just for fun, we have included another business method invocation on line 57. This invocation will throw an exception.

Because we are striving for simplicity, all exceptions are handled together at the end of the procedure. This strategy may or may not be the best approach for your own program. If you need to provide detailed exception handling for each individual method, it may be in your best interest to enclose each method in its own try/catch block.

Deploying the Example

The deployment requirements for this example are straightforward. In your deployment descriptor, you need to specify the following:

- The name of the bean's home interface class, `book.chap04.bag.BagHome`.
- The name of the bean's remote interface class, `book.chap04.bag.Bag`.
- The name of the bean's implementation class, `book.chap04.bag.BagBean`.

- The name by which you will look up the bean's home interface using JNDI, `BagHome`.
- The bean's isolation level, `TRANSACTION_SERIALIZABLE`.
- The bean's transaction attribute, `TX_REQUIRES_NEW`, which means that each method invocation will occur in a new transaction context. As a result, a rollback from another method will not affect the state of our transaction.
- The environment property `bagBean.databaseURL`, `jdbc:weblogic:jts:ejbPool`. This database URL has already been created for some of the WebLogic examples; for our example, we simply added some new tables to the database.
- The environment property `bagBean.JDBCDriverName`, `weblogic.jdbc.jts.Driver`.
- A state management type, `STATEFUL_SESSION`.

In addition to the usual steps required in deploying the bean, you must create the tables used by this bean. With WebLogic, you can use an evaluation version of the Cloudscape database as your underlying database. With other environments, you must find another database. The SQL statements required to create the tables was given earlier; you can run them to create the tables.

Summing Up the Stateful Session Bean Example

As mentioned earlier in this chapter, Session beans are not guaranteed to survive a server crash or restart, and they can be destroyed after a configurable timeout elapses. In the real world, however, server crashes and restarts should be relatively rare events, and you can always set the timeout value high enough to avoid beans timing out in the midst of a session. For these reasons, we have left the state of the application as part of the Session bean.

Stateless Session Bean Example

Let's build another shopping bag example—this time, implement it using a stateless Session bean. This approach will allow us to point out some key differences in the design and implementation of the two strategies.

Requirements

Our requirements for the stateless Session example can be stated as follows:

- Do the same stuff as the stateful example.
- Use stateless Session beans instead.

We will implement the same example again to give a sense of some of the similarities and differences of stateful and stateless bean implementations. Implementing two solutions to the same problem should help to illustrate these similarities and differences.

Design

Because this example uses stateless Session beans, we decide where to keep state. As it cannot reside in the Session bean itself, it must reside either in the client or in the database. To keep the client simple, we put the state in the database. Instead of holding finalized orders, the ORDERS table holds the interim orders, which were placed in a hash table in the previous example. Because we still need a place to put finalized orders, we create a new table called FINAL_ORDERS that will be updated from the ORDERS table when the user finalizes his or her order. The data definition language for the FINAL_ORDERS table is as follows:

```
create table FINAL_ORDERS (
CUST_ID SMALLINT ,
ITEMCODE VARCHAR(5) ,
QUANTITY SMALLINT );
```

Note that the columns, column names, and column types match those used in the ORDERS table. The ORDERS table, the CUSTOMERS table, and the INVENTORY table are used as well, unchanged from the previous example.

Another design implication of using a stateless Session bean is that information such as the customer ID, which was previously retained as part of the state of the Session bean, must now be stored somewhere else. In this example, we will keep this information on the client. This choice is reflected in changes to the remote interface.

Implementation

The Home Interface

The classes and interfaces for the second example will reside in the package book.chap04.bag2. This home interface resembles the one used in the previous example, with an important exception. According to the EJB specification, a stateless Session bean can only have one create() method, and this method must take no arguments. Because of this requirement, we cannot use the create() method to create a new customer. This constraint is not a huge problem, though; we can simply create a new method in the remote interface that imparts the same functionality.

The Remote Interface

Listing 4.1 gives the code for our remote interface.

Listing 4.1   Remote Interface for a Stateless Session Bean

```
1    package book.chap04.bag2;
2    import javax.ejb.EJBObject;
3    import java.rmi.RemoteException;

4    public interface Bag2 extends EJBObject
5    {
6        //get list of inventory
7        public InventoryItem[] getInventory() throws
         RemoteException;
8        //add an item to the bag
9        public void addItem(int custid, String itemcode, int
         quantity) throws RemoteException;
10       //remove an item from the bag
11       public void removeItem(int custid, String itemcode, int
         quantity) throws RemoteException, ItemNotFoundException;
12       //list the contents of the bag
13       public InventoryItem[] getBagContents(int custid) throws
         RemoteException;
14       //execute the order
15       public void finalizeOrder(int custid) throws
         RemoteException;
16       //get customer ID
17       public int newCustomer(String name, String addr) throws
         RemoteException;
18   }
```

The remote interface here is roughly similar to the one used in the previous example. Some notable differences exist, however:

- We have modified the addItem(), removeItem(), getBagContents(), and finalizeOrder() methods to take an additional argument, the customer ID.
- A new method, newCustomer(), creates a new entry in the CUSTOMERS table and returns the new customer ID.
- No getCustID() method exists; because we cannot retain state as part of the bean, we cannot obtain the customer ID from the bean. We cannot obtain it from the database, either, because other customers might be inserted into the database after our client calls newCustomer(). As a result, the client must keep track of the customer ID itself.

The Bean Implementation

The full text of this class appears in Appendix A. The following discussion focuses on selected snippets from it.

```
64  public void addItem(int custid, String itemcode, int
    quantity)
65  {
66      try{
67      Connection c = DriverManager.getConnection(getDBURL());
68      int quantityOrdered = getItemCount(custid, itemcode, c);
69      if (quantityOrdered > 0)
70      {
71          //update
72          String query = "update orders set quantity = " +
            (quantityOrdered + quantity )+ "where cust_id = " +
            custid + " and itemcode = '" + itemcode + "'";
73
74          Statement s = c.createStatement();
75          s.executeUpdate(query);
76          s.close();
77      }
78      else
79      {
80          //insert
81          String query = "insert into orders(cust_id,
            itemcode, quantity) values( ? , ? , ?)";
82          PreparedStatement ps = c.prepareStatement(query);
83          ps.setInt(1, custid);
84          ps.setString(2, itemcode);
85          ps.setInt(3, quantity);
86          ps.executeUpdate();
87          ps.close();
88      }
89      //insert rows into table
90          c.close();
91          }catch(SQLException e){
92              log("SQL exception in addItem: " + e);
93          }
94  }
```

Lines 64–94 contain the stateless implementation of the addItem() method. On line 67, this method creates a new JDBC Connection object from the database URL obtained in the getDBURL() method. If you carefully analyze the life cycle of a stateless Session bean, you'll see that ejbCreate() and setSessionContext() are always called at the beginning of a stateless Session bean's life, and ejbRemove() is always called at the end of it. As a result, you can create a Connection object in either ejbCreate() or setSessionContext() and then remove it in ejbRemove() when you discard the bean. You should be aware, however, potentially many clients with different identities will use this connection over its lifetime. For the purposes of this example, we will create a new Connection object in each method. This approach slows each method down, but allows us to release the database connections at the end of each method—a somewhat more resource-friendly strategy.

On line 68, the addItem() method invokes the getItemCount() method, which returns the number of items that are currently on order. If the number of items is greater than 0, a row will exist in the ORDERS table for this item. We can therefore update the QUANTITY column in this row to reflect the fact that the customer has ordered more items. If the number of items equals 0, no row exists in the ORDERS database for this particular item and customer ID, so we insert one in lines 78–88.

```
95   public int getItemCount(int custid, String itemcode,
     Connection c) throws SQLException
96   {
97        //Note: For our example, the business rule is that, if
98        //no items are ordered, the row is deleted. In other
99        //cases, you may want to throw an exception rather
100       //than simply returning 0, to differentiate between
101       //cases where a row exists with a field containing 0,
          and a case where no row exists.
102       String query = "select quantity from orders where
          cust_id = "+ custid +" and itemcode ='"+itemcode+"'";
103       Statement s = c.createStatement();
104       ResultSet rs = s.executeQuery(query);
105       boolean more = rs.next();
106       int quantity;
107       if (!more)
108       {
109           quantity = 0;
110       }
111       else  //more rows
112       {
113           quantity = rs.getInt(1);
114       }
115       rs.close();
116       s.close();
117       return quantity;
118  }
```

Lines 95–118 implement the getItemCount() method that is invoked by the addItem() method. Note that the getItemCount() method reuses the Connection object created by the addItem() method. Also note the comment. In the general case, you would probably want to throw an exception if you expect to find a row and find none. This strategy allows you to differentiate between a row with a quantity field containing 0 and the situation where no row is found. Our business rules dictate that, when the quantity field reaches 0, the row is removed from the ORDERS table, allowing us to treat both cases the same way.

```
119  public void deleteRow(int custid, String itemcode,
     Connection c) throws SQLException
120  {
```

```
121      String query = "delete from orders where cust_id = "+
         custid +" and itemcode ='"+itemcode+"'";
122      Statement s = c.createStatement();
123      int count = s.executeUpdate(query);
124      s.close();
125  }
```

Lines 119–125 implement the deleteRow() method, which the remove-Item() method uses when the customer has requested to remove all instances of an item from his or her shopping bag. This method simply executes an SQL delete call that removes the row containing that item for the particular customer ID.

```
126  public void updateRow(int custid, String itemcode,
         Connection c, int oldQuantity, int itemsToRemove) throws
         SQLException
127  {
128      Statement s = c.createStatement();
129      String query = "update orders set quantity = " +
         (oldQuantity - itemsToRemove) + " where cust_id = "+
         custid +" and itemcode = '"+itemcode+"'";
130      int count = s.executeUpdate(query);
131      s.close();
132  }
```

Lines 126–132 implement the updateItem() method, which the remove-Item() method uses when the customer wants to remove only a few items from his or her order. This method invokes an SQL update routine that decreases the number of a particular item in the order by the argument value.

```
133  public void removeItem(int custid, String itemcode, int
         quantity) throws ItemNotFoundException
134  {
135      try{
136      Connection c = DriverManager.getConnection(getDBURL());
137      int numOrdered = getItemCount(custid, itemcode, c);
138      if (numOrdered == 0)
139      {
140      c.close();
141      throw new ItemNotFoundException();
142      }
143      log ("numOrdered = " + numOrdered);
144      if (numOrdered <= quantity)
145      {
146      //   remove table entry
147      deleteRow(custid, itemcode, c);
148      }
149      else
150      {
151      //   update table with reduced amount
```

```
152         updateRow(custid, itemcode, c, numOrdered, quantity);
153       }
154       c.close();
155       }catch(SQLException e){
156           log("SQL exception in removeItem: " + e);
157       }
158  }
```

Lines 133–158 implement the removeItem() method. This method first uses getItemCount() to count the quantity of the item currently contained in the shopping bag. If the item is not found in the shopping bag, the program throws an ItemNotFoundException. If the item is found, the action taken depends on how many of the item appear in the shopping bag. If the request indicates that all items should be removed, it calls the deleteRow() method. If only a portion of the items should be removed, it invokes the updateItem() method instead.

```
159  public InventoryItem[] getBagContents(int custid)
160  {
161       InventoryItem[] inventory;
162       //query database to get count of inventory objects
163       String query = "select count(*) from orders where
             cust_id = " + custid;
164       try
165       {
166       Connection c = DriverManager.getConnection(getDBURL());
167       Statement stmt = c.createStatement();
168       ResultSet rs = stmt.executeQuery(query);
169       rs.next();
170       int count = rs.getInt(1);
171       //query database to load inventory table
172       inventory = new InventoryItem[count];
173       query = "select itemcode, quantity from orders where
             cust_id = " + custid + "";
174       rs = stmt.executeQuery(query);
175       rs.next();
176       for (int i = 0; i < count; i++)
177       {
178           inventory[i] = new InventoryItem();
179           inventory[i].itemCode = rs.getString(1);
180           inventory[i].quantity = rs.getInt(2);
181           rs.next();
182       }
183       rs.close();
184       stmt.close();
185       c.close();
186       return inventory;
187       }//end try block
188       catch (SQLException e)
189       {
190       log("initInventory:SQLException: " + e);
```

```
191      return null;
192      }
193  }
```

Lines 159–193 implement the getBagContents() method. Because we are storing the contents of our bag in a database table, the routine first selects the count of items in the database for the specified customer. It then uses this count to construct an array of InventoryItems and retrieves the contents of the database into this InventoryItem array. Finally, it returns the array to the client.

```
194  public int newCustomer(String name, String address)
195  {
196      //given a name and address, create a customer
197      //in the database, and return the customer identifier
198      try
199      {
200          String query = "insert into customers (cust_id,
                 cust_name, cust_addr) values ((select max(cust_id)
                 from customers) + 1, '" +name + "', '" + address +
                 "')";
201          Connection c = DriverManager.getConnection(getDBURL());
202          Statement stmt = c.createStatement();
203          int count = stmt.executeUpdate(query);
204          stmt.close();
205          stmt = c.createStatement();
206          query = "select max(cust_id) from customers";
207          ResultSet rs = stmt.executeQuery(query);
208          rs.next();
209          int custid = rs.getInt(1);
210          rs.close();
211          stmt.close();
212          c.close();
213          return custid;
214      }
215      catch (SQLException e)
216      {
217          log("SQLException in createCustomer: " + e);
218          return 0;
219      }
220  }
```

Lines 194–220 implement the newCustomer() routine. This routine replaces the ejbCreate() constructor from the first example that was used to create a new customer. The SQL statement in this routine resembles that used in the internal createCustomer() method in the stateful Session bean. First, a new row is inserted into the CUSTOMERS table; then the CUSTOMERS table is queried to find the value of CUST_ID that was inserted (remember, we're within a transaction and using the TRANSACTION_SERIALIZABLE isolation level, so no one can interpose another customer insertion routine). Because we can't store the value of CUST_ID in an object variable, we return it to the client.

```
228  public void finalizeOrder(int custid)
229  {
230      //update another table from the ORDERS table for the
         custid
231      try{
232      //insert rows into table
233      Connection c = DriverManager.getConnection(getDBURL());
234      String query = "insert into final_orders (cust_id,
         itemcode, quantity) select cust_id, itemcode, quantity
         from orders where cust_id = " + custid + "";
235
236      Statement stmt = c.createStatement();
237      stmt.executeUpdate(query);
238      stmt.close();
239      //get rid of info in the ORDERS table
240      query = "delete from orders where cust_id = " + custid
         + "";
241      stmt = c.createStatement();
242      stmt.executeUpdate(query);
243      stmt.close();
244      c.close();
245      }catch(SQLException e){
246          log("SQL exception in finalizeOrder: " + e);
247      }
248  }
```

Lines 228–248 implement the stateless version of the finalizeOrder()
method. First, the routine inserts all the rows for the customer specified in the
argument into the FINAL_ORDERS table. Next, it deletes these rows from the
ORDERS table.

```
249  public InventoryItem[] getInventory()
250  {
251      //query database to get count of inventory objects
252      String query = "select count(*) from inventory";
253      try
254      {
255      Connection c = DriverManager.getConnection(getDBURL());
256      Statement stmt = c.createStatement();
257      ResultSet rs = stmt.executeQuery(query);
258      rs.next();
259      int count = rs.getInt(1);
260      System.out.println("count is " + count);
261      rs.close();
262      //query database to load INVENTORY table
263      InventoryItem []inventory = new InventoryItem[count];
264      query = "select itemcode, itemdesc, quantity, price
         from inventory";
265      rs = stmt.executeQuery(query);
266      rs.next();
267      for (int i = 0; i < count; i++)
268      {
```

```
269              inventory[i] = new InventoryItem();
270              inventory[i].itemCode = rs.getString(1);
271              inventory[i].itemDesc = rs.getString(2);
272              inventory[i].quantity = rs.getInt(3);
273              inventory[i].price = rs.getDouble(4);
274              rs.next();
275          }
276      rs.close();
277      stmt.close();
278      c.close();
279      return inventory;
280      }//end try block
281      catch (SQLException e)
282      {
283      log("initInventory:SQLException: " + e);
284      return null;
285      }
286      }
287  }
```

Finally, the last routine implemented in this class is the getInventory() method. This method performs a query against the INVENTORY table, populates an array of InventoryItem objects with the resulting information, and returns the array to the client.

A note on the SQL is in order. In our select statement, we said "select itemcode, itemdesc, quantity, price from inventory" rather than "select * from inventory", even though itemcode, itemdesc, quantity, and price are the only columns present in the table. Why did we do this? In real life, database tables can change over the life of a system. In particular, a new column may be added to a table, and the order of columns within a table may change. If you specify the exact set of columns needed, your application will be able to continue to function even if new columns are added to the underlying table. We strongly recommend that you avoid using "select *" except for casual interactive queries.

The Client

The client used to test the Bag2Bean project is very similar to the original BagClient program; it appears in its entirety in Appendix A. The major difference is that it must pass the customer ID to the various methods.

Deploying the Example

The deployment requirements for this example are straightforward. In your deployment descriptor, you need to specify the following:

- The name of the bean's home interface class, `book.chap04.bag2.Bag2Home`.
- The name of the bean's remote interface class, `book.chap04.bag2.Bag2`.
- The name of the bean's implementation class, `book.chap04.bag2.Bag2Bean`.
- The name by which you will look up the bean's home interface using JNDI, `Bag2Home`.
- The bean's isolation level, `TRANSACTION_SERIALIZABLE`.
- The bean's transaction attribute, `TX_REQUIRES_NEW`, which means that each method invocation will occur in a new transaction context. Note that stateless Session beans cannot preserve an open transaction across method invocations.
- The environment property `bagBean.databaseURL`, `jdbc:weblogic:jts:ejbPool`. This database URL has already been created for some of the WebLogic examples; here we simply added some new tables to the database.
- The environment property `bagBean.JDBCDriverName`, `weblogic.jdbc.jts.Driver`.
- A state management type, `STATELESS_SESSION`.

Conclusion

In this chapter, we've covered stateful and stateless Session beans in detail. In Chapter 5, we'll look at Entity beans.

CHAPTER 5

Writing EJB Entity Beans

In earlier chapters, we touched on Entity beans to some degree. To recap, Entity beans are beans that persist across multiple sessions and multiple users. Typically, an Entity EJB maps directly to a row in an underlying database (or, more generally, to an entity that exists in persistent storage), though it is also possible to create more complex Entity EJBs that map to join across several tables or even to map Entity EJBs to data elements stored in previous applications. The EJB 1.0 specification does not require support for Entity beans for EJB compliance, but most of the currently available implementations of EJB nevertheless support them. The EJB 2.0 specification will require support for Entity EJBs.

When to Use Entity Beans

To understand Entity beans, a brief recap of Session beans is helpful. Session beans are

- Intended to be used by a single client;
- Relatively short-lived—they are intended to last for the duration of the client's session with the server;
- Not able to survive a server crash; and
- Capable of interacting with shared data in a database.

Entity beans, by contrast,

- Can be used concurrently by several clients;
- Are relatively long-lived—they are intended to exist beyond the lifetime of any single client;

- Will survive a server crash; and
- Directly represent data in a database.

We'll address each of these points in detail here.

Concurrent Use by Several Clients

For a Session bean, it is an error for more than one client to access the same Session bean. For an Entity bean, on the other hand, it is assumed that more than one client will have access to the bean concurrently. Although the clients all think that they're accessing the bean freely, in reality this interaction is interposed by the container so as to guarantee the integrity of the database. A container may interpose on client interactions with an Entity bean in two ways to guarantee database integrity:

- The container can directly interpose, queuing client requests and allowing only one request at a time to be executed.
- The container can create an instance of the bean for each client that wishes to use it, and then allow the underlying database to deal with synchronization issues.

Long Lifetime

As noted, Entity EJBs represent data in an underlying database. Therefore, their lifetime matches the lifetime of the underlying data itself. Entity EJBs may continue to exist for days, months, or even years. No upper limit exists on the lifetime of entity EJBs, and they can be removed in only two ways:

- A client explicitly invokes the `remove()` method on the bean's remote interface or home interface.
- Someone deletes the bean's data from the underlying database.

Another interesting fact about an Entity bean's lifetime is that an Entity bean does not necessarily need to provide a `create()` method in its home interface. If the Entity EJB does not implement a `create()` method, a client will not be able to create a new Entity EJB via the bean's home interface. Nevertheless, one can create a new Entity EJB by directly inserting a row of data into its underlying database. Even without a `create()` method, a client can still obtain a reference to an existing Entity EJB by using one of its **finder** methods.

Survival of Server Crashes

Chapter 4 noted that a Session bean could be irrevocably destroyed in three ways:

- The client connection to the bean can time out.
- The server can be restarted.
- The server can crash.

None of these three problems applies to Entity beans.

- There is no timeout period associated with Entity EJBs.
- Entity EJBs are guaranteed to survive an orderly server restart.
- Entity EJBs are guaranteed to survive a server crash.

Direct Representation of Data in an Underlying Database

Typically, an Entity EJB maps directly to a row in an underlying database. For example, imagine that we have a table called CUSTOMERS with the following columns:

- An integer called CUST_ID that represents a unique ID for each customer
- A string called CUST_NAME that contains the customer's name
- A string called CUST_ADDR that contains the customer's address

We can create an Entity EJB called "customer" that contains three instance variables:

- cust_id
- cust_name
- cust_addr

These variables map directly to the columns in the underlying CUSTOMERS table. A client application can then interact with the customer EJBs to modify these fields, update the underlying database, or perform any other business logic necessary on the customer object.

Bean-Managed Versus Container-Managed Persistence

Within the world of Entity beans, there are two main types of beans:

- Entity beans with bean-managed persistence
- Entity beans with container-managed persistence

An Entity bean with bean-managed persistence contains code that updates the underlying database. In contrast, an Entity bean with container-managed persistence contains no such code; instead, it relies on the container to update the database as necessary. Later in this chapter, we'll see examples of both the bean-managed and the container-managed approach. For now, it suffices to note that this dichotomy exists. In general, Entity beans with container-managed persistence are simpler to implement (because they do not require any database code), but require a higher degree of functionality from their container (that is, the container provider must support container-managed persistence). Beans with bean-managed persistence, on the other hand, are slightly more complex to implement (because they contain additional code), but do not require extra support from the container.

As an example, imagine that you have a logical entity for which you'd like to create an Entity EJB. This entity is created via joins on several underlying tables. You might therefore lean toward a bean-managed implementation, because support for creating such objects may be lacking in several early implementations of EJB.

Primary Keys

Each Entity bean instance has an associated **primary key.** Logically, a primary key is a value or combination of values that allows you to uniquely specify a row of data. As an example, refer back to the CUSTOMERS table. Because CUST_ID is guaranteed to be unique for each customer (and therefore for each row in the CUSTOMERS table), it makes a good primary key. In EJB, the primary key is represented by a Java class that contains whatever unique data are necessary to look up a particular entity EJB. For example, here's a primary key class for a hypothetical customer Entity EJB:

```
1  package book.chap05.customer;

2  public class CustomerPK implements java.io.Serializable
3  {
4      public int custid;
5  }
```

According to the EJB specification, a primary key class must implement the java.io.Serializable interface (so that it can be sent over the wire). This class simply carries the value for the primary key from the client to the server. The server inspects the class and uses the values it contains to perform a database lookup for the object of the requested primary key.

Another thing to note about primary keys is that, if two Entity EJBs have the same home interface and the same primary key, they are considered to be identical.

Entity Bean Life Cycle

Figure 5.1 illustrates the various states of existence that an entity bean can have, as well as the transitions from one state to another. As shown in the figure, an Entity EJB can have one of three states:

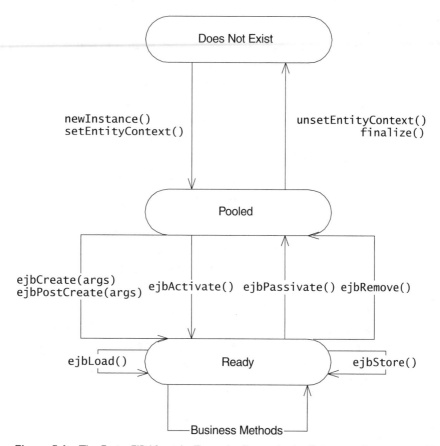

Figure 5.1 The Entity EJB life cycle (From the Enterprise JavaBeans specification, page 61, copyright 1998, Sun Microsystems, used with permission.)

- Nonexistence
- Pooled
- Ready

Nonexistence

When an Entity EJB is in the state of nonexistence, it doesn't exist (naturally enough). A bean leaves this state and enters the pooled state when it is added into the pool by the container, at which point newInstance() and setEntityContext() are invoked on it. It enters the state of nonexistence when the container removes it from the pool, at which point unsetEntityContext() and finalize() are called on it. The unsetEntityContext() method has no counterpart in Session EJBs; it's used to eliminate the Entity bean's EntityContext reference.

The Pooled State

Entities in the pooled state have no identity; for all intents and purposes, they are identical. When an `ejbFind()` method is invoked, the container uses an EJB instance from the pooled state to handle the request. Therefore, you cannot assume that any of the Entity EJB's instance variables have been set when writing the implementation of a finder method.

A bean transitions from the pooled state to the ready state when one of two things happens:

- The container selects the instance to handle an `ejbCreate()` request, at which point `ejbCreate()` and `ejbPostCreate()` are invoked on the object.
- The container selects the instance to be activated (that is, to be assigned an identity so as to handle a client request), at which point `ejbActivate()` is invoked on the instance.

The `ejbPostCreate()` method takes the same arguments as the `ejbCreate()` method. It is invoked only after `ejbCreate()` has reached completion successfully (that is, after the bean has been assigned an identity). You can use `ejbPostCreate()` to perform any special processing needed after the bean is created, but before it becomes available to the client. If you don't need to do any such processing, you can simply implement it as a skeletal method. You must provide at least a skeletal implementation, however, as the container expects it to be there.

A bean transitions from the ready state to the pooled state when one of two things happens:

- The container selects the instance for passivation, at which point `ejbPassivate()` is called on the object.
- The client invokes a `remove()` method on the instance, at which point the instance's `ejbRemove()` method is invoked.

When a bean returns to the pooled state, it once again loses its identity and becomes one of several available instances in the pool.

The Ready State

When the bean is in the ready state, it is able to accept invocations of its business methods. It can also process invocations of its `ejbLoad()` and `ejbStore()` methods. The container these methods invoke keep the state of the object consistent with its representation in the database; `ejbLoad()` reads data from the database and uses it to populate instance variables, and `ejbStore()` writes data from the instance variables to the database. (In the case of container-managed persistence, `ejbLoad()` is invoked after the container has loaded the object's data, and `ejbStore()` is invoked before the object's data are written to the database. Typically, if you use container-managed persistence, you won't need to provide more than a skeletal implementation of the `ejbLoad()` and `ejbStore()` methods.)

When a bean is **activated,** the container automatically invokes its `ejbLoad()` method. Similarly, before a bean becomes passivated, its `ejbStore()` method is invoked. As a result, you need not put any logic in `ejbActivate()` or `ejbPassivate()` to handle state synchronization between the object and the database.

Reentrant Instances

It is possible, in narrow circumstances, to make an Entity EJB reentrant. Basically, the only circumstance in which you should take this step is if your Entity bean uses another Entity bean as a client, and the remote Entity bean must perform a callback to your bean. The EJB specification emphasizes that you must be very careful in coding a reentrant instance.

Example: Container-Managed Persistence

The first example in this chapter provides an implementation of an Entity bean with container-managed persistence.

Requirements

The requirements are straightforward:

- Create an Entity EJB that uses container-managed persistence.
- Reuse as much code as possible from earlier examples.

Those requirements should be a piece of cake. Because Entity beans represent objects in a database, and we already have some databases, we'll simply map the Entity beans to an existing table.

Design

For this example, we'll reuse the ORDERS table from the example in Chapter 4. We'll create an Order interface that allows the user to manipulate the values of the fields in a row in the ORDERS table.

Implementation

Now that requirements and design are set, let's get started with the implementation.

The Home Interface

Listing 5.1 gives the code for our example's home interface.

Listing 5.1   Home Interface for an Entity Bean with Container-Managed Persistence

```
1    package book.chap05.order;
2    import javax.ejb.EJBHome;
3    import java.rmi.RemoteException;
4    import javax.ejb.CreateException;
5    import javax.ejb.FinderException;

6    public interface OrderHome extends EJBHome
7    {

8        public Order create(int custid, String itemcode, int
         quantity) throws RemoteException, CreateException;
9        public Order findByPrimaryKey(OrderPK pk) throws
         RemoteException, FinderException;
10       public java.util.Enumeration findByCustID(int custid)
         throws RemoteException, FinderException;
11   }
```

By now, most of the items in the home interface should be quite familiar to you. Both Session and Entity beans inherit from the EJBHome interface. Some of the key differences are described here.

Line 5 imports the FinderException, which is new to us. The Finder-Exception is an exception that can be thrown by a finder method to indicate that a problem occurred.

Line 8 declares the create() method for this bean. Entity EJBs can have zero or more create() methods (as discussed earlier, you might implement an Entity bean without a create() method if new instances should be created only via updates to the underlying database). As with Session beans, all create() methods must be declared as throwing both RemoteException and Create-Exception. The return type of the create() method in the home interface is the remote interface of the bean—in this case, the Order interface. Note that, in the implementation class, the return type of the ejbCreate() method will differ from the return type of the create() method in the home interface. For container-managed Entity EJBs, the ejbCreate() method has a return type of void, because the container is solely responsible for creating the bean. For bean-managed Entity EJBs, the return value of ejbCreate() is an instance of the bean's primary key class, which the container uses to create an actual instance.

Line 9 declares the `findByPrimaryKey()` method. All Entity EJBs must provide a `findByPrimaryKey()` method in their home interface. Clients use this **finder method** to locate existing Entity EJBs based on their primary key. The implementation details of the finder methods also vary depending on whether the bean has bean-managed or container-managed persistence. If the bean has bean-managed persistence, you must implement a finder method in the bean for each finder method that you declare in the home interface. If the bean has container-managed persistence, the container will provide implementations of the finder methods; you don't have to implement them in your implementation class.

The container can easily generate an implementation of the `findBy-PrimaryKey()` method, because it knows exactly what it needs to do and receives the primary key class. For other finder methods, such as the method `findByCustID()` shown on line 10, the situation is less clear-cut. The container typically does not receive enough information from the method signature alone to provide an implementation. So how do you tell the container how to implement your finder method? Unfortunately, the EJB specification does not outline this process; it says only that the bean provider should provide the deployer with information about how to implement any custom finder methods. The specification does not identify the form that this information should take.

BEA WebXpress WebLogic, for example, provides a syntax in its Entity deployment descriptor that allows you to specify SQL-like conditions to be used by your finder method. This approach is not likely to be universally used, however, so you should include detailed instructions on how to create any finder methods that are required if you are using container-managed persistence. A future version of the EJB specification will provide a definite syntax for describing container-managed finder methods.

Before leaving line 10, note that the return type of the `findByCustID()` method is `java.util.Enumeration`. If a finder method returns a single entity as its result, its return type should be the same as the type of the remote interface. If the finder method can return two or more Entity EJBs, it should return an enumeration in its declaration in the home interface. For bean-managed persistence, the implementation of a finder method that returns multiple Entity EJBs should return a collection of primary keys; the container will interpose and transform this collection of primary keys into a collection of remote interfaces. (By "collection," we do not mean only Java 2 collection classes. Support for these classes will be included in a future version of the EJB specification; as of version 1.0, however, the `java.util.Enumeration` interface is used to implement collections in EJB.) That is, your bean implementation returns a `java.util.Enumeration` of primary keys, which the container transmogrifies into a `java.util.Enumeration` of remote interfaces.

The Remote Interface

Listing 5.2 gives the code for our remote interface.

Listing 5.2   Remote Interface for an Entity Bean with Container-Managed Persistence

```
1    package book.chap05.order;
2    import javax.ejb.EJBObject;
3    import java.rmi.RemoteException;
4    public interface Order extends EJBObject
5    {
6         //note: no setCustID or setItemCode-these are part of
          the primary key
7         public void setQuantity(int quantity) throws
          RemoteException;
8         public int getCustID() throws RemoteException;
9         public String getItemCode() throws RemoteException;
10        public int getQuantity() throws RemoteException;
11   }
```

The code for this example's remote interface is not dramatically different from the code for the remote interfaces seen in earlier examples in this book. This particular remote interface doesn't provide much in the way of business logic. Certainly, it is possible to implement any business logic you want in an Entity EJB. In the interests of brevity here (which you'll certainly appreciate after the lengthy examples found in Chapter 4), we will stick to a simple set of getter/setter methods for this example. In "plain old" JavaBeans, it is common to use pairs of methods to provide access to a field in a bean. We will use that paradigm in the current example, with two exceptions—there are no setCustID() or setItemCode() methods. These fields are used as the primary key, so modifying them would change the identity of the object.

The Implementation Class

The full source code for this class appears in Appendix B. The implementation of this class is so simple that it reminds one of the "hello world!" example from Chapter 2. Do not be deceived, however; this class comes with persistence, free of charge.

Before we examine the description of what this class does, note that no implementations of finder methods appear in this class, not even skeletal ones. The container is solely responsible for generating the finder methods for a class with container-managed persistence. As discussed earlier, the container needs a little help from the deployer, but the overall message is that you don't have to provide an implementation for the finder methods in your class.

The first thing that this class does is to implement the EntityBean interface. The EntityBean interface has the following methods:

- `ejbActivate()`
- `ejbPassivate()`
- `ejbLoad()`
- `ejbStore()`
- `ejbRemove()`
- `setEntityContext()`
- `unsetEntityContext()`

```
7     transient private EntityContext ctx;
8     public int custid;
9   public String itemcode;
10  public int quantity;
```

Next, lines 7–10 declare the instance variables. The `EntityContext` variable is similar in purpose to the `SessionContext` variable discussed in Chapter 4. It allows the bean to make requests of the container. In addition to the core methods of the EJBContext interface (also discussed in the previous chapter), the EntityContext interface provides two methods:

- `getEJBObject()`, which returns a reference to the Entity bean's EJBObject
- `getPrimaryKey()`, which returns an object that contains the primary key for this Entity object

An important note about lines 8–10: These variables are all declared as public. Beans that use container-managed persistence must declare all fields that the container should manage to be public.

Next, the class implements the `setEntityContext()` and `unsetEntity-Context()` methods. Note that the `EntityContext` is not a reference to a static class; rather, it is dynamically updated by the container. Even though a given Entity bean may be invoked by many clients over its lifetime, the container ensures that the `EntityContext` contains current data for each invocation.

```
19  public void ejbCreate(int custid, String itemcode, int
    quantity) throws CreateException
20  {

21    this.custid = custid;
22    this.itemcode = itemcode;
23    this.quantity = quantity;

24
25  }
```

Lines 19–25 implement the `ejbCreate()` method. This method has a return type of void, as discussed earlier; the container itself will create the appropriate reference to return to the client. This `ejbCreate()` method simply initializes the instance variables with the argument instance variables and then returns.

Only skeletal implementations of the `ejbPostCreate()`, `ejbActivate()`, `ejbPassivate()`, `ejbRemove()`, `ejbLoad()`, and `ejbStore()` methods are provided. For beans with container-managed persistence, these methods serve merely as notification callbacks; you can add code to them if the program should take some action when they are invoked, but you are not required to do so.

The Primary Key Class

Listing 5.3   The Primary Key Class

```
1   package book.chap05.order;

2   public class OrderPK implements java.io.Serializable
3   {
4       public int custid;
5       public String itemcode;
6   }
```

Listing 5.3 gives the implementation of the primary key class. Because the primary key of the `ORDERS` table is composed of both the customer ID and the item code, this class must include both. Also note that the class implements the `java.io.Serializable` interface.

The Client

The client is a straightforward test client that creates a few bean instances and exercises the available functionality. Appendix B gives the full source code for the client.

In general, the sort of fine-grained access used for this client (getter and setter methods for each data element) is not recommended in the context of distributed programming. Each remote method invocation carries quite a bit of communication overhead. Remember the walkthrough of a distributed invocation from Chapter 2? As you'll recall from that discussion, each method invocation must perform the following tasks:

- Serialize all arguments on the client side
- Transmit the arguments to the server
- Deserialize the arguments on the server
- Invoke the remote method

- Serialize the return value on the server
- Transmit the return value to the client
- Deserialize the return value on the client side

One way to pare down the number of remote method invocations required is to include a data structure that contains all data for a particular instance. Instead of querying for each bit of data piecemeal, the client simply calls a `getData()` method and receives all of the class's data in a single chunk.

Deployment

The process for packaging the Entity bean for deployment is similar to that for deploying a Session bean (discussed in detail in Chapter 4; Chapter 7 will discuss deployment descriptors in even greater detail). Some key similarities are as follows:

- You must include the names of your home interface, remote interface, and implementation class.
- You must set the isolation level and transaction attribute for your bean.

Some key differences also exist:

- Your deployment descriptor must be of type `javax.ejb.deployment.EntityDescriptor`.
- You must include the name of your primary key class (in this case, `OrderPK`).
- You must provide a list of container-managed fields.
- You must specify whether the class is reentrant. As discussed earlier, it's generally a good idea to specify that your classes are nonreentrant.
- You must provide a description of your finder methods, so that the deployer can use the container to generate them.

The following line from the author's deployment descriptor specifies how to implement the `findByCustID()` custom finder method. This syntax is specific to BEA WebXpress's WebLogic, though it is likely that your EJB container will provide something similar.

```
"findByCustID(int custidnum)" "(= custid $custidnum)"
```

where

- `findByCustID` is the name of the method;
- The method takes one integer argument, called `custidnum`; and

- The expression "(= custid $custidnum)" is a prefix-notation expression that indicates that the method should return all instances where the database column that maps to the field custid matches the argument of the finder method exactly.

The resulting JDBC code ends up in a file called OrderPSJDBC.java in this example. You can see this file if you invoke the EJB compiler with the -keepgenerated parameter, as in the following code:

```
java weblogic.ejbc -keepgenerated order.jar
```

The SQL generated by WebLogic looks like this:

```
"select CUST_ID, ITEMCODE, QUANTITY from orders where
(CUST_ID = ? )";
```

The question mark is a placeholder used to represent a parameter that will be passed into a PreparedStatement object.

Now that we've wrapped up the container-managed example, let's look at a bean-managed example.

Example: Bean-Managed Persistence

In this example, we implement a bean using bean-managed persistence.

Requirements

The requirements are again straightforward:

- Create an Entity EJB that uses bean-managed persistence.
- Reuse the infrastructure from the earlier example.

Design

Once again, we will reuse a table from the examples in Chapter 4. For this example, we'll reuse the CUSTOMERS table. To refresh your memory, the CUSTOMERS table was specified as follows:

```
create table CUSTOMERS (
CUST_ID SMALLINT ,
CUST_NAME VARCHAR(64) ,
CUST_ADDR VARCHAR(64) );
```

We'll now create an Entity bean with bean-managed persistence that represents rows of data in the CUSTOMERS table.

Implementation

Let's get on to the implementation. As usual, we'll start with the home interface.

The Home Interface

Listing 5.4 gives the code for our new home interface.

Listing 5.4   Home Interface for an Entity Bean with Bean-Managed Persistence

```
1   package book.chap05.customer;
2   import javax.ejb.EJBHome;
3   import java.rmi.RemoteException;
4   import javax.ejb.CreateException;
5   import javax.ejb.FinderException;

6   public interface CustomerHome extends EJBHome
7   {
8       public Customer create(String custname, String custaddr)
            throws RemoteException, CreateException;
9       public Customer findByPrimaryKey(CustomerPK pk) throws
            RemoteException, FinderException;
10      public java.util.Enumeration findByName(String name)
            throws RemoteException, FinderException;
11  }
```

This home interface is quite similar to the home interface for the last example, with the following exceptions:

- The arguments to the `create()` method are different, as they represent a row in the CUSTOMERS table rather than a row in the ORDERS table.
- The primary key used in `findByPrimaryKey()` is of type `CustomerPK` rather than `OrderPK`, for similar reasons.
- The interface uses a different custom finder method, `findByName()`. This method takes a name or substring thereof and queries the database for customers matching the argument. More about this method later.

The Remote Interface

Listing 5.5 gives the code for our remote interface.

Listing 5.5   Remote Interface for an Entity Bean with Bean-Managed Persistence

```
1   package book.chap05.customer;
2   import javax.ejb.EJBObject;
3   import java.rmi.RemoteException;
```

```
 4   public interface Customer extends EJBObject
 5   {
 6       public String getName() throws RemoteException;
 7       public void setName(String name) throws RemoteException;
 8       public String getAddress() throws RemoteException;
 9       public void setAddress(String addr) throws
         RemoteException;
10       public int getCustID() throws RemoteException;
         //read-only
11   }
```

As in the previous example, the remote interface merely provides a set of getter and setter methods that can be used to view and modify the values in the instance class.

The Implementation Class

Because Entity beans with bean-managed persistence must provide their own database updates, the implementation of a bean-managed Entity bean is a bit more involved than that of a container-managed Entity bean. Nevertheless, the individual steps of implementation are all quite straightforward. The full source code for this class appears in Appendix B; the following discussion will merely highlight relevant snippets of code.

```
17   transient private EntityContext ctx;
18   private int custid;
19   private String name;
20   private String addr;
```

Lines 17–20 declare the instance variables. Just to make a point, we have declared the member variables of this class as private. You are required to make them public only if you're using container-managed persistence.

```
41   public void setEntityContext(EntityContext ctx)
42   {
43       this.ctx = ctx;
44       Properties props = ctx.getEnvironment();
45       String JDBCDriverName = (String)
         props.get("customerBean.JDBCDriverName");
46       //load the JDBC driver

47       try
48       {
49       Class.forName(JDBCDriverName).newInstance();
50       }
51       catch (Exception e)
52       {
```

```
53      }

54   }
```

The `setEntityContext()` method of this bean also loads the JDBC driver. Remember that finder methods are invoked on entity EJBs in the pool, so you must make sure to load your JDBC driver before invoking the finder method.

```
59   public CustomerPK ejbCreate(String custname,
     String custaddr) throws CreateException
60   {
61     //create customer as in Session bean
62     try
63     {
64     //given a name and address, create a customer
65     //in the database, and return the customer identifier
66     String query = "insert into customers (cust_id,
       cust_name, cust_addr) values ((select max(cust_id) from
       customers) + 1, '" +custname + "', '" + custaddr + "')";
67     Connection c = DriverManager.getConnection(getDBURL());
68     Statement stmt = c.createStatement();
69     int count = stmt.executeUpdate(query);
70     stmt.close();
71     stmt = c.createStatement();
72     query = "select max(cust_id) from customers";
73     ResultSet rs = stmt.executeQuery(query);
74     rs.next();
75     int custid = rs.getInt(1);
76     rs.close();
77     stmt.close();
78     c.close();
79     this.custid = custid;
80         this.name = custname;
81         this.addr = custaddr;
82         CustomerPK custPK = new CustomerPK();
83         custPK.custid = custid;
84     return custPK;
85     }
86     catch (Exception e)
87     {
88     throw new CreateException();
89     }
90
91   }
```

Lines 59–91 implement the `ejbCreate()` method. The logic in this method is similar to that used in the `newCustomer()` method of the `Bag2Bean` class used in Chapter 4. First, a new customer ID is created in the database, equal to the current maximum customer ID in the database plus 1. This approach ensures that the new customer will have a unique ID. The database is then queried to find the newly assigned customer ID. In lines 79–81, the instance variables are set to the values of the argument variables. In line 82, a new `CustomerPK` instance is created and initialized with the new customer ID. Line 84 returns this new `CustomerPK` instance. The container will take this instance and transmogrify it into a remote reference to this Entity bean instance.

```
101  public void ejbRemove()
102  {
103  //delete row by custid
104      try
105      {

106          String query = "delete from customers where cust_id =
             " + this.custid;
107          executeUpdate(query);

108      }
109      catch (Exception e)
110      {
111      }
112  }
```

Lines 101–112 contain the implementation of the `ejbRemove()` method. It is necessary to implement this method because bean-managed Entity beans are entirely responsible for their own database management. This method formulates an appropriate SQL delete clause in line 106, then invokes a method called `executeUpdate()` that performs the necessary JDBC operations to establish a connection, invoke the method, and close the connection again.

```
113  public void ejbLoad()
114  {

115      //read in values from database

116      try
117      {
118      CustomerPK pk = (CustomerPK)ctx.getPrimaryKey();
119      this.custid = pk.custid;

120      Connection c = DriverManager.getConnection(getDBURL());
121      //update
122      String query = "select cust_name, cust_addr from
             customers where cust_id = " + this.custid;
123      Statement s = c.createStatement();
124      ResultSet rs = s.executeQuery(query);
125      boolean more = rs.next();
126      if (more)
127          {
```

```
128              this.name = rs.getString(1);
129              this.addr = rs.getString(2);
130              }
131          rs.close();
132          s.close();
133          c.close();
134          }
135          catch (SQLException e)
136          {
137          }
138  }
```

Lines 113–138 implement the ejbLoad() method. Recall that, for the container-managed example, we did not have to provide an implementation for this method. If an Entity bean uses bean-managed persistence, however, you must implement this method. The ejbLoad() method simply performs a query against the database based on the primary key (in this case, the customer ID), retrieves the values for the other columns in the table, and sets the instance variables of this instance to the values from the database table. The ejbLoad() method is called when an Entity bean transitions from the pooled state to the ready state and needs an identity; it is also called at various times throughout the life of an Entity bean in the ready state to ensure that the values in the Entity bean's instance variables match those in the database.

Note lines 118 and 119, which read the primary key in from the Entity-Context and set the class's primary key variable accordingly. When the container decides to create a new entity instance from the available pool, no special method is called to set the primary key of the new instance. Rather, the container simply sets the primary key in the EntityContext and assumes that the bean will retrieve this value in the ejbLoad() method.

```
139  public void ejbStore()
140  {
141      //write out values to database
142      try
143      {
144      String query = "update customers set cust_name = '"+
           this.name +"', cust_addr = '" + this.addr + "' where
           cust_id = " + this.custid;
145      executeUpdate(query);
146      }
147      catch (Exception e)
148      {
149      }

150  }
```

Lines 139–150 implement the `ejbStore()` method, which is the counterpart of the `ejbLoad()` method; it updates the underlying database with the values contained in the EJB object. Here, `ejbLoad()` is implemented as an SQL update statement, which updates the database row corresponding to the primary key of the EJB instance with the values of the instance's variables.

```
151   public void executeUpdate(String SQLCommand) throws
      SQLException
152   {
153       Connection c = DriverManager.getConnection(getDBURL());
154       //update
155       String query = SQLCommand;
156       Statement s = c.createStatement();
157       s.executeUpdate(query);
158       s.close();
159       c.close();
160       }
```

Lines 151–160 implement the `executeUpdate()` method, which is simply a convenience method that encapsulates the mechanics of invoking an SQL update command on a database. Actually, this method can be used to invoke any SQL command that doesn't return a result set.

```
168   public CustomerPK ejbFindByPrimaryKey(CustomerPK pk) throws
      FinderException
169   {
170       //query database for primary key
171       int count = executeCountQuery("select count(*) from
      customers where custid = " + pk.custid);
172       if (count == 1)
173       {
174           return pk;
175           }
176       else if (count < 1)
177           {
178           throw new FinderException("row not found for
      custid " + pk.custid + ";count was " + count);
179           }
180       else // (count > 1)
181           {
182           throw new FinderException("more than one row found
      for custid " + pk.custid + ";count was " + count);
183
184           }
185       //throw finder exception if not found
186   }
```

Lines 168–186 implement the `ejbFindByPrimaryKey()` method. This method takes a primary key as an argument, and returns a primary key representing the argument as its return value. Before returning the primary key, the ejbFindByPrimaryKey() method checks the underlying data store to ensure that the key already exists in the database. If the query doesn't find a row, or if it finds duplicate rows for the primary key, a FinderException is thrown to inform the caller that an error has occurred. After a primary key is returned, the container will perform the appropriate magic to provide the client with a suitably initialized instance. Remember that finder methods are invoked on beans that are in the pooled state; thus, when you're implementing a finder method, you shouldn't try to access the object's state.

```
187  public Enumeration ejbFindByName(String name)
188  {
189       //do query for pks
190       try
191       {
192       Connection c = DriverManager.getConnection(getDBURL());
193       //update
194       String query = "select cust_id from customers where
                 cust_name like '%" + name + "%'";
195       Statement s = c.createStatement();
196       ResultSet rs = s.executeQuery(query);
197       //create enumeration object
198       Vector v = new Vector();
199       CustomerPK pk;
200       //populate with pks
201       boolean more = rs.next();
202       while (more)
203       {
204           pk = new CustomerPK();
205           pk.custid = rs.getInt(1);
206           v.addElement(pk);
207           more = rs.next();
208       }
209       rs.close();
210       s.close();
211       c.close();
212       return v.elements(); //vector returns an enumeration
                 of all values in the table
213       }//end try
214       catch (SQLException e)
215       {
216           return null;
217       }
218  }
```

Lines 187–218 implement the custom finder method, findByName(). This method takes a String as its argument; this String represents a name or a substring of a name. In line 194, an SQL query is constructed using the SQL "like" operator, which can carry out wildcard matching. The bean executes this query on line 196, then loops through the ResultSet in lines 202–208. For each key in the ResultSet, the bean creates a new CustomerPK object, sets its custid field to the value returned from the database, and adds the CustomerPK object to a vector. Once the ResultSet has been read through, the method closes its database connections and uses the Vector class's elements() method (which returns a java.util.Enumeration of all elements in the vector) to return an enumeration of all the primary keys in the result set.

The Primary Key Class

```
1   package book.chap05.customer;
2   public class CustomerPK implements java.io.Serializable
3   {
4       public int custid;
5   }
```

The preceding code gives the primary key class for the customer example. As CUST_ID is the only field that makes up the primary key in the database, custid is the only field in the primary key class.

The Client

Appendix B provides the source code for the client. The client code is straightforward and requires no explanation.

Deployment

The deployment descriptor for this bean is quite similar to the bean in the previous example, with the following exceptions:

- Because the bean uses bean-managed persistence, the deployment descriptor should not specify any container-managed fields.
- The deployment descriptor does not need to contain any information on finder methods, because we have already implemented them.

Conclusion

Entity beans are a potent tool in the toolbox of the EJB developer. They can be used to wrap existing data in objects or to allow newly created objects to be saved to persistent storage with little trouble.

CHAPTER 6

EJB Clients

This chapter discusses how to write client programs that access EJBs. Rather than trying to lump everything into one or two large examples, the chapter is split into a number of discrete examples that demonstrate the various bits of functionality. A small, well-defined example that demonstrates one particular thing is often clearer than a large, amorphous example that attempts to demonstrate many things.

An EJB Bean as a Client to Another Bean

The first example focuses on how an EJB bean interacts with another bean. As noted earlier in the book, EJB beans use exactly the same API as any other client when they access an EJB. The example here will demonstrate this point.

The Home Interface

The code for the EJB client bean's home interface is presented in Listing 6.1. The client bean is a stateless Session bean, so it needs only a single `create()` method that takes no arguments. In fact, as you'll recall from Chapter 4 on Session beans, a stateless Session bean can have only one `create()` method. Session beans of any kind cannot declare finder methods, so the home interface for this bean is quite simple.

Listing 6.1 Home Interface for an EJB Client Bean

```
1   package book.chap06.bean;
2   import javax.ejb.*;

3   public interface ClientHome extends EJBHome
```

```
4   {
5       public Client create() throws java.rmi.RemoteException,
        javax.ejb.CreateException;
6   }
```

The Remote Interface

Because we are striving to keep the examples in this chapter short and to the point, the remote interface is correspondingly simple. The client performs all of its interactions with the remote EJB in the run() method.

```
package book.chap06.bean;
import javax.ejb.*;
import java.rmi.*;

public interface Client extends EJBObject
{
    void run() throws RemoteException;
}
```

The EJB Client Bean

The code for the EJB client bean is provided in Listing 6.2. It's just a simple stateless Session bean, so we won't go over the basics again.

Listing 6.2   EJB Client Bean

```
1   package book.chap06.bean;
2   import javax.ejb.SessionBean;
3   import javax.ejb.SessionContext;
4   import java.rmi.RemoteException;
5   import javax.naming.NamingException;
6   import javax.ejb.CreateException;
7   import javax.ejb.RemoveException;
8   import java.util.Properties;
9   import javax.naming.Context;
10  import javax.naming.InitialContext;
11  import book.chap05.order.Order;
12  import book.chap05.order.OrderHome;

13  public class ClientBean implements SessionBean
14  {
15      SessionContext ctx;
16      public void ejbCreate()
17      {
18      }

19      public void run()
20      {
```

```
21          try
22          {
23      Properties p = new Properties();
24          p.put(Context.INITIAL_CONTEXT_FACTORY,
25              "weblogic.jndi.TengahInitialContextFactory");
26          InitialContext ic = new InitialContext(p);

27          OrderHome oh = (OrderHome) ic.lookup("OrderHome");
28          Order o1 = oh.create(1, "1," 1);
29          Order o2 = oh.create(1, "2," 1);
30          o1.remove();
31          o2.remove();
32          }
33          catch(NamingException e){}
34          catch(CreateException e){}
35          catch(RemoveException e){}
36          catch(RemoteException e){}

37      }

38      public void ejbRemove()
39      {
40      }
41      public void ejbActivate()
42      {
43      }
44      public void ejbPassivate()
45      {
46      }

47      public void setSessionContext(SessionContext ctx)
48      {
49          this.ctx = ctx;
50      }

51  }
```

The only noteworthy thing about the rest of the program is that, in lines 11 and 12, we import the Order and OrderHome interfaces from Chapter 4. We use the Order bean as the target bean for this client.

Lines 23–26 set up an initial naming context. This example employs an idiom that was not used in previous clients. In the clients described in earlier chapters, we used a command-line parameter to define the initial naming factory. For example,

```
java -Djava.naming.factory.initial=weblogic.jndi.
T3InitialContextFactory ClientClient
```

In this example, we don't have access to the command line; the bean is started by the bean container, without the developer's intervention. To define an environment property, we therefore have two options:

- We can set up an environment property in the deployment descriptor.
- We can create a new `Properties` object in the client and pass it to the `InitialContext` constructor.

The first option is generally preferable to the second, because it allows the bean's deployer to configure the property at deployment time so as to point to an appropriate factory. As we have already covered setting environment properties in deployment descriptors, let's show an example of the second approach.

All of the EJB client interaction in this bean happens between lines 23 and 31. On line 23, an empty `Properties()` object is created.

On lines 24 and 25, the program uses the static final variable `Context.INITIAL_CONTEXT_FACTORY` (which holds the string `"java.naming.factory.initial"`) to set the value of the initial naming factory to `"weblogic.jndi.TengahInitialContextFactory"` in the Properties array from line 23.

On line 26, a new `InitialContext` object is created, and the `Properties` array is passed to the constructor as an argument. The constructor reads the values from this array and uses them to obtain a reference to a real `Initial-ContextFactory`.

As noted earlier in this book, you should not hard-code any vendor-specific information in your EJB code. This consideration is especially important if you wish to deploy your beans under more than one EJB container, or if you wish to be able to resell your beans.

Once the initial context is obtained, the bean looks up a reference to the OrderHome interface from Chapter 5, creates a couple of beans, and then immediately removes them. (I like to undo any changes I've performed when I'm writing examples, so that it's possible to run those examples again without getting errors because of an attempt to insert a row with a duplicate primary key.)

The Client

The client program in Listing 6.3 is about as short and simple as an EJB client program can possibly be. We declare the `main()` routine as throwing Exception, which means that we are not required to catch any exceptions in the code. It also means that any exceptions that do occur will terminate the program; for such a brief example, however, we can ignore this eventuality.

In lines 1–3, the client imports the EJB client program's home and remote interfaces, as well as `InitialContext`. It uses this context to look up the ClientHome interface (for this client, we pass in the value of `java.naming.context.initial` on the command line, so you don't see a reference to it in the code). From there, the client creates an instance of a Client bean, invokes its `run()` method, and removes the instance.

Listing 6.3   EJB Client

```
1   book.chap06.bean.ClientHome;
2   import book.chap06.bean.Client;
3   import javax.naming.InitialContext;

4   public class ClientClient{

5   public static void main(String[] args) throws Exception {

6   InitialContext ic = new InitialContext();
7   ClientHome ch = (ClientHome) ic.lookup("ClientHome");
8   Client c = ch.create();
9   c.run();
10  c.remove();
11  System.out.println("Client is done");
12  }
13  }
```

Serializing a Handle

The next example shows how to serialize a handle to a bean. A handle is a serializable reference to a bean; that is, you can obtain a handle from a bean's remote interface, write it out to persistent storage, and then close the program down. At some later time, you can read the handle in and use it to obtain a new reference to a remote bean.

Before delving too deeply into the example, you should learn some details about handles. In particular, the handle mechanism allows you to serialize a remote reference to the bean—but not to recreate the bean itself. Thus, if you save a reference via a handle and the bean is later removed by another process (or, in the case of a Session bean, by a server crash, shutdown, or timeout), the handle will throw a NoSuchObjectException when you attempt to reobtain a reference. That is, for the handle to work, the server-side object must still exist when you attempt to reobtain the reference. If you're not sure that the object will still be there, a better approach might be to simply recreate the object at a later time by storing the initialization data on the client and invoking the bean's create() or find() method. A good strategy is to attempt to reestablish your connection in a try block, and then include the necessary code to recreate the reference if the handle fails to do so.

The Client

As you will see in Listing 6.4, there are two paths through the client program. If the client is called with the command-line argument of "write," it obtains a reference to an Order bean, obtains a handle to the reference, and writes the handle to a file. If it is called with the command-line argument of "read," it reads the handle back in from the file, reobtains the remote reference, and uses this reference to finish its work.

Listing 6.4 EJB Client Using a Handle

```
1   import book.chap05.order.Order;
2   import book.chap05.order.OrderHome;
3   import javax.ejb.Handle;
4   import javax.ejb.CreateException;
5   import javax.ejb.RemoveException;
6   import java.rmi.RemoteException;
7   import javax.naming.InitialContext;
8   import javax.naming.NamingException;
9   import java.io.ObjectInputStream;
10  import java.io.ObjectOutputStream;
11  import java.io.FileInputStream;
12  import java.io.FileOutputStream;
13  import java.io.IOException;

14  public class HandleClient
15  {
16      static Handle myHandle;
17      public static void main (String[] argv)
18      {
19          if (argv[0].equalsIgnoreCase("read"))
20          {
21              readHandle();
22              finishWork();
23          }
24          else if (argv[0].equalsIgnoreCase("write"))
25          {
26              beginWork();
27              writeHandle();
28          }
29          else
30          {
31              System.out.println("usage: java HandleClient
                \"read\" | \"write\" ");
32          }
33      }
34      static void writeHandle()
35      {
36          System.out.println("called writeHandle");
37          try
38          {
39              FileOutputStream fos = new FileOutputStream
                ("beanhandle.ser");
40              ObjectOutputStream oos = new ObjectOutputStream
                (fos);
41              oos.writeObject(myHandle);
42              oos.flush();
43              oos.close();
```

```
44              }
45              catch(IOException e)
46              {
47                  System.out.println("Exception occurred in
                    writeHandle: " + e);
48              }
49          }

50          static void readHandle()
51          {
52              System.out.println("called readHandle");
53              try
54              {
55              FileInputStream fis = new FileInputStream
                ("beanhandle.ser");
56              ObjectInputStream ois = new ObjectInputStream
                (fis);
57              myHandle = (Handle)ois.readObject();
58              ois.close();
59              }
60              catch(Exception e)
61              {
62                  System.out.println("Exception occurred in
                    readHandle: " + e);
63              }
64      }
65      static void beginWork()
66      {
67          System.out.println("called beginWork");
68          try
69          {
70          InitialContext ic = new InitialContext();
71          System.out.println("looked up initial context");
72          OrderHome oh = (OrderHome) ic.lookup("OrderHome");
73          System.out.println("looked up home interface");
74          Order o1 = oh.create(1, "1," 1);
75          myHandle = o1.getHandle();
76          }
77          catch (CreateException e)
78          {
79              System.out.println("CreateException occurred:
                " + e);
80          }
81          catch (RemoteException e)
82          {
83                  System.out.println("CreateException occurred:
                    " + e);
84          }
85          catch (NamingException e)
86          {
87                  System.out.println("NamingException occurred:
                    " + e);
88          }
```

```
89        }

90        static void finishWork()
91        {
92            System.out.println("called finishWork");
93            try
94            {
95            System.out.println("using handle to obtain
                 reference");
96            Order o1 = (Order) myHandle.getEJBObject();
97            System.out.println("removing");
98            o1.remove();
99            //could also use remove method on home interface
                 with handle as argument
100           System.out.println("removed");
101           }
102           catch(RemoteException e)
103           {
104               System.out.println("RemoteException occurred:
                     " + e);
105               e.printStackTrace();
106           }
107           catch(RemoveException e)
108           {
109               System.out.println("RemoveException occurred:
                     " + e);
110               e.printStackTrace();
111           }
112       }
113   }
```

Lines 1–13 in Listing 6.4 are the import statements for the various classes that will be used. Note that we also import several classes from the java.io package; these classes will be used to store and retrieve the handle.

In line 16, the class declares a static variable of type Handle named myHandle. This variable will hold the value of the handle; it is static because the program is written using only static methods. (Note that Enterprise JavaBeans cannot have static variables, except for static final variables, because they would interfere with the container's ability to manage EJB instances. No such prohibition applies to client programs that make calls to EJB objects, however, unless the client programs are also EJB objects, as in the first example in this chapter.)

Lines 17–33 comprise the main routine of the program. As discussed earlier, this procedure checks for a command-line argument of "read" or "write" (note that it uses the equalsIgnoreCase() string comparison method to correctly interpret an argument such as "Read" or "READ" as being equivalent to "read"). If "read" or "write" is found on the command line, the routine invokes the appropriate procedures. If neither "read" nor "write" is found, it prints a usage message and exits.

Lines 34–49 implement the writeHandle() method, which writes the object stored in myHandle to a file.

In line 39, the method creates a FileOutputStream to a file named beanhandle.ser. This file will contain the serialized handle.

In line 40, the FileOutputStream from line 39 is wrapped in an ObjectOutputStream object. The ObjectOutputStream class includes the writeObject() method, which is a handy way to write a serializable object to persistent storage.

In line 41, the writeObject() method of the ObjectOutputStream class writes the value of myHandle to the file beanhandle.ser. Line 42 flushes the output stream, and line 43 closes the output stream. Output streams will be flushed automatically when they are closed, but good programming practice is to flush the streams when you have finished with them.

Lines 50–64 implement the readHandle() method, which reads the handle back in from persistent storage. Line 55 opens the file beanhandle.ser for reading. Line 56 wraps the FileInputStream in an ObjectInputStream, which provides the readObject() method. In line 57, the ObjectInputStream's readObject() method reads the value of myHandle in from the file. Note that a cast is used in line 57; the return value of readObject is of type Object and must be cast to the appropriate type before it can be used. Line 58 closes the input stream.

Lines 65–89 implement the beginWork() method. Lines 70–74 show a typical EJB client interaction:

- Creating an initial naming context
- Using the naming context to look up the home interface
- Using the home interface to create a bean

In line 75, the getHandle() method of the bean's remote interface obtains a handle and stores it in the myHandle static class variable. The writeHandle() method later uses this value to write the object out to persistent storage.

Lines 90–112 implement the finishWork() method. This method assumes that the readObject() method has been called before it is invoked and that the value stored in myHandle will be a valid handle to a remote bean. In line 96, it invokes the Handle object's getEJBObject() method, which returns a remote reference to the object. Again, note that you must cast the reference to the appropriate type, because it returns an object of type EJBObject by default. After the reference is obtained from the handle, the client calls the remote EJB object's remove() method to discard it. As the comment on line 99 indicates, we could have passed the handle itself as an argument to a remove() method on the bean's home interface; instead, we decided to show, however briefly, that the reactivated reference can be used just the same way as it was before it was serialized.

Invoking the Client

To invoke this client, first call

```
java -Djava.naming.factory.initial=weblogic.jndi.
T3InitialContextFactory HandleClient write
```

to write out a serialized handle. Next, call

```
java -Djava.naming.factory.initial=weblogic.jndi.
T3InitialContextFactory HandleClient read
```

to read the handle back in and finish working with it.

Transactions in Clients

We have briefly alluded to the idea that a client can create its own transaction context and use it to manage transactions across multiple invocations. Now, let's demonstrate exactly how to perform this task in Listing 6.5.

Listing 6.5   Client-Created Transaction Context

```
1   //this example illustrates how to obtain and use
2   //a transaction context in a client
3   import book.chap05.order.Order;
4   import book.chap05.order.OrderHome;
5   import javax.ejb.CreateException;
6   import javax.ejb.RemoveException;
7   import java.rmi.RemoteException;
8   import javax.naming.InitialContext;
9   import javax.naming.NamingException;
10  import java.io.ObjectInputStream;
11  import java.io.ObjectOutputStream;
12  import java.io.FileInputStream;
13  import java.io.FileOutputStream;
14  import java.io.IOException;
15  import javax.jts.UserTransaction;

16  public class ClientTx
17  {
18    public static void main (String[] argv)
19    {
20        UserTransaction utx = null;
21        try
22        {
23        InitialContext ic = new InitialContext();

24        System.out.println("looked up initial context");
```

```
25        OrderHome oh = (OrderHome) ic.lookup("OrderHome");
26        System.out.println("looked up home interface");
27        utx = (UserTransaction)ic.lookup("javax.jts.
          UserTransaction");
28        utx.begin();
29        Order o1 = oh.create(1, "1," 1);
30        Order o2 = oh.create(1, "2," 1);
31        utx.commit(); //or utx.rollback();
32        }
33        catch (CreateException e)
34        {
35            System.out.println("CreateException occurred:
             " + e);
36            if (utx != null)
37            {
38                utx.rollback();
39            }
40        }
41        catch (RemoteException e)
42        {
43            System.out.println("CreateException occurred:
             " + e);
44            if (utx != null)
45            {
46                utx.rollback();
47            }
48        }
49        catch (NamingException e)
50        {
51            System.out.println("NamingException occurred:
             " + e);
52            if (utx != null)
53            {
54                utx.rollback();
55            }
56        }
57    }
58 }
```

The initial import statements are similar to those given in the previous example; once again, we use the Order bean from Chapter 5 as the server-side EJB object. In line 15, we import the interface `javax.jts.UserTransaction`. This interface is part of the Java Transaction Services (JTS) specification. It's not necessary to get into JTS in much detail here, except to note that it is based on CORBA's Object Transaction specification, and that it's used by Enterprise JavaBeans that do bean-managed transactions and by EJB clients (such as this one) that take care of their own transactions. When the EJB specification is next updated, it will reflect the fact that `javax.jts.UserTransaction` has been moved to a package named `javax.transaction.UserTransaction`. Even though this class may move, its functionality remains the same.

Most of the `main()` method of this program is similar to many methods you've seen before, so our discussion will focus on the transaction code. Line 20 creates a variable of type `UserTransaction` to hold the reference to the object we'll obtain. The value of this variable is initialized to null. Later, in the exception-handling routines, we test the value of this variable to make sure that it's not null before invoking the `rollback()` method.

Line 27 obtains a reference to an object that implements the User-Transaction interface by doing a JNDI lookup on the name `javax.jts.User-Transaction`. The mechanism by which a client obtains a reference to a transaction is not outlined in the EJB specification (in fact, the specification virtually ignores the client side of EJB), but the various vendors apparently agree that a JNDI lookup will be a useful and portable way to obtain such a reference. Consult your documentation for specifics on how your vendor has implemented client-side transaction references.

After obtaining a reference, using the `UserTransaction` object is quite simple. In line 28, we invoke `utx.begin()` to begin a transaction. We then create two beans and call `utx.commit()` to commit our changes. The exception-handling methods call `utx.rollback()` to roll back the transaction if any exceptions are thrown. This step is not required; not all exceptions dictate that a transaction be rolled back. Some guidelines for the handling of exceptions in transactions follow:

- Throwing a TransactionRolledbackException indicates that the transaction has been rolled back and cannot be recovered. In this event, you should not try to recover the transaction, although you can begin a new one from scratch and attempt the transaction again from the beginning.
- If a RemoteException occurs during a transaction, the client should roll back the transaction. Recovering from a RemoteException is somewhat dicey, because the client generally can't tell whether the method has been completed. To preserve database consistency, it's best to roll back and start over.
- A RemoteException generally indicates some sort of system-level failure (for example, a server crash). These events do not mark the transaction for rollback automatically, but the client should carefully consider what sort of exception has occurred before attempting to move forward. For example, if the RemoteException occurred because of a loss of network connectivity, it may be pointless to attempt to continue work until the underlying cause of the problem is fixed.

Authentication in Clients

The EJB specification does not dictate the mechanism by which clients are authenticated by the EJB server. Although it goes into some detail about server-side access control lists (which we'll discuss in Chapter 7 on bean deployment and management), it never specifies exactly how information about a client's identity is passed from the client to the remote server. Authentication is sufficiently important to merit an example, however, even though the example may not work under all implementations. The example in Listing 6.6 will work under BEA WebXpress WebLogic, and presumably other EJB vendors offer a similar means of authentication.

Listing 6.6   Client Authentication Program

```
1
2
3    import book.chap05.order.Order;
4    import book.chap05.order.OrderHome;

5    import java.util.Properties;
6    import javax.naming.Context;

7    import javax.ejb.CreateException;
8    import javax.ejb.RemoveException;
9    import java.rmi.RemoteException;
10   import javax.naming.InitialContext;
11   import javax.naming.NamingException;
12   import java.io.ObjectInputStream;
13   import java.io.ObjectOutputStream;
14   import java.io.FileInputStream;
15   import java.io.FileOutputStream;
16   import java.io.IOException;
17   import javax.jts.UserTransaction;

18   public class AuthClient
19   {
20     public static void main (String[] argv)
21     {
22         try
23         {

24         Properties p = new Properties();
25         p.put(Context.INITIAL_CONTEXT_FACTORY,
26         "weblogic.jndi.T3InitialContextFactory");
27         p.put(Context.PROVIDER_URL, "t3://localhost:7001");
28         p.put(Context.SECURITY_PRINCIPAL, "myUser");
29         p.put(Context.SECURITY_CREDENTIALS, "myPassword");

30         InitialContext ic = new InitialContext(p);
```

```
31      System.out.println("looked up initial context");
32      OrderHome oh = (OrderHome) ic.lookup("OrderHome");
33      System.out.println("looked up home interface");
34      UserTransaction utx = UserTransaction)ic.lookup
        ("javax.jts.UserTransaction");
35      utx.begin();
36      Order o1 = oh.create(1, "1," 1);
37      Order o2 = oh.create(1, "2," 1);
38      utx.commit(); //or utx.rollback();
39      }
40      catch (CreateException e)
41      {
42          System.out.println("CreateException occurred:
            " + e);
43      }
44      catch (RemoteException e)
45      {
46          System.out.println("CreateException occurred:
            " + e);
47      }
48      catch (NamingException e)
49      {
50          System.out.println("NamingException occurred:
            " + e);
51      }
52  }
53  }
```

In WebLogic, authentication is carried out via JNDI. The authentication portion of this example is found in lines 24–30 of Listing 6.6.

Lines 25 and 26 set up a property entry for the InitialContextFactory.

Line 27 gives a URL with which to check the authentication information. This URL specifies the t3 protocol (which is specific to BEA WebXpress's WebLogic product) running on port 7001 of the local host.

Line 28 specifies the security principal. In this case, the principal is a user named myUser.

Line 29 specifies the security credential used to authenticate the user. In this case, a password is used, and the value of the password is myPassword. You might also use certificates to authenticate a user, but passwords are much simpler to demonstrate in a short example.

The authentication takes place in line 30, when the initial context is created. If the user ID and password given do not satisfy the server, the creation of the InitialContext will fail and throw an exception.

For this example to work, you must add the user myUser and the password myPassword to WebLogic's authentication. The most straightforward way to accomplish this task is to add a line in the weblogic.properties file stating the following:

```
weblogic.password.myUser=myPassword
```

This line creates the entity `myUser` and assigns it the password of `myPassword`. (For real-world usage, WebLogic provides the ability to set up a database to maintain user ID/password pairs. For purposes of a quick-and-dirty example, however, using the `weblogic.properties` file is sufficient.)

To enable this example to work, you should not specify any access control entries in the deployment descriptor of the Order bean. If you do, WebLogic will check whether the user `myUser` is a member of the access control lists you've specified; it will reject your login if it is not. Chapter 9 explains how to set up access control lists; for now, just leave access as wide-open.

Getting Metadata

Some clients may need to obtain **metadata** about the bean. If you've used JDBC extensively, the idea of metadata is probably not a new one. In JDBC, two metadata classes are frequently used:

- `DatabaseMetaData`, which allows the client to query for information about the database and the sorts of operations that it supports
- `ResultSetMetaData`, which allows the client to dynamically discover metadata about a `ResultSet`, such as the number of columns that it contains, the name and type of each column, and so forth.

Enterprise JavaBeans also provides clients with the ability to obtain metadata; in EJB, this retrieval takes place via the `getMetaData()` method provided as part of a bean's home interface. The container generates the `getMetaData()` method at deployment time. Typically, this method will be used by clients that wish to automatically discover information about a bean—for example, development environments that wish to make it easy to link beans together will often call this method. Typically, EJB metadata will be used by tool builders who wish to automatically generate connections among groups of already-installed beans. We will discuss EJB metadata, as shown in Listing 6.7, because you may eventually need to use it.

Listing 6.7   EJB Metadata Example

```
1
2
3    import book.chap05.order.Order;
4    import book.chap05.order.OrderHome;

5    import javax.ejb.CreateException;
6    import javax.ejb.RemoveException;
```

```
7   import java.rmi.RemoteException;
8   import javax.naming.InitialContext;
9   import javax.naming.NamingException;
10  import javax.ejb.EJBMetaData;
11  import javax.ejb.EJBHome;

12  import java.lang.reflect.*;

13  public class Metadata
14  {
15    public static void main (String[] argv)
16    {
17        try
18        {
19        InitialContext ic = new InitialContext();
20        System.out.println("looked up initial context");
21        OrderHome oh = (OrderHome) ic.lookup("OrderHome");

22        //get metadata from remote interface
23        EJBMetaData emd = oh.getEJBMetaData();
24        printMetaData(emd);
25        }
26        catch (RemoteException e)
27        {
28            System.out.println("CreateException occurred:
            " + e);
29        }
30        catch (NamingException e)
31        {
32            System.out.println("NamingException occurred:
            " + e);
33        }

34    }

35    public static void printMetaData(EJBMetaData emd)
36    {
37        EJBHome eh = emd.getEJBHome();
38        printEJBHomeInterface(eh);
39        Class hi = emd.getHomeInterfaceClass();
40        printClass(hi);
41        Class pk = emd.getPrimaryKeyClass();
42        printClass(pk);
43        boolean isSession = emd.isSession();
44        if (isSession)
45        {
46            System.out.println("\n\nThe bean is a Session
            bean");
47        }
48        else
49        {
50            System.out.println("\n\nThe bean is not a Session
            bean");
```

```
51            }
52    }

53            public static void printEJBHomeInterface(EJBHome eh)
54            {
55                System.out.println("\n\nHome interface: " + eh);

56            }
57            public static void printClass(Class c)
58            {
59                System.out.println("\n\nDisplaying information on
                  class: " + c.getName());
60        Class [] array = c.getInterfaces();
61        System.out.println("Interfaces");
62        printClassArray(array);
63        array = c.getClasses();
64        System.out.println("Classes");
65        printClassArray(array);
66        System.out.println("Fields");
67        Field[] f = c.getFields();
68        printFields(f);
69        System.out.println("Methods");
70        Method[] m = c.getMethods();
71        printMethods(m);
72        System.out.println("Constructors");
73        Constructor[] co = c.getConstructors();
74        printConstructors(co);
75        }
76            public static void printClassArray(Class[] ca)
77            {
78                System.out.println("-------------------------");
79                if (ca.length == 0)
80                {
81                    System.out.println("none");
82                }
83                else
84                {
85                    for (int i = 0; i < ca.length; i++)
86                    {
87                        System.out.println(":" + ca[i]);
88                    }

89            }
90
91            System.out.println("-------------------------");

92            }
93            public static void printMethods(Method[] ma)
94        {
95            System.out.println("-------------------------");
96            if (ma.length == 0)
97            {
98                System.out.println("none");
```

```
 99            }
100            else
101            {
102                for (int i = 0; i < ma.length; i++)
103                {
104                    System.out.println(":" + ma[i]);
105                }
106            }
107            System.out.println("--------------------------");

108            }

109        public static void printFields(Field[] fa)
110        {
111          System.out.println("--------------------------");
112          if (fa.length == 0)
113          {
114                System.out.println("none");
115          }
116          else
117          {
118                for (int i = 0; i < fa.length; i++)
119                {
120                    System.out.println(":" + fa[i]);
121                }
122          }
123          System.out.println("--------------------------");

124        }

125        public static void printConstructors(Constructor[] ca)
126        {
127          System.out.println("-------------------------");
128          if (ca.length == 0)
129          {
130                System.out.println("none");

131          }
132          else
133          {
134                for (int i = 0; i < ca.length; i++)
135                {
136                    System.out.println(":" + ca[i]);
137                }
138          }
139          System.out.println("---------------------");
140        }
141 }
```

The example in Listing 6.7 is quite straightforward. In line 23, we call getEJBMetaData() on the Order bean's home interface. The rest of the example is largely devoted to printing out the results. For the purposes of this example, we merely print out the various `Field` and `Method` objects using their default string representations. It's also possible to do a more detailed inspection of these values, however.

The `printMetaData()` method (lines 35–52) is the "meat" of this example, showing what sort of information is available as part of the EJBMetaData interface.

- In lines 37 and 38, the method obtains the bean's home interface and prints it.
- In lines 39 and 40, it obtains the class that represents the home interface and prints it.
- In lines 41 and 42, it obtains the class that represents the primary key for this bean and prints it.
- In line 43, it calls the Boolean method `isSession()` to discover whether the bean is a Session or an Entity bean.

A Servlet Client

For our next trick, let's call an EJB bean from a servlet. **Servlets** are basically Java's answer to CGI programming. These small programs are invoked by a Web server. Servlets offer several advantages over CGI programs:

- Each time a CGI program is invoked, the Web server must spawn a new process to handle the invocation. Servlets, on the other hand, do not require a new process for each invocation; they are invoked as part of a new thread, which is a considerably lighter-weight operation in terms of server resources.
- Servlets have a fairly straightforward interface for input and output. In CGI scripting, interface libraries have evolved over the years that make input and output more straightforward, but they are not necessarily built into the Web server. With servlets, you can depend on the existence of the servlet API.
- Servlets allow you to write in Java. I'm rather fond of Java, and many readers probably are, too. It's possible—though painful—to write a CGI program using Java, but several hacks are involved. Servlets are a much cleaner way to use Java for server-side web programming, as you can see in Listing 6.8.

Listing 6.8 Servlet Example

```
1    package book.chap06.servlet;
2    import java.io.*;
3    import javax.servlet.*;
4    import javax.servlet.http.*;
```

```
5   import book.chap05.order.Order;
6   import book.chap05.order.OrderHome;
7   import javax.ejb.CreateException;
8   import javax.ejb.RemoveException;
9   import java.rmi.RemoteException;
10  import javax.naming.InitialContext;
11  import javax.naming.NamingException;

12  public class ServletClient extends HttpServlet {
13  OrderHome oh;

14  public void init()
15  {
16    try
17    {
18    //do naming lookup on load
19    InitialContext ic = new InitialContext();
20    oh = (OrderHome) ic.lookup("OrderHome");
21    }
22    catch(NamingException e)
23    {
24        //exception handling code here
25    }

26  }
27  public void service(HttpServletRequest req, HttpServlet
    Response res)
28    throws ServletException, IOException
29    {

30    PrintWriter out = res.getWriter();
31    int custid = Integer.parseInt(req.getParameter("custid"));
32    String itemcode = req.getParameter("itemcode");
33    int quantity = Integer.parseInt(req.getParameter
      ("quantity"));
34    out.println("<HTML>");
35    out.println("<HEAD>");
36    out.println("<TITLE>");
37    out.println("Servlet as an EJB Client example");
38    out.println("</TITLE>");
39    out.println("</HEAD>");
40    out.println("<BODY>");
41    out.println("This example illustrates a servlet calling
      an EJB bean<br>");
42    try
43    {
44        Order o1 = oh.create(custid, itemcode, quantity);
45        out.println("Created bean<br>");
46        o1.remove();
47        out.println("Removed bean<br>");
48        out.println("<p>The example has completed
          successfully<br>");
49    }
```

```
50      catch(Exception e)
51      {
52          out.println("An exception occurred: " + e);
53      }
54      finally
55      {
56          out.println("</BODY>");
57          out.println("</HTML>");
58          out.close(); //if you don't do this, your data will
                not be sent to the browser
59      }
60  }

61  public String getServletInfo()
62  {
63      return "ServletClient: a servlet that acts as an
            Enterprise JavaBeans client";
64      }
65  }
```

The first 11 lines of Listing 6.8 import the various classes needed.

Line 12 declares this class as extending the class HttpServlet. We could have used another class, GenericServlet, but since we are dealing with HTTP, we'll use HttpServlet.

Line 13 declares a variable of type OrderHome to hold a reference to the home interface.

Lines 14–25 implement the init() method, which is called once, when the servlet is first initialized. This method obtains a reference to the OrderHome interface. After the init() method is called, the servlet may have its service() method invoked many times by many different clients; thus you should not put anything in the init() method that is intended to service any particular client. Because many clients may reuse the reference to the home interface, it's acceptable to put this reference in the init() method.

Lines 27–60 implement the service() method of this bean. This method acts similarly to a classical CGI program; it is invoked in response to a client request, takes whatever input the client has sent, and generates Hypertext markup Language (HTML) that is returned to the client. Note the arguments that the method takes:

- An object of type HttpServletRequest, which contains the information from the client request
- An object of type HttpServletResponse, which is used to create a response and send it to the client

On line 30, the method invokes the getWriter() method of the Http-ServletResponse object. This method returns an object of type PrintWriter that sends its output to the client's browser. This `PrintWriter` object will be used to write the response HTML page.

Lines 31–33 use the `HttpServletRequest` object's `getParameter()` method to retrieve the values that were passed in from the HTML form (the code for the HTML form appears later in this section). The three parameters—`custid`, `itemcode`, and `quantity`—correspond to the arguments to the Order bean's `create()` method. Note that `getParameter()` always returns a string; in lines 31 and 33, the static method `Integer.parseInt()`transforms this string into an integer value. (You can also obtain an integer value by creating a new Integer object—use the string as a constructor argument and then call the `valueOf()` method of the instantiated Integer class. Using `parseInt()` is less expensive in terms of object creation and a bit more straightforward to read, however.)

Lines 34–41 use the `PrintWriter` object obtained from the `HttpServlet-Response` object to write some boilerplate HTML to the browser. Lines 42–48 create a bean and then remove it, also writing HTML to the browser. If an exception occurs while the bean is being used, lines 50–53 catch the exception, and the information about the exception is written to the browser.

Lines 54–59 contain the `finally` clause for the `try` block that begins on line 42. As you may remember from learning Java fundamentals, the `finally` block always executes, regardless of whether the `try` block completes normally or an exception is thrown. As a result, the `finally` clause is a good place to close system resources and the like. In our example, the finally clause writes the end of the HTML document and closes the `PrintWriter` stream. As the comment indicates, if you do not close the `PrintWriter` stream, the HTML will not show up in the user's browser; instead, the user will likely get a message such as "Document contains no data." If this message appears, you most likely haven't properly closed your output stream.

Lines 61–65 implement the `getServletInfo()` method. This method is similar to the `getAppletInfo()` method in the Applet class and returns a brief chunk of text describing the servlet and its purpose.

HTML to Make a Call to the Servlet

Listing 6.9 gives the HTML needed to call our servlet.

Listing 6.9   HTML to Call the Servlet

```
1   <HTML>
2   <HEAD>
3   <TITLE>Servlet as EJB client</TITLE>
4   </HEAD>
5   <BODY>
6   <p>
7   <H1>Servlet as EJB client</H1>
```

```
8   <p>
9   This test page invokes a servlet that, in turn, invokes
10  an EJB bean. There are two forms below: the first sends the
11  request via HTTP GET, and the second uses HTTP POST.
12  <hr>
13  HTTP GET example<br>

14  <FORM method=GET action="http://localhost:7001/
    ServletClient">
15  <table border>
16  <tr>
17  <td>
18  Customer ID:
19  </td>
20  <td>
21  <input type=text name=custid value=1>
22  </td>
23  </tr>
24  <tr>
25  <td>
26  Item code:
27  </td>
28  <td>
29  <input type=text name=itemcode value=1>
30  </td>
31  </tr>
32  <tr>
33  <td>
34  Quantity:
35  </td>
36  <td>
37  <input type=text name=quantity value=1>
38  </td>
39  </tr>
40  <tr>
41  <td>
42  <input type=submit>
43  </td>
44  <td>
45  <input type=reset>
46  </td>
47  </tr>
48  </table>
49  </form>
50  <hr>
51  HTTP POST example<br>

52  <FORM method=POST action="http://localhost:7001/
    ServletClient">
53  <table border>
54  <tr>
55  <td>
```

```
56 Customer ID:
57 </td>
58 <td>
59 <input type=text name=custid value=1>
60 </td>
61 </tr>
62 <tr>
63 <td>
64 Item code:
65 </td>
66 <td>
67 <input type=text name=itemcode value=1>
68 </td>
69 </tr>
70 <tr>
71 <td>
72 Quantity:
73 </td>
74 <td>
75 <input type=text name=quantity value=1>
76 </td>
77 </tr>
78 <tr>
79 <td>
80 <input type=submit>
81 </td>
82 <td>
83 <input type=reset>
84 </td>
85 </tr>
86 </table>
87 </form>

88 </BODY>
89 </HTML>
```

This chunk of HTML invokes the servlet shown in Listing 6.8. This page contains two CGI forms. The first form, found in lines 14–49, invokes the servlet using the HTTP GET protocol. In the HTTP GET protocol, the input parameters are stored in an environment variable called QUERY_STRING. In a CGI program, the program itself would decode the values in QUERY_STRING; with servlets, the servlet environment takes care of the decoding.

The second form, found in lines 52–87, invokes the same servlet via the HTTP POST protocol. In this protocol, a CGI program would have to open standard input for reading, read in the parameters using a function similar to the C read() function, decode the parameters, and then use them.

This example includes both a GET and a POST request to demonstrate that the servlet will work without you taking any special action for either a GET or a POST. By the time the servlet is called, the data have already been read in, decoded, and made available in the HttpServletRequest object.

If you plan to run your servlet on another machine, you must alter the "action" parameters of both forms to point them to the correct target. Currently, they both point to

```
http://localhost:7001/ServletClient
```

Setting Up WebLogic Servlets

To install a servlet in BEA WebXpress WebLogic, add the following line to your `weblogic.properties` file:

```
weblogic.httpd.register.ServletClient=book.chap06.servlet.
ServletClient
```

This line tells the server several things:

- The server should use the alias `ServletClient` for invocation. You can precede this alias with path entries if you wish. For example, if the class should be invoked as `http://localhost:7001/foo/bar/ServletClient`, you would say `weblogic.httpd.register.foo.bar.ServletClient=book.chap06.servlet.ServletClient`.
- WebLogic should use the class `book.chap06.servlet.ServletClient`. This class must be installed somewhere in WebLogic's class path. For example, assuming that a directory called `c:\weblogic\classes` appears in your class path, you would install the ServletClient class in the directory `c:\weblogic\classes\book\chap06\servlet`.

An Applet Client

You can also access EJB server objects from within an applet, as shown in Listing 6.10.

Listing 6.10   An Applet Client

```
1   //this example illustrates how to obtain and use
2   //a transaction context in a client
3   import book.chap05.order.Order;
4   import book.chap05.order.OrderHome;

5   import java.applet.Applet;
6   import java.awt.Graphics;

7   import javax.ejb.CreateException;
8   import javax.ejb.RemoveException;
9   import java.rmi.RemoteException;
10  import javax.naming.Context;
```

```
11  import javax.naming.InitialContext;
12  import javax.naming.NamingException;
13  import javax.jts.UserTransaction;
14  import java.util.Properties;
15  public class EJBApplet extends Applet implements Runnable
16  {
17    String message;
18    Thread t;
19    public void init()
20    {
21        message = "Initializing applet";
22    }
23    public void doEJBStuff()
24    {
25        try
26        {
27        Properties p = new Properties();
28        p.put(Context.INITIAL_CONTEXT_FACTORY,
29            "weblogic.jndi.TengahInitialContextFactory");
30        p.put(Context.PROVIDER_URL, "t3://" +
            getCodeBase().getHost() + ":7001/");
31        InitialContext ic = new InitialContext(p);

32        message = "looked up initial context";
33        OrderHome oh = (OrderHome) ic.lookup("OrderHome");
34        message = "looked up home interface";
35        UserTransaction utx = (UserTransaction)ic.lookup
            ("javax.jts.UserTransaction");
36        message = "looked up UserTransaction";
37        utx.begin();
38        message = "began transaction";
39        Order o1 = oh.create(1, "1," 1);
40        message = "created an order";
41        Order o2 = oh.create(1, "2," 1);
42        message = "created another order";
43        utx.commit(); //or utx.rollback();
44        message = "committed transaction; done";
45        ic.close();

46        }
47        catch (CreateException e)
48        {
49            message = "CreateException occurred: " + e;
50        }
51        catch (RemoteException e)
52        {
53            message = "CreateException occurred: " + e;
54        }
55        catch (NamingException e)
56        {
57            message = "NamingException occurred: " + e;
58        }
```

```
59  }
60  public void paint(Graphics g)
61  {
62      g.drawString(message, 10, 10);
63  }
64  public void start()
65  {
66      t = new Thread(this);
67      t.start();
68  }
69  public void stop()
70  {
71      t.stop();
72      t = null;
73  }
74  public void run()
75  {
76      doEJBStuff();
77      while (true)
78      {
79          repaint();
80          try
81          {
82          Thread.sleep(500);
83          }
84          catch (Exception e)
85          {
86              System.out.println ("exception occurred" + e);
87          }
88      }
89  }
90  }
```

The applet in Listing 6.10 again reuses the Order bean from Chapter 5 as its target. Lines 27–45 contain the EJB-specific code. Not much has changed from the other client examples, except that lines 28 and 29 specify the initial context class (because we can't pass it in via the command line; we could have passed it in as an applet parameter, however) and the URL for JNDI to use. (We used `getCodeBase().getHost()` to ensure that we obtained a reference to the host from which the applet was downloaded.)

This example has been tested in Netscape 4.05 and appletviewer, but does not appear to work in Internet Explorer. BEA WebXpress recommends that you use the Java Plug-in when using WebLogic as applets. The Java Plug-in (formerly known as the Java Activator) is a Java Virtual Machine (VM) that can be used instead of the browser's own virtual machine. It acts as a plug-in under Netscape and as an ActiveX control under Internet Explorer. The Java Plug-in does not rely on the browser's own virtual machine, so you can run a current VM even in old browsers. For example, you might run a JDK 1.1 applet using

RMI in Internet Explorer 3.02 if you have installed the Java Plug-in. Using the Java Plug-in requires you to wrap your applet tags in some fairly strange-looking HTML so as to invoke the plug-in instead of the browser's own VM. When downloading the plug-in, you can also download an HTML converter that will automate this process.

Another significant benefit of using the Java Plug-in is that, if you need signed applets, you can sign them one way. Netscape, Internet Explorer, and HotJava all support signed applets. Each uses a completely different approach to code signing, however, so that you must either sign your code three different ways or specify a particular browser and ignore the other two. The Java Plug-in provides a third option—sign your code so that it works with the plug-in, and then use the plug-in in any client browsers.

Why would you want to sign your code? Two general reasons are usually cited:

- Signing your code provides the user with some evidence that you are who you say you are. The user can then make an informed decision about whether to allow your code to run.
- Signed applets can potentially do more than unsigned applets. In JDK 1.1, a signed applet is granted the same level of privilege as a locally running Java application. In Java 2, the permissions granted to a signed applet are specified at a finer level of granularity, but you can still grant a signed applet virtually any permission to which the user agrees.

If your applet requires the ability to do things that are not ordinarily permitted for applets (such as connecting to more than one host, writing to a local file, and so forth) you may need to sign your applets to make this ability become reality.

The Applet Tag

The following applet tag is used to run the applet:

```
<APPLET code=EJBApplet.class codebase="/classes" width=2000
height=100> </APPLET>
```

Note that the codebase parameter is set to "/classes." WebLogic creates the "/classes" alias to point to all classes in its class path. Thus, by adding this alias to your tag, you can ensure that the applet gains access to all classes that it needs.

In fact, the applet needs quite a few classes to run EJB successfully. Consequently, an EJB applet can take some time to start. WebLogic includes a tool called the Applet Archiver that will run an applet and create a .jar or .cab file containing all of the required classes. You can then place this .jar or .cab file in an archive field in your applet tag, and the browser will download all of the classes at once. This approach saves on the overhead (you don't need to make a separate request for each class that must be downloaded) and so speeds up the start-up time for your applets.

CORBA Client Example

Listing 6.11 is a CORBA client that accesses EJB beans. The story behind this example goes as follows: I couldn't gain access to an EJB server that implemented the EJB-to-CORBA mapping in time to put this example together. Fortunately, the folks at Inprise Corporation (who were then putting the finishing touches on their CORBA-aware EJB product) came to the rescue. Inprise's Jonathan K. Weedon took the order example from Chapter 5 and the client transaction example from Listing 6.5 and e-mailed back a CORBA-ized version of the client transaction program, as well as some execution traces showing that the program had actually been run. The CORBA client is shown in Listing 6.11.

Listing 6.11 CORBA Client

```
1   //this example illustrates how to obtain and use
2   //a transaction context in a client
3
4   import book.chap05.order.*;
5   import org.omg.CosNaming.*;
6   import org.omg.CosTransactions.*;
7
8   import java.util.Enumeration;
9   import org.omg.CORBA.ORB;
10
11  public class CorbaClientTx {
12
13  public static void main (String[] argv) throws Exception {
14
15  System.out.printIn("client is running");
16  ORB orb=ORB.init(argv, null);
17
18  NamingContext context=NamingContextHelper.narrow
19  (orb.resolve_initial_references("NameService"));
20  System.out.printIn("looked up initial context");
21
22  OrderHome oh;
23  {
24     NameComponent nameComponent=new NameComponent
        ("OrderHome","");
25     NameComponent[] nameComponents={ nameComponent };
```

```
26    oh=OrderHomeHelper.narrow(context.resolve
      (nameComponents));
27    System.out.printIn("looked up home interface");
28  }
29
30  //get the transaction current (analogous to UserTransaction)
31  Current current=CurrentHelper.narrow
32  (orb.resolve_initial_references("TransactionCurrent"));
33
34  current.begin();
35  Order o1=oh.create(1, "1", 1);
36  Order o2=oh.create(1, "2", 1);
37  //commit the transaction, reporting heuristic failures
38  current.commit(true); //or current.rollback();
39
40  }
41
42  }
```

We selected the client transaction program for use as the CORBA client because two key differences exist between "normal" EJB clients and CORBA EJB clients:

- Instead of JNDI, CORBA clients use COS naming to look up home interfaces.
- CORBA clients that employ client-demarcated transactions use CORBA Object Transaction Service (OTS) transactions.

Listing 6.11 illustrates both of these cases.

The import statements include two packages that we haven't seen in other examples:

- org.omg.CosNaming, which contains classes used in CORBA's naming service
- org.omg.CosTransactions, which contains classes used in CORBA transactions

In addition, we import the class org.omg.CORBA.ORB. This class represents the client-side CORBA ORB. In line 16, this class is used to initialize an instance of an ORB in the client.

Lines 18–19 obtain a reference to a CORBA naming context. The string "NameService" maps to an implementation of the naming context. Lines 23–28 use this reference to locate the Order bean's home interface in the COS Naming namespace. A new name component is created in line 24, and this component is looked up in the name service on line 26. (The curly braces on lines 23 and 28 are used to limit the scope of the variables to the enclosed block. This step is not required, but some programmers prefer to keep the scope of their variables as limited as possible.)

The transaction context is obtained similarly. Lines 31–32 obtain a transaction context, which is then used on lines 34 and 38 to begin and commit the transaction.

Listing 6.12 gives the IDL generated for the order bean.

Listing 6.12   IDL Generated for the Order Bean

```
1    #include <ejb.idl>
2
3    module book {
4    module chap05 {
5    module order {
6    valuetype OrderPK {
7    public long custid;
8    public string itemcode;
9    };
10   interface Order : ::javax::ejb::EJBObject {
11   readonly attribute string itemCode;
12   attribute long quantity;
13   readonly attribute long custID;
14   };
15   interface OrderHome : ::javax::ejb::EJBHome {
16   ::book::chap05::order::Order findByPrimaryKey (in
     ::book::chap05::order::OrderPK arg0)
17   raises (::javax::ejb::FinderEx);
18   ::book::chap05::order::Order create (in long arg0), in string
     arg1, in long arg2)
19   raises (::javax::ejb::CreateEx);
20   ::java::util::Enumeration findBYCustID (in long arg0)
21   raises (::javax::ejb::FinderEx);
22   };
23   };
24   };
25   };
```

As discussed earlier, IDL is a language- and platform-independent language used to specify interfaces. The `#include <ejb.idl>` statement acts as a C or C++ `include` statement; it inserts the contents of the file `ebj.idl` (which contains IDL definitions of the various EJB components). The rest of the file provides IDL definitions for the `OrderPk`, `Order`, and `OrderHome` classes from the Chapter 5 Order example. Note how the java package `book.chap05.order` maps to the nested "module" statements on lines 3–5. Also note the `raises` syntax, which is used to declare exceptions (in lines 17, 19, and 21). Most CORBA-oriented EJB tools will probably generate IDL for you, rather than requiring you to write it yourself.

Before leaving the subject of CORBA clients, note that the "pure CORBA client" approach is not the only way to use CORBA to connect to EJB beans. Some vendors (such as Gemstone) have taken the approach of keeping the client API code the same as that used with RMI, but using CORBA and IIOP "under the covers" for the conversation between client and server. Inprise's product also includes this functionality, allowing the developer to choose between an RMI-over-IIOP approach and a "pure CORBA client" approach.

What to Look for in a CORBA-Compliant EJB Implementation

As CORBA-compliant EJB implementations become available, you should look for a specific set of features to make your life easier:

- The CORBA implementation should provide IDL for the core EJB classes.
- A tool to generate IDL directly from your EJB interface classes would be helpful.
- The environment should support COS naming and provide a method of mapping from JNDI names to COS names.
- The environment should support OTS transactions.

HTTP Tunneling and SSL

HTTP tunneling and Secure Sockets Layer (SSL) support are two features that are not specified in the EJB specification itself, but should be widely implemented in various vendor-specific ways.

HTTP tunneling is a way to allow objects to communicate through a firewall. In HTTP tunneling, the various method invocations are translated into a series of HTTP requests and responses. This translation occurs transparently to the application. That is, you don't have to decompose your method invocations into HTTP—it's handled for you by the protocol handler.

SSL is a standard for encryption. Like HTTP, SSL translation occurs "under the covers," and the application program should not need to take special steps to use it.

Unfortunately, the EJB specification steers clear of issues involving the transport layer, so no standard approach to either HTTP tunneling or SSL exists at this time. Presumably, some vendors will support one or the other. If you need either SSL or HTTP tunneling right now, one option is to use servlets as wrappers for your EJB classes. You can then communicate purely over HTTP and use the SSL support provided by the browser itself.

RMI 1.2 includes expanded capabilities for extending the underlying transport protocol; in particular, it allows a VM to support multiple RMI protocols. The next generation of environments may provide more built-in support for HTTP tunneling and SSL.

Conclusion

This chapter covered a wide variety of operations that you can do in EJB clients. Most of these options are not mutually exclusive. For example, you can build a client that uses handles for persistent references, takes advantage of EJB metadata to discover information about its target bean, and then sends the results to beans within a transaction. Feel free to mix and match as necessary.

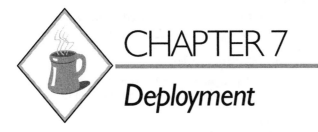

CHAPTER 7

Deployment

If you've been working through the examples shown thus far in the book, you've already had some experience with deploying EJBs. In this chapter, we discuss the deployment descriptor in great detail. We focus on each field of the base `DeploymentDescriptor` class, as well as the specialized fields that pertain only to the `SessionDescriptor` and `EntityDescriptor` classes. The generation of these classes is included in the role of "bean developer." In addition, we discuss the actual deployment and management of beans within the server, addressing the roles of "deployer" and "server administrator." After finishing this chapter, you should have a solid understanding of all elements of the EJB deployment process.

The DeploymentDescriptor Class

The `DeploymentDescriptor` class is the base class used by both the `SessionDescriptor` and the `EntityDescriptor` classes. It provides functionality that is common to all types of deployment descriptors.

Before getting too deep into the details, it's important to note that this class is the main way in which information is communicated from the EJB developer to the deployer and to the container in which the bean will be deployed. Typically, the bean developer uses the "setter" methods of this class to initialize the various properties of this class, and the deployment environment uses the "getter" methods to read these values at deployment time.

All currently available EJB tools provide graphical user interface (GUI) tools to allow the developer and/or deployer to generate `Deployment-Descriptors` and their associated classes via pointing and clicking. It is unlikely that you will ever need to modify these classes directly via Java code. Because each development environment uses a somewhat different tool to generate these classes, however, the best way to discuss deployment is to start with a discussion of the underlying classes. Once you understand these classes, it should be a snap to use any deployment tool to generate the desired results.

Listing 7.1 gives the code for the `DeploymentDescriptor` class.

Listing 7.1   The `DeploymentDescriptor` Class

```
1   public class javax.ejb.deployment.DeploymentDescriptor
2   extends java.lang.Object implements java.io.Serializable
3   {
4   protected int versionNumber;
5   public DeploymentDescriptor();
6   public AccessControlEntry[] getAccessControlEntries();
7   public AccessControlEntry getAccessControlEntries(int
    index);
8   public Name getBeanHomeName();
9   public ControlDescriptor[] getControlDescriptors();
10  public ControlDescriptor getControlDescriptors(int index);
11  public String getEnterpriseBeanClassName();
12  public Properties getEnvironmentProperties();
13  public String getHomeInterfaceClassName();
14  public boolean getReentrant();
15  public String getRemoteInterfaceClassName();
16  public boolean isReentrant();
17  public void setAccessControlEntries(AccessControlEntry
    values[]);
18  public void setAccessControlEntries(int index,
    AccessControlEntry value);
19  public void setBeanHomeName(Name value);
20  public void setControlDescriptors(ControlDescriptor
    value[]);
21  public void setControlDescriptors(int index,
    ControlDescriptor value);
22  public void setEnterpriseBeanClassName(String value);
23  public void setEnvironmentProperties(Properties value);
24  public void setHomeInterfaceClassName(String value);
25  public void setReentrant(boolean value);
26  public void setRemoteInterfaceClassName(String value);
27  }
```

Line 1 gives the class's name. Note that this class is part of the package `javax.ejb.deployment`, and not simply `javax.ejb` (as were most of the other classes examined so far).

Line 2 tells us that the deployment descriptor inherits from `java.lang.Object` and that it is serializable. Serialization is important for deployment descriptors. As we've seen in previous examples, the author of a bean provides a serialized deployment descriptor as one of the files shipped with the final product. Before serializing it, the bean developer must fill in all necessary values in the class. During serialization of the class, these values are saved to persistent storage. Upon later deployment of the bean, the class is deserialized and the data are read in from persistent storage; thus the bean deployer is provided with an already-initialized deployment descriptor that contains the bean developer's default information about how to deploy the bean. Typically, the EJB container will provide the ability to edit and modify some values of the deployment descriptor to more closely suit the deployment environment.

Line 4 contains a version number. In section 3.1.5, the EJB specification indicates that a container should provide support for versioning, and gives the example that, if a new version of a bean is installed, an older version should also continue to run. The version number provides a mechanism for discriminating among otherwise-identical beans.

Line 5 is the public no-argument constructor for this class.

The AccessControlEntry Class

Line 6 provides a getter method to obtain the access control entries for this bean. An AccessControlEntry is another class in the javax.ejb.deployment package; the purpose of this class is to pair a given method in your bean with a list of identities. Listing 7.2 gives the code for the AccessControlEntry class.

Listing 7.2 The AccessControlEntry Class

```
1    public class javax.ejb.deployment.AccessControlEntry
2    extends java.lang.Object implements java.io.Serializable
3    {
4    public AccessControlEntry();
5    public AccessControlEntry(Method method);
6    public AccessControlEntry(Method method, Identity
     identities[]);
7    public Identity[] getAllowedIdentities();
8    public Identity getAllowedIdentities(int index);
9    public Method getMethod();
10   public void setAllowedIdentities(Identity values[]);
11   public void setAllowedIdentities(int index, Identity value);
12   public void setMethod(Method value);
13   }
```

Note that the class consists mainly of **getter** and **setter methods** (also known as **accessor** and **mutator methods**) that allow you to associate a set of identities with a particular method.

Lines 1 and 2 define the class AccessControlEntry. Note two points about this class:

- This class is part of the package javax.ejb.deployment.
- The class is serializable.

Lines 4–6 provide constructors for the AccessControlEntry class.

Lines 7 and 8 provide methods to set the identities allowed so as to execute a particular method. If you set up an access control entry for a given method, then only the accounts that correspond to the specified identities will be allowed to invoke that method. Typically, the `Identity` objects correspond to roles (for example, "user," "administrator," and so on) rather than to the identities of particular users. At deployment time, the EJB deployer establishes access control lists that relate sets of actual accounts to the roles provided in the deployment descriptor. Later in this chapter, we'll see a WebLogic example of this sort.

A default access control entry provides access control for the entire bean. In WebLogic, the default access control entry is signified by providing "null" as the value of the method field. If both a default `AccessControlEntry` and an `AccessControlEntry` exist for a particular method, the method's `Access-ControlEntry` takes precedence over the defaults during invocation of the method.

Line 9 allows the container to retrieve the method to which this particular `AccessControlEntry` corresponds. Note that this method does not simply return a string; rather, it returns a `java.lang.reflect.Method` object, which carries a great deal of information about the method: its parameters and their types, its return type, the types of exceptions it throws, and other information that is useful to automated tools.

In lines 10 and 11, the bean developer can create an array of `Identity` objects that are allowed to invoke this particular method. If a user that does not map to one of these identities attempts to execute the method, a Security-Exception will be thrown.

Line 12 allows the bean developer to set the `Method` to be associated with the `AccessControlEntry`.

Our discussion of the `AccessControlEntry` class is now complete. Let's return to discussion of the `DeploymentDescriptor` class.

Back to the `DeploymentDescriptor` Class (I)

Line 7 in Listing 7.1 provides another version of the `getAccessControl-Entries()` method. This method takes an index as an argument and returns a single `AccessControlEntry` that corresponds to the index in the array of `AccessControlEntry` objects. In the JavaBeans world, this type of accessor method is referred to as an **indexed property**. For example, given the `DeploymentDescriptor` accessor method,

```
public AccessControlEntry getAccessControlEntries(int index);
```

invoking this method with an argument of 4 would return the fifth element in the array of access control entries (the index starts at 0).

Line 8 in the listing for the DeploymentDescriptor class is the getBean-HomeName() method. This method returns a javax.naming.Name object representing the name that the container should make available for clients that wish to use the bean. The container is responsible for placing this name into the JNDI namespace. Clients then use the JNDI InitialContext.lookup() method, with this name as the argument, to find the bean's home interface.

Line 9 is a getter method for ControlDescriptors.

The ControlDescriptor *Class*

Listing 7.3 provides the code for the ControlDescriptor class.

Listing 7.3   The ControlDescriptor Class

```
1   public class javax.ejb.deployment.ControlDescriptor
2   extends java.lang.Object
3   implements java.io.Serializable
4   {
5   public final static int CLIENT_IDENTITY;
6   public final static int SPECIFIED_IDENTITY;
7   public final static int SYSTEM_IDENTITY;
8   public final static int TRANSACTION_READ_COMMITTED;
9   public final static int TRANSACTION_READ_UNCOMMITTED;
10  public final static int TRANSACTION_REPEATABLE_READ;
11  public final static int TRANSACTION_SERIALIZABLE;
12  public final static int TX_BEAN_MANAGED;
13  public final static int TX_MANDATORY;
14  public final static int TX_NOT_SUPPORTED;
15  public final static int TX_REQUIRED;
16  public final static int TX_REQUIRES_NEW;
17  public final static int TX_SUPPORTS;
18  public ControlDescriptor();
19  public ControlDescriptor(Method method);
20  public int getIsolationLevel();
21  public Method getMethod();
22  public Identity getRunAsIdentity();
23  public int getRunAsMode();
24  public int getTransactionAttribute();
25  public void setIsolationLevel(int value);
26  public void setMethod(Method value);
27  public void setRunAsIdentity(Identity value);
28  public void setRunAsMode(int value);
29  public void setTransactionAttribute(int value);
30  }
```

The ControlDescriptor class serves a function roughly similar to that of the AccessControlEntry class; it associates information with a particular method. Like the AccessControlEntry class, the ControlDescriptor class can be used both to specify properties of a particular method and to specify default properties for the bean as a whole (by setting the value of Method to "null"). As with the AccessControlEntry class, properties specified for a particular method override any defaults that may be in effect. Unlike the AccessControlEntry class, which is concerned solely with security and identity, the Control-Descriptor has three concerns:

- The method's transaction attribute
- The method's isolation level
- The method's "run-as" mode

In previous chapters, we discussed transaction attributes (TX_BEAN_MANAGED, TX_MANDATORY, TX_NOT_SUPPORTED, TX_REQUIRED, TX_REQUIRES_NEW, and TX_SUPPORTS) and isolation levels (TRANSACTION_READ_COMMITTED, TRANSACTION_READ_UNCOMMITTED, TRANSACTION_REPEATABLE_READ, and TRANSACTION_SERIALIZABLE) at length, so we won't cover them again here. Instead, we'll focus on "run-as" modes.

"Run-as" Modes

"Run-as" modes specify the identity that the bean should have at runtime. The run-as mode is important mainly if you have set up an access-control scheme for your beans and need to call one bean from another. The run-as mode specifies the type of identity that the calling bean should pass to the called bean. Three run-as modes exist:

- CLIENT_IDENTITY, which means that the bean will use the identity of the client as its own identity when it makes calls to other beans.
- SYSTEM_IDENTITY, which means that the bean will use the identity of a "system" account when invoking other beans. Generally, the bean deployer must configure this account in the container.
- SPECIFIED_IDENTITY, which means that the bean will use specific identity. This identity is found in the RunAsIdentity property, which is applicable only if the bean is using SPECIFIED_IDENTITY.

Lines 5–17 of Listing 7.3 define the various constants used. Lines 18 and 19 provide constructors for this class. Lines 20–24 provide accessor methods for the various properties associated with this class:

- getIsolationLevel(), to get the isolation level
- getMethod(), to get the Method
- getRunAsIdentity()
- getRunAsMode()
- getTransactionAttribute()

Lines 25–29 provide mutator methods that correspond to the accessor methods in lines 20–24.

Back to the DeploymentDescriptor *Class (II)*

Now let's finish our discussion of the DeploymentDescriptor class.

Line 10 of the DeploymentDescriptor class (Listing 7.1) provides an indexed-property-style accessor method for the array of ControlDescriptors.

Line 11 provides a method to return the name of the class used to implement the Enterprise JavaBean. For the Order example from Chapter 5, this field would be set to book.chap05.order.OrderBean.

In line 12, we find a method to return an array of environment properties. In previous chapters, we used environment properties to carry information such as the name of the JDBC driver and the name of the JDBC data source. Properties are useful for holding information that may be modified at deployment time. In this sense, they roughly correspond to Microsoft Windows .ini files.

Line 13 provides a method to return the home interface name. Referring back to the Order example from Chapter 5 again, this method would return book.chap05.order.OrderHome.

The getReentrant() method, which returns a Boolean value indicating whether the bean is reentrant, appears in line 14. Reentrancy in beans was introduced in Chapter 5. To jog your memory, here are a few important points about reentrancy:

- Only Entity beans can be reentrant; Session beans can never be reentrant.
- Reentrancy introduces the possibility of several sorts of concurrency-related problems. Think twice before using it. Then think again. Then find another way to do it.

Line 15 of Listing 7.1 provides a method to return the remote interface name. In the Order example from Chapter 5, this method would return book.chap05.order.Order.

The isReentrant() method in line 16 essentially duplicates the functionality of the getReentrant() method on line 14. As mentioned earlier, by a JavaBeans design convention, when a property is a Boolean value, you should also include an accessor method prefixed with "is".

Lines 17–26 provide setter (mutator) methods for the properties discussed above.

The SessionDescriptor Class

The DeploymentDescriptor class is never used by itself. Rather, you use a SessionDescriptor to contain information about Session beans, and an Entity descriptor to contain information about Entity beans. Both `SessionDescriptor` and `EntityDescriptor` inherit from `DeploymentDescriptor`; each provides all the functionality of a `DeploymentDescriptor`. The `SessionDescriptor` and `EntityDescriptor` classes also provide specialized methods for their particular type of bean, however. First, let's look at the `SessionDescriptor` in Listing 7.4.

Listing 7.4   The SessionDescriptor Class

```
1    public class javax.ejb.deployment.SessionDescriptor
2    extends javax.ejb.deployment.DeploymentDescriptor
3    {
4    public final static int STATEFUL_SESSION;
5    public final static int STATELESS_SESSION;
6    public SessionDescriptor();
7    public int getSessionTimeout();
8    public int getStateManagementType();
9    public void setSessionTimeout(int value);
10   public void setStateManagementType(int value);
11   }
```

In lines 1 and 2 of Listing 7.4, note that the `SessionDescriptor` class extends the `EntityDescriptor` class. As a result, `SessionDescriptor` provides all the functionality of a `DeploymentDescriptor` (including serializability).

Lines 4 and 5 declare two constants, STATEFUL_SESSION and STATELESS_SESSION. The `StateManagementType` property uses these constants to convey whether the bean is stateful or stateless.

Line 6 is a **no-argument constructor** for this class.

Line 7 returns the value of the `SessionTimeout` property. The int value represents the number of seconds that a Session bean can be inactive before the container is allowed to destroy it. A value of zero indicates that the bean should use the container's default value (which the container administrator may specify) for the timeout value. Note that the Java int is a 32-bit signed integer, so you can specify timeout values as large as several years. The duration of the timeout value must take into account how the user will typically interact with the application. Discussions with the EJB specification authors indicate that they originally intended the timeout to be an absolute upperbound on the bean's life, measured from the time the bean is created. However, most implementations use timeout as elpased time since last usage. A future version of the specification will state which approach should be used. Generally, a smaller timeout value will allow the server more freedom in reclaiming resources, and a longer timeout may potentially result in many orphan beans waiting on the server to die (assuming that their clients don't invoke their remove() methods for some reason).

In line 8, Listing 7.4 provides an accessor method for the Session-ManagementType. It can return only one of two values: STATEFUL_SESSION or STATELESS_SESSION.

Lines 9 and 10 are mutator methods that correspond to the accessor methods in lines 7 and 8.

The EntityDescriptor Class

Listing 7.5 gives the code for the EntityDescriptor class.

Listing 7.5   The EntityDescriptor Class

```
1   public class javax.ejb.deployment.EntityDescriptor
2   extends javax.ejb.deployment.DeploymentDescriptor
3   {
4   public EntityDescriptor();
5   public Field[] getContainerManagedFields();
6   public Field getContainerManagedFields(int index);
7   public String getPrimaryKeyClassName();
8   public void setContainerManagedFields(Field values[]);
9   public void setContainerManagedFields(int index, Field
    value);
10  public void setPrimaryKeyClassName(String value);
11  }
```

Like the SessionDescriptor class, the EntityDescriptor class inherits from the DeploymentDescriptor class.

Line 4 of Listing 7.5 is the no-argument constructor for this class.

Line 5 returns an array of java.lang.reflect.Field() methods that indicate the container-managed fields. You must set the container-managed fields only if the bean uses container-managed persistence. A bean with bean-managed persistence should not specify any container-managed fields; in fact, doing so may result in confusion for the container and produce some quite strange error messages.

The Field class is similar to the Method class discussed in connection with the AccessControlEntry class. Instead of carrying information about a particular method, however, it provides information about a particular field. Remember that container-managed fields must be declared as public, so that the container can access them.

Line 6 is an indexed-property accessor for the array of container-managed fields. It returns the appropriate Field object from the array of Field objects that the class contains.

Line 7 returns a string representation of the name of the class used as the primary key. In the Order example from Chapter 5, calling this method on the EntityDescriptor for the Order bean would return book.chap05.order. OrderPK.

Why return a string instead of the class itself? The environment can use this string to load an instance of the class using the Class.forName() method.

Example Program

To better frame our discussion of deployment issues and runtime identities, let's build a very simple bean. The purposes of this bean are twofold:

- To provide a framework for discussing deployment issues
- To experiment with roles and identities

The Home Interface

Listing 7.6   Home Interface for a Stateless Session Bean

```
1    package book.chap07.id;
2    import javax.ejb.EJBHome;
3    import java.rmi.RemoteException;
4    import javax.ejb.CreateException;
5    public interface IDHome extends EJBHome
6    {
7    public ID create() throws RemoteException, CreateException;
8    }
```

The bean in Listing 7.6 is a stateless Session bean. Thus it needs only a single, no-argument create() method.

The Remote Interface

Listing 7.7   Remote Interface for a Stateless Session Bean

```
1    package book.chap07.id;
2    import javax.ejb.EJBObject;
3    import java.rmi.RemoteException;
4    import java.security.Identity;
5    public interface ID extends EJBObject
6    {
7      public Identity getCallerIdentity() throws
         RemoteException;
8      public boolean isCallerInRole(Identity id) throws
         RemoteException;
9      public void myProtectedMethod() throws RemoteException;
10   }
```

The bean's remote interface, shown in Listing 7.7, contains three methods:

- getCallerIdentity(), which is a "wrapper" method that invokes the bean's getCallerIdentity() method and returns the result. It allows the client to see how the bean has identified the client.
- isCallerInRole(), which is another wrapper method. It allows the client to pass in an Identity object and see whether the bean thinks that the caller is in that role.

- `myProtectedMethod()`, which is a do-nothing method included to illustrate how `AccessControlDescriptors` are used to control access to particular methods.

The Bean Implementation Class

Listing 7.8 Stateless Session Bean Implementation Class

```
1    package book.chap07.id;
2    import javax.ejb.SessionBean;
3    import javax.ejb.SessionContext;
4    import javax.ejb.CreateException;
5    import java.security.Identity;

6    public class IDBean implements SessionBean
7    {
8        transient private SessionContext ctx;

9        public void setSessionContext(SessionContext ctx)
10       {
11           this.ctx = ctx;
12       }
13       public void ejbCreate() throws CreateException
14       {

16       }
17       public void ejbActivate()
18       {
19       }
20       public void ejbPassivate()
21       {
22       }
23       public void ejbRemove()
24       {
25       }
26       public Identity getCallerIdentity()
27       {
28           return ctx.getCallerIdentity();
29       }
30       public boolean isCallerInRole(Identity i)
31       {
32           return ctx.isCallerInRole(i);
33       }
34       public void myProtectedMethod()
35       {
36           //doesn't do anything; just a demonstration of ACLs
37       }
38   }
```

The bean implementation in Listing 7.8 does not really introduce anything new. In fact, it's almost as straightforward as the "Hello, EJB" example we developed in Chapter 3. There are only a few items to study closely:

- Lines 26–29 implement the getCallerIdentity() wrapper method, which invokes the SessionContext's getCallerIdentity() method and returns the result.
- Lines 30–33 implement the isCallerInRole() method, which invokes the SessionContext's isCallerInRole() method and returns the result.
- Lines 34–37 implement the myProtectedMethod() method, which doesn't do much, but will be useful later when we discuss access control lists.

The Client

Listing 7.9   Client for a Stateless Session Bean

```
1    import book.chap07.id.ID;
2    import book.chap07.id.IDHome;
3    import book.chap07.id.MyIdentity;
4    import javax.naming.InitialContext;
5    import javax.naming.NamingException;
6    import java.rmi.RemoteException;
7    import javax.ejb.RemoveException;
8    import javax.ejb.CreateException;
9    import java.security.Identity;
10   import javax.naming.Context;
11   import java.util.Properties;
12   public class IDClient
13   {
14
15       public static void main(String[] argv)
16       {
17           try
18           {
19           doConnection(argv[0], argv[1]);
20           }
21           catch(Exception e)
22           {
23           System.out.println("Exception occurred: " + e);
24           }
25   }
26       public static void doConnection(String username, String
         password) throws NamingException
27       {
28           InitialContext ic = null;
29
30           System.out.println("client is running");
31           try
32           {
33           Properties p = new Properties();
34           p.put(Context.INITIAL_CONTEXT_FACTORY,
35           "weblogic.jndi.T3InitialContextFactory");
36           p.put(Context.PROVIDER_URL, "t3://localhost:7001");
```

```
37        p.put(Context.SECURITY_PRINCIPAL, username);
38        p.put(Context.SECURITY_CREDENTIALS, password);
39        ic = new InitialContext(p);
40        System.out.println("looked up initial context");
41        IDHome ih = (IDHome) ic.lookup("IDHome");
42        System.out.println("looked up home interface");
43        ID id = ih.create();
44        System.out.println("created remote interface");
45        Identity callerID = id.getCallerIdentity();
46        System.out.println("Identity is " +
          callerID.getName());
47        ReadDD.printIdentity(callerID);
48        Identity mpID = new MyIdentity("mypeople");
49        ReadDD.printIdentity(mpID);
50        Identity suID = new MyIdentity("superusers");
51        ReadDD.printIdentity(suID);
52        boolean isInRole = id.isCallerInRole(mpID);
53        System.out.println("result of isCallerInRole
          'mypeople' is "+ isInRole);
54        isInRole = id.isCallerInRole(suID);
55        System.out.println("result of isCallerInRole
          'superusers' is " + isInRole);
56        System.out.println("invoking superuser method");
57        id.myProtectedMethod();
58        System.out.println("invoked superuser method");
59        id.remove();
60        ic.close();
61        System.out.println("done with IDClient");
62        }
63        catch (NamingException e)
64        {
65            System.out.println("NamingException caught");
66            e.printStackTrace();
67            ic.close();
68        }
69        catch (RemoteException e)
70        {
71            System.out.println("RemoteException caught");
72            e.printStackTrace();
73            ic.close();
74        }
75        catch (RemoveException e)
76        {
77            System.out.println("RemoveException caught");
78            e.printStackTrace();
79            ic.close();
80        }
81        catch (CreateException e)
82        {
83            System.out.println("CreateException caught");
84            e.printStackTrace();
85            ic.close();
86        }
```

```
87    }
88  }
```

The `IDClient` class in Listing 7.9 is relatively straightforward. Although we won't discuss every line of it, we will highlight a few salient points.

On line 3, we import the class `MyIdentity`. The `java.security.Identity` class is declared as abstract class, so we can't simply say the following:

```
Identity id = new Identity("MyID")
```

Instead, we must create a wrapper class to provide the `Identity` class's functionality. Fortunately, this task is quite straightforward.

```
1    package book.chap07.id;
2    import java.security.Identity;

3    public class MyIdentity extends Identity
4    {
5        public MyIdentity(String id)
6        {
7            super(id);
8        }
9    }
```

Two `Identity` classes are considered identical if they share the same name and the same scope. In WebLogic, the `Identity` classes have a null scope, so they should be considered equivalent if their names are equal.

Lines 15–25 of the client provide the `main()` method of this class. The `main()` method simply invokes the `doConnection()` method with a username and password that are supplied on the command line.

Lines 26–87 implement the `doConnection()` method.

Lines 33–39 create an `InitialContext`. Note especially lines 37 and 38, where the username and password are passed to the `InitialContext`. This chunk of code is WebLogic-specific; an update to the EJB specification will outline a canonical method for passing the client's ID to the server.

In lines 40–44, we go through the usual process of looking up the home interface and creating a remote interface. By now, this approach should be old hat to you—in fact, you're probably yawning right now. Wake up! Things are about to get interesting.

Line 45 invokes the `getCallerIdentity()` remote method, which in turn invokes the `SessionContext`'s `getCallerIdentity()` method. Note that, even though `Identity` is an abstract class, we can declare a variable of type `Identity` to hold the return value of `getCallerIdentity()`. It's acceptable to use a variable typed as an abstract class to hold a reference to an object that implements the abstract class, in the same way that you might use a variable typed as an interface to hold a reference to an object that implements the interface.

In line 47, the `PrintIdentity` method of the `ReadDD` class prints out the values of the various properties of the `Identity` object. The `ReadDD` class was originally written to read in and print a serialized deployment descriptor; as it uses static methods to print various values, it can be employed to print out the `Identity` class as well. The source code for the `ReadDD` class appears later in this chapter.

In lines 48–51, we create two new `Identity` objects (actually, `MyIdentity` objects—remember that you can't directly instantiate the `Identity` class) to represent two new user classes. The creation of these classes will be discussed later.

Lines 52–55 check whether the caller is in either the role `mypeople` or `superusers` and print a Boolean value to report the result.

Line 57 attempts to invoke the `myProtectedMethod()` method. Only members of the `superusers` group can access this method. When a client with an identity that's not part of the `superusers` group attempts to invoke the method, a SecurityException will be thrown.

The rest of the class contains the usual cleanup and exception-handling code. By now you've seen this code so often that you can probably write it in your sleep—no need to discuss it in any detail.

Using Roles at Runtime

You can also use `isCallerInRole()` within your beans to allow a method to respond differently based on the role of the user who invokes it. For example, if a `getAccountInformation()` method returns information about accounts, you might want to provide two types of functionality for this method:

- When it is invoked by a normal user, the method could display information about the user's account.
- When it is invoked by a superuser, it might display information about all accounts.

To bestow such functionality, you could write the following code:

```
Identity su = new MyIdentity("superuser");
if (ctx.isCallerInRole(su))
    {
    //return a list of all accounts
    }
else
{
//return only the caller's account info
}
```

The ReadDD Class

Listing 7.10   The ReadDD Class

```
1   //readDD.java
2   //reads in a session or entity descriptor
3   import javax.ejb.deployment.*;
4   import java.io.*;
5   import java.security.*;
6   import java.lang.reflect.*;
7   public class ReadDD
8   {
9      static SessionDescriptor sd;
10     static EntityDescriptor ed;
11     public static void main(String[] argv)
12     {
13         if (argv.length != 2)
14             {
15             System.out.println("usage: java ReadDD s|e
                   <descriptor filename>");
16             return;
17             }
18         if (argv[0].equals("e"))
19             {
20             readEntity(argv[1]);
21             printEntityDescriptor();
22         }
23         else if (argv[0].equals("s"))
24             {
25             readSession(argv[1]);
26             printSessionDescriptor();
27             }
28         else
29             {
30             System.out.println("usage: java ReadDD s|e
                   <descriptor filename>");
31             return;
32         }
33     }
34     public static Object readDescriptor(String filename)
35     {
36         Object retval;
37         System.out.println("called readHandle");
38         try
39         {
40             FileInputStream fis = new FileInputStream(
                   filename);
41             ObjectInputStream ois = new ObjectInputStream(
                   fis);
42             retval = ois.readObject();
43             ois.close();
44             return retval;
45         }
```

```
46          catch(Exception e)
47          {
48              System.out.println("Exception occurred reading
                descriptor: " + e);
49              return null;
50          }
51      }
52      public static void readSession(String filename)
53      {
54          sd = (SessionDescriptor) readDescriptor(filename);
55
56      }
57      public static void readEntity(String filename)
58      {
59          ed = (EntityDescriptor) readDescriptor(filename);
60      }
61      public static void printSessionDescriptor()
62      {
63          printDD(sd);
64          //print session-specific stuff
65      }
66      public static void printEntityDescriptor()
67      {
68          printDD(ed);
69          //print entity-specific stuff
70      }
71      public static void printDD(DeploymentDescriptor dd)
72      {
73          AccessControlEntry [] ace;
74          ace = dd.getAccessControlEntries();
75          printAccessControlEntries(ace);
76
77      }
78      public static void printAccessControlEntries(
        AccessControlEntry[] ace)
79      {
80          for (int i = 0; i < ace.length; i++)
81          {
82              printAccessControlEntry(ace[i]);
83          }
84      }
85      public static void printAccessControlEntry(
        AccessControlEntry ace)
86      {
87        Method m = ace.getMethod();
88        printMethod(m);
89        Identity[] i = ace.getAllowedIdentities();
90        printIdentities(i);
91      }
92      public static void printMethod(Method m)
93      {
94        System.out.println("method: " + m);
95      }
```

```
96        public static void printIdentities(Identity[] ia)
97        {
98           for(int i = 0; i < ia.length; i++)
99           {
100          printIdentity(ia[i]);
101          }
102       }
103       public static void printIdentity(Identity i)
104       {
105          System.out.println("identity: " + i);
106          System.out.println("\tName = " + i.getName());
107          System.out.println("\tInfo = " + i.getInfo());
108          System.out.println("\tPublicKey = " +
             i.getPublicKey());
109          System.out.println("\tScope = " + i.getScope());
110          System.out.println("\tCertificates follow");
111          printCertificates(i.certificates());
112       }
113       public static void printCertificates(Certificate[] c)
114 {
115          for (int i = 0; i < c.length; i++)
116          {
117              printCertificate(c[i]);
118          }
119       }
120       public static void printCertificate(Certificate c)
121       {
122
123          System.out.println("\t\tFormat = " + c.getFormat());
124          System.out.println("\t\tPublic key = " +
             c.getPublicKey());
125          System.out.println("\t\tGuarantor = " +
             c.getGuarantor());
126          System.out.println("\t\tPrincipal = " +
             c.getPrincipal());
127          System.out.println("\t\tformat = " + c.getFormat());
128          System.out.println("\t\tformat = " + c.getFormat());
129       }
130 }
```

As an added bonus, we have provided the source code for the ReadDD class in Listing 7.10. This class is intended to be run from the command line with two arguments:

- An "s" or an "e" to indicate whether the descriptor is a Session or an Entity descriptor. You could also identify this characteristic at runtime using the instanceOf operator.
- The name of a serialized deployment descriptor.

The ReadDD class is not fully implemented. It doesn't print out all of the information contained in a deployment descriptor (doing so is left as an exercise for the reader; it's basically just a tedious series of System.out.println statements), for example, but it does fully display information related to the AccessControlEntries array. Also, because all the methods are static, this class can be conveniently used in other programs to print out detailed information about Identity objects, Certificate objects, and AccessControlEntry objects.

The Deployment Descriptor

So far, we have seen how the bean interacts with its access control lists using isCallerInRole() and getCallerIdentity(), but we haven't seen how to set up those access control lists. Setting up these lists is a two-part process:

- When the bean is written, AccessControlEntry objects need to be established for the various categories of users that are allowed to access the methods.
- At deployment time, these categories of users must be mapped to actual users.

To take care of the first part of this process, add the following code to the deployment descriptor:

```
1   (accessControlEntries
2   DEFAULT [superusers mypeople]
3   myProtectedMethod [superusers]
4   ); end accessControlEntries
```

This snippet is specific to WebLogic; other tools may use a different syntax to set these values. The end result will be the same, however.

Lines 1 and 4 delimit the AccessControlEntries block of the deployment descriptor.

Line 2 sets the default access permissions for this bean. According to this line, only members of the groups superusers and mypeople are allowed to access any methods on this bean. If a client who is not a member of one of these groups attempts to invoke one of the bean's methods, a SecurityException will be thrown.

Line 3 sets up access permissions for myProtectedMethod(). Only members of the superusers group will be allowed to access these methods.

When distributing your beans, you should include a clear description of the roles supported. This precaution will allow the deployer to make informed decisions about which users should be in which roles.

Setting Up Access Control Lists

The specifics of how access control lists are created in the container will vary from implementation to implementation. Our example will focus on the Web-Logic option. Your implementation should provide similar functionality.

In WebLogic, you have two ways of setting up access control lists:

- You can set them up in the `weblogic.properties` file.
- You can create an authentication database and set up your user identities there.

The second option is probably the better approach for production usage. The first is more straightforward, however, so we'll use it in this example. The following excerpt from a `weblogic.properties` file sets up the `superusers` and `mypeople` groups:

```
1    weblogic.password.superuser1=superpassword1
2    weblogic.password.superuser2=superpassword2
3    weblogic.security.group.superusers=superuser1,superuser2
4    weblogic.password.myUser=myPassword
5    weblogic.password.myUser2=myPassword2
6    weblogic.security.group.mypeople=myUser,myUser2
```

In lines 1 and 2, we create two new user IDs, `superuser1` and `superuser2`, and assign passwords to them. To create a `userid` in WebLogic, you use the syntax

```
weblogic.password.<userid>=<password>
```

where `<userid>` and `<password>` are the actual `userid` and `password`, respectively.

In line 3, we create a new group called `superusers`, and add the `userids` `superuser1` and `superuser2` as members. To create a group in WebLogic, you use the following syntax:

```
weblogic.security.group.<groupname>=<userid1>,..<useridn>
```

replacing `<groupname>` with the actual name of the group and `<userid1>,..` `<useridn>` with the list of actual `userids` that the group should contain.

After you've made these entries to your `weblogic.properties` file, restart WebLogic. The entries will then be active.

Container-Managed Finder Methods

Recall from Chapter 5 that finder methods for container-managed Entity beans are created at deployment time, and that the EJB specification does not mandate any particular format that the bean developer must use to describe the finder methods to the bean deployer. A revised version of the EJB specification should soon be available that provides a standard method for specifying finder methods; the standard is not here yet, however. As a bean developer, you should provide a full and complete description of exactly how to implement your finder methods, if you use container-managed Entity beans. An SQL-like syntax is probably the least ambiguous way to describe these finder methods. For example, if you need a finder method called `findDelinquentAccounts()` that returns a list of overdue accounts, you might provide a description like the following:

> `findDelinquentAccounts()`—This method retrieves a list of all accounts where the due date is greater than the argument value. A sample SQL statement to implement this functionality is:

```
select *
from accounts
where date_today - date_due > $argument
```

With luck, a standard method of specifying finder methods for container-managed Entity beans will become available soon. Having such a standard syntax would allow the bean provider to send a description directly to the container and allow the container to directly implement the finder methods without intervention by the deployer. The online supplement to this book will track specification changes and provide up-to-date information on this subject.

Other Deployment Issues

In this section, we focus on some additional deployment issues.

Caching Issues

Typically, your container will allow you to make decisions at deployment time (and modify them later, if necessary) concerning the system resources allocated to your bean. Examples of these decisions include the following:

- The number of Entity beans to maintain in the pool
- The number of instances of a Session bean to allow before the container begins to passivate beans
- A time interval after which inactive beans will be passivated by the container

Consult your implementation's documentation for more information on the configuration paramaters available to you.

Persistent Storage

The container may require the deployer to create a particular database table to be used for persistent storage of Entity EJBs. It also may require information about the mechanism employed to passivate stateful Session EJBs temporarily.

Properties

If environment properties must be set for the bean, the deployer should examine the properties and ensure that they are set correctly.

Other Administrative Issues

There are a few things to keep in mind in the day-to-day operation of an EJB container. Paying attention to these issues should help your programs run smoothly.

Don't Reboot

The edict "don't reboot" might seem a bit strong, but generally you should try to avoid rebooting an EJB server unless absolutely necessary. As noted in Chapter 4, Session beans typically do not survive a system reboot. If a user is in the middle of a task involving stateful Session beans and the server is rebooted, the user will lose his or her work. EJB servers are more similar to database servers than to Web servers. Rebooting a Web server is generally not a major event, because Web clients are not connection-oriented. Users will simply notice a lost request or two, but then the server comes back online and everything functions as before. EJB clients, on the other hand, maintain continuous connections to the server. A reboot will, at the very least, knock off all the current users and require them to reestablish their connections. If you must reboot an EJB server, try to schedule the procedure for off-hours when few or no users will be connected to the server.

Watch for Churning

Churning occurs when a server does not have sufficient memory to handle its load of clients. When a server runs out of memory, it begins to passivate beans to temporary storage. Normally, passivation affects only beans that have remained inactive for some time. If, on the other hand, the system beans are being passivated many times in a relatively short period of time, the system may be experiencing churning. Churning could potentially result either from a configuration problem (that is, the server is configured so as to allow too few concurrent instances of a bean) or from a resource-limitation problem (that is, the machine does not have enough memory to hold all active instances). If churning results from a configuration problem, simply increase the number of concurrent instances allowed for the beans that are having the problem. If a resource-limitation problem is the culprit, you have two choices:

- Add more physical memory to the machine.
- Add another server and move some of the beans to the second server to lighten the load.

Adjust the Timeout Value of Your Session Beans Appropriately

A too-long timeout value could clutter the server with many orphaned beans that are simply waiting to die. As noted earlier, a well-behaved client will remove a stateful Session bean when it has finished with it—but not all clients are well behaved. Also, if a client loses contact with the server before the bean has been removed, the bean may persist unnecessarily on the server.

A too-short timeout value could cause users to lose their beans if they wander off for a coffee break. Consider the usage patterns for the application, and set your timeout interval accordingly.

Monitor the Number of Aborted Transactions

The number of transactions that must be rolled back should generally remain small. If a large number of rollbacks occurs, your system may be experiencing a problem. The situation may be caused by configuration problems (for example, if an underlying database table has run out of space, failed attempts to insert data to the table may cause the rollbacks) or bugs in the implementation of the beans. Whatever the cause, a high incidence of rollbacks points to a problem.

Watch for SecurityExceptions

Your EJB server should add an entry to its log for each SecurityException that occurs. Review this log frequently to spot users who are attempting to access things that they ought not access. Don't rely exclusively on this log, however; really skilled hackers may go to great lengths to avoid leaving footprints in logs. If a large number of SecurityExceptions appears in your log, however, you should investigate further.

Be Parsimonious with Permissions

Grant your users the minimal permissions they need to do their jobs.

Be Parsimonious with Services

In a production environment, if a given service is not required for production, it's generally a good idea to shut it down. For example, WebLogic provides an HTTP server. If you're using WebLogic purely as an EJB server, deactivating the HTTP server would be a good idea. The fewer services that a machine runs, the fewer potential holes are available for hackers to exploit.

Check for Default Accounts and Obsolete Accounts

Default accounts are a favorite tool of hackers. If your EJB server comes with a "guest" account or something similar, remove this account before you put the server into production.

Know Your System

As an administrator, you should be well acquainted with the capabilities provided by your system, its limitations, and its normal usage patterns. Possessing this awareness, you should be able to notice potential problems before they become full-blown crises.

Conclusion

We have now concluded our whirlwind tour of deployment and administration issues in EJB. By this time, deployment should hold no surprises for you, and you should be able to administer an EJB server. The next chapter offers some pointers for building distributed systems.

CHAPTER 8

Tips, Tricks, and Traps for Building Distributed and Other Systems

The Hagakure is a book that records a relatively disjointed series of epigrams, stories, and bits of advice from an old samurai. This chapter is sort of like that, with the following exceptions:

- I'm not a samurai; I'm an MIS developer.
- I'm not that old.

This chapter provides a list of rules of thumb and things to consider in developing distributed and other systems. It is basically a "brain dump" of useful and/or important issues in developing systems; you may find this information useful as well. Generally, each of the points mentioned has been backed up with much sweat and toil, and, by reading this chapter, perhaps you'll be able to save some sweat and toil as well.

Expect Your Network Connections to Fail

One thing that makes designing distributed systems so much fun is that a very real possibility exists that you will lose network connectivity at any point in time. In the real world, this type of failure happens infrequently, but it does occur:

- Cables are cut, chewed by rats (yes, it happened to the author), or otherwise damaged.
- Routers die.
- Ethernet cards go bad.
- Fuses blow.

- People trip over power cords and knock out servers.
- Janitors plug their vacuum cleaners into the wrong outlets.

Remember that every method in your remote interface is declared as throwing RemoteException; this step is taken because a network failure can potentially occur at any time. Decide early in the design phase how your system should behave if its network connectivity becomes severed.

And don't just protect the client-to-EJB-server connection. You should also play "what-if" games with your EJB server's connection to the database and to any other EJB servers involved in the system.

On the other hand, you don't necessarily have to design a system that's impervious to nuclear attack; perhaps it is acceptable that your system goes offline if the database fails. At the requirements stage, you should establish the required level of uptime for the system, and your design should reflect this requirement. Not all systems require 24×7 uptime or fault tolerance, but if your system does, you need to design it with that consideration in mind.

Test Catastrophic Failure

After you've designed your failure-handling mechanism, don't assume it will work—test it to be sure. Start a transaction and then yank the network cable out. Pull out the power cord on your EJB server. These sorts of failures happen, and you should know in advance how your system will behave.

Avoid Remote Method Invocations Where Possible

What?! You may have thought that the point of this book was to learn how to do remote method invocations. Indeed, remote method invocations do make distributed systems possible. Nevertheless, a remote invocation is typically several hundred times more costly in terms of time and instructions executed than a local procedure call. Keep this expense in mind when designing your system. If your system performs a half-dozen remote calls to accomplish a single logical unit of work, you should reevaluate your design and find a way to reduce the number of remote calls.

Treat Transactions and Database Connections as Precious Resources

There are costs involved in maintaining an open transaction or database connection. Database connection pools can alleviate some of the overhead involved in maintaining a database connection, because, strictly speaking, you don't maintain one. Nevertheless, if you've performed a query, go through the `ResultSet` and retrieve your data, and then close the `ResultSet`.

Monitor the Granularity of Objects

How large should your EJB objects be? No hard and fast rule has been established, but a good rule of thumb is "not so large that they overwhelm the server, but larger is generally better." Although this point should not be taken as a blanket endorsement of the "one mammoth object" school of software development, the fact is that very fine-grained objects are troublesome for distributed systems for several reasons:

- They generally increase the number of remote invocations necessary to accomplish a particular unit of work.
- Each object carries some degree of administrative overhead. A multitude of small objects can generate an unnecessarily high degree of overhead.

Monitor the Granularity of Methods

Similarly, the methods in your EJB objects should generally accomplish some useful unit of work. In particular, you should generally avoid using getter/ setter methods as part of your remote interface. If you must send information to a remote object or retrieve results from it, bundle several chunks of information into a single method call, rather than calling a number of small methods sequentially.

Isolate Vendor-Specific Code

If you must use vendor-specific code in your system, isolate it and document it. Consider using the Facade pattern (discussed later in this chapter) to insulate your application from direct interaction with vendor-specific code. If you must later move to another platform, it's much easier to modify a few objects than to go through the entire system's source code.

Avoid Making Entity Beans Reentrant

The EJB specification allows an Entity bean to be made reentrant, but strongly advises against it. Reentrancy is permitted only where a bean calls another bean, and the called bean wishes to make a loopback call to the calling bean. Reentrancy is discouraged because the container cannot generally distinguish between a legitimate loopback call and an illegal concurrent call to the bean from within the same transaction context. Thus, allowing reentrancy can potentially permit illegal calls to your bean.

Observe Programming Restrictions on EJB Beans

The EJB specification places several restrictions on beans:

- Beans are not allowed to start new threads, terminate threads, or use thread synchronization primitives.
- Beans cannot have read/write static fields.
- Only beans with the `TX_BEAN_MANAGED` transaction specifier are allowed to interact directly with the transaction manager, and then only through the `javax.jts.UserTransaction` interface.
- A bean cannot change its `java.security.Identity`.
- Only beans using the `TX_NOT_SUPPORTED` transaction specifier are allowed to invoke JDBC `commit()` or `rollback()` methods.

These restrictions are part of the specification and will affect any EJB-compliant container you use. Don't try to fight them; rather, embrace them. They can make the container's job easier, and the container's job is to make your job easier.

Don't Implement the Bean's Remote Interface in Its Implementation Class

It's possible to implement the bean's remote interface in its implementation bean. For example, using the order example from Chapter 5, it is permissible to say the following:

```
public class OrderBean implements Order
```

However, it is preferable not to do this. Why? Because the EJB architecture assumes that all calls to your implementation class are interposed by the container. This interposition gives the server the freedom to manage the running instances of EJB objects and to provide the implementation of the declarative transaction management scheme. If a bean implements its own remote interface, it could inadvertently return a reference to itself to a client, and the client could potentially make calls to the bean without the interposition of the container.

Of course, it's nice to have the type checking entailed in implementing an interface. One approach that protects against inappropriate calls to your bean while still providing type checking is as follows:

- Create a nonremote interface that includes all of your method signatures, and declare your bean as implementing the interface.
- Declare your remote interface as extending this interface as well as the EJBRemote interface. An interesting fact: Although Java prohibits multiple inheritance for implementation classes, it's perfectly legal to have an interface inherit from multiple parent interfaces. Using this approach, you realize the familiar security of compile-time type checking without running the risk of exposing your bean to direct contact with the outside world.

Use Relatively Small and Well-Defined Queries

There are few circumstances in which you can justify retrieving thousands of rows of data from a database and sending them to the client. Large queries are expensive in terms of database and network resources. Don't grab an entire table and ship it down to the client; grab only the data in which the client is interested.

Don't Keep Database Cursors Open

Perform your query and then release your cursors. Database cursors can interfere with the ability of other processes to access the table. More specifically, many implementations of cursors place read locks on the tables and rows in your ResultSet. If a read lock exists on a table, another program that wishes to write to the table cannot do so until the read lock is removed.

Minimize Transactions

Transactions carry some level of overhead with them. They are vital for guaranteeing database integrity when updating a database. If your method merely reads data and returns it, however, you might consider calling it outside a transaction scope (that is, setting the method's transaction attribute to TX_NOT_SUPPORTED). Of course, if you perform a read outside of a transaction, you may see some potentially inconsistent data depending on the isolation level of the transaction. For example, you may read a row that was inserted by a transaction that later rolls back. In this case, the row you read will no longer exist in the database.

Minimize Distributed Transactions

Distributed transactions carry quite a bit of overhead. They also tie up resources on several servers at once. Design your system to minimize the necessity for using distributed transactions.

Avoid Indexing Your Tables

EJB is an OLTP-oriented system, so providing indices on your underlying tables could be bad for performance. By "bad," we mean "potentially several orders of magnitude worse." Each time a row is inserted into an indexed table, the database must add the row to its index. As an extreme example, the author once used a piece of beta software that required the underlying tables to be indexed before making bulk data inserts. Under this regime, a typical bulk insert took more than a day to run. A later version of the software allowed bulk inserts without requiring indexes on the tables; with this version, a typical bulk insert took only a few hours.

Not all indices are a bad thing, however. On the contrary, they can improve the performance of queries by orders of magnitude. Nevertheless, when the table in question is the target of frequent inserts and updates, indices can actually slow performance and should generally be avoided.

Remember That Memory Is Cheap

If your system is experiencing performance problems caused by a lack of memory, the simplest solution is to add more memory. Memory is cheap, and there's no reason not to add more if you need it. You should check your system to ensure that a lack of memory is indeed the problem before throwing hardware at it. The typical symptom indicating that you need more memory involves extensive paging by the operating system; that is, the operating system spends a significant percentage of its time swapping things into and out of memory because not enough physical memory is available to hold all running programs.

Build in Upward-Scalability

Your system may be initially intended as a small departmental application. Later, it may well be deployed at an enterprise level. Build the initial application with an increased user load in mind. In the context of distributed systems, this consideration typically means designing your system so that different components can be moved to different servers. EJB makes this task relatively straightforward because JNDI is used to provide a location-independent method of obtaining references to beans.

Wrap Entity Beans with Session Beans

One of the earliest design patterns to emerge in EJB is the idea of hiding Entity beans by wrapping them in Session beans. The Session bean provides an interface for the client, but all references to Entity beans remain hidden within the Session bean. The idea here is to minimize the number of remote references. Of course, this approach assumes that your Session bean and its contained Entity beans reside on the same container.

Chapter 9 provides an example of the Session-wraps-Entity pattern. The rough idea is similar to the stateful Session example from Chapter 4, except that the state is maintained in Entity beans rather than in the Session bean itself.

Streamline Your Middleware Methods

Life is easier for your EJB container if your methods are relatively short and to the point. This idea may seem to contradict the earlier point about making your methods large enough to do something useful, but really it doesn't. The earlier point suggested setting a lower bound on method size; you don't want to write your objects so that the client has too many relatively trivial methods to accomplish a task. This point, on the other hand, establishes an upper bound for method size; you don't want your methods to run for seconds or minutes at a time.

Put Your Business Logic in the Middle Tier

This idea is the raison d'être for Enterprise JavaBeans; they exist to provide a middle-tier location for business logic. Use them for that purpose. If you find yourself putting business logic in the client, take a step back and reevaluate your design.

Understand the Tradeoffs Between Isolation Level and Concurrency

Typically, the higher the degree of isolation associated with a query, the more it interferes with the execution of other queries. High levels of isolation typically mandate high levels of locking on the underlying database, which can cause other user transactions to be blocked until your transaction completes. Experiment with isolation levels until you find one that suits your needs.

Avoid Extensive Object Allocation and Deallocation

In the pre-Java world, the classic way for a long-running process to die was as a result of a memory leak. Java provides garbage collection to protect against memory leaks. Allocating and freeing a large number of objects, however, creates more work for the garbage collector. Garbage collection is not a silver bullet. You will make the garbage collector's life easier if you avoid unnecessary creation and deletion of objects.

Prototype, Prototype, Prototype

Prototyping is important. It's especially critical if you haven't built a distributed system before, because distributed components in the real world can interact in strange and unforeseen ways.

Early prototyping and testing are exceedingly important steps in the EJB world, because many of the EJB products on the market are brand-new, and hence include a slew of bugs. The earlier in the development process you find a bug, the earlier you can obtain a fix from the vendor (or, if the vendor is unresponsive, the earlier you can switch to another EJB container).

Another benefit of early prototyping is that it allows your developers to gain experience in working with EJB. In learning about any new product, you will inevitably make mistakes. It's best to make most of the mistakes at an early stage, before development begins in earnest.

Do Load Testing

Find a load-testing tool and challenge your application with it. See how it stands up to a load. If no load-testing tool is available, you can make one by taking the sort of simple client interactions demonstrated in this book and creating a wrapper object for them that spawns many such events.

The typical pattern of system performance is that the system performs well up to some load, and then performance degrades markedly. You want to find that point in advance, estimate whether you'll reach it in the course of normal operations, and have a plan ready for when you do reach it.

Monitor the Size of Your User Base
When Designing an Architecture

Something that works fine for 50 users may not do so well for 5,000 users. Pick tools that have been shown to work under the conditions under which your application will run. These days, "enterprise" is the hot buzzword, and virtually every vendor will insist that it has an "enterprise-ready" solution that will handle your every need. Don't believe the hype. Find some customers who are already using the tools, and see what they have to say.

Separate Transaction-Processing Tables from Reporting Tables

Two basic classes of database applications exist:

- OLTP (online transaction processing) systems, which mostly insert or update data
- OLAP (online analytical processing) systems, which mainly perform read-only queries

These two types of systems have conflicting needs. OLTP systems, because they modify data, typically require fast performance on inserts, updates, and deletes, and perform only relatively simple queries. Speedy response time is essential for OLTP systems. OLAP systems, on the other hand, generally do not modify data, but perform potentially large and complex queries against existing data. Because OLAP queries generate read locks, they can potentially interfere with an OLTP system's ability to establish write locks.

Enterprise JavaBeans is fundamentally OLTP-oriented. If you need to provide OLAP functionality, a good solution is to perform periodic extracts from the OLTP tables and then move them to a more stable OLAP platform. Next, fully index the tables and allow OLAP users to query away to their heart's content.

If a Database Query Runs Slowly, Review Its Query Plan

The **query plan** is the actual set of operations that the database performs to execute your SQL query. The query plan contains detailed information about the order in which tables are joined, whether table scans are used, and so on. Sometimes slight modifications to the query can produce dramatic improvements in performance.

Keep Joins Simple

In a relational database, joins that involve multiple tables can result in very long-running queries. A good rule of thumb is to avoid joining more than three tables in a single "where" clause.

Have a Database Administrator

It may seem self-evident, but if you have a database, you should have a database administrator (DBA) to manage it. Databases are finicky creatures, and the performance differences between a well-tuned database and a badly tuned one can be considerable. If you can't justify having a full-time DBA as part of your staff, at least hire a consultant to help install and set up your database and to provide you with scripts for routine maintenance, backups, and other such administrative tasks. DBAs are highly paid because their expertise is valuable.

Use Prepared Statements

JDBC Prepared Statements can improve performance under some circumstances. A Prepared Statement improves performance by creating a temporarily stored procedure on the first invocation, then invoking the stored procedure for subsequent invocations. Like any language, SQL must be translated into some lower-level representation before it can be executed. With a Prepared Statement, this translation takes place only once (for the initial call), rather than once per query.

Have Your Development Environment Mirror Your Production Environment

If your production environment will entail three machines (a client, an EJB server, and a back-end database), then your development environment should also have three machines. Having identical development and deployment environments ensures that you don't make the wrong assumptions about communication costs.

During Load Testing, Use a Sniffer to Monitor Network Traffic

A sniffer is a tool that can intercept packets and generate statistics on network utilization. Make sure that you're not swamping the network with packets. If so, you may need to reconfigure your network to isolate your application's traffic.

Use the Facade Pattern for Interfacing with Legacy Systems

If you have not read the book, *Design Patterns; Elements of Reusable Object-Oriented Software* (Gamma, Helm, Johnson, Vlissides), you should definitely pick up a copy. **Design patterns** are designs that have been found to work well for particular problems. If you are unfamiliar with patterns, you will likely experience a strong sense of déjà vu when reading Gamma et al.'s book, because the types of patterns that it discusses are found throughout the Java Development Kit (JDK).

- The Bridge pattern is used in the old Abstract Windows Toolkit (AWT) peer mechanism.
- The Abstract Factory and FactoryBuilder patterns are often used to generate new classes.
- The Observer pattern is used in JavaBeans' bound and constrained properties and is implemented directly in the `java.util.Observer` class.
- The Adapter pattern is used in the JDK 1.1 AWT event model and by JavaBeans development environments to provide linkage between beans.

The **Facade** pattern describes how to provide interfaces to complex subsystems without requiring detailed knowledge of these subsystems from the rest of the application. Basically, the idea of the Facade is to create a single wrapper that makes calls to the underlying subsystems. Thus the underlying complexity of the subsystems remains hidden behind a simpler facade.

Use Patterns

A small but growing pool of literature focuses on the subject of design patterns and analysis patterns. The aforementioned book by Gamma et al. (often called "the Gamma book," the "Gang of Four book," or "the GoF book") is absolutely not to be missed. In addition, Martin Fowler has written a book on Analysis patterns, called *Analysis Patterns*, that raises the level of abstraction to the world of analysis. Jim Coplien's book on C++ idioms gives examples of how patterns translate into implementation.

The patterns movement is intended to give you, the developer, some well-described solutions to common problems, so that you don't have to reinvent the wheel.

Keep Network Topology in Mind

All remote method invocations are not created equal. An invocation to a machine on the other side of the continent may be orders of magnitude more expensive than one to a machine on the same network segment.

Design Security in from the Start

Your security mechanisms should not be grafted onto your application as an afterthought; rather, they should inform your design from its earliest stages. Typically, an MIS application has three types of users:

- Basic users, who use the system's core functionality
- Managers, who may use core functionality, but also typically require some types of reporting functionality so that they can keep tabs on how work is progressing
- Administrators, who can modify permissions for the other users and perform system maintenance

Early in the design stage, you should identify the classes of users for your system and design your interfaces accordingly. The access control list mechanism is a handy way of implementing this sort of role-based security.

Work Closely with Network Personnel

As mentioned several times in this book, network topology and network load are important issues. Likewise, security is an important issue. In a typical MIS shop, one group takes charge of network topology and security. You should work with these people over the course of your design, to ensure that no unpleasant surprises emerge at deployment time. Typically, the network personnel have access to specialized hardware such as sniffers that may help you in development. Cultivate a good working relationship with them.

Be Aware of the Internal Politics

Although you shouldn't necessarily rush out to buy a copy of Machiavelli's *The Prince* (a pretty good read, nevertheless), you should keep an eye out for organizational and political issues that may affect the development of your system. Who is in favor of the system? Does anyone actively oppose it? Is anyone developing a competing system?

Be Aware of the Organizational Culture

This idea is an extension of the point about being aware of the political situation. Different organizations have different cultures. Does your customer typically use cutting-edge technology, or is it still mainly a COBOL shop? Does it embrace or scorn object-oriented technology? Such preferences are important to recognize. If an organization is brand-new to object-oriented technology, for example, you often must spend a fair amount of time convincing key players of the usefulness of object-oriented technology. On the other hand, if the organization has been using this technology for 10 years, you face a smoother road.

Be Prepared for Requirements Changes

Everybody knows that changes in requirements tend to lead to schedule slippage; still, requirements changes happen. Iterative prototyping is a good way to minimize late requirements changes. In the iterative prototyping approach, the development team meets with customer representatives and extracts requirements from them. The team then builds a prototype that implements some of the required functionality and shows it to the customer. The customer either gives its approval or requests changes. If changes are requested, the modifications are made, and the process is repeated until the customer accepts the functionality. The next piece of system functionality is then incorporated, and the process begins again.

Iterative prototyping allows you to build your system bit by bit, obtaining feedback at every step. The feedback alone is reason enough to take this approach. Typically, late requirements changes happen either because the customer forgot to mention some piece of required functionality or because it assumed that the developer would implement some piece of functionality differently. In the iterative prototyping approach, the customer has many opportunities to review the design and ensure that nothing has been forgotten.

Another desirable aspect of the iterative approach is that it doesn't assume that you do a perfect job at any step of the development process. The classic "waterfall" approach (requirements analysis, design, implementation, maintenance) assumes that each step of the process is fully complete before the next step begins, and consequently tends to punish revisions to requirements rather severely. In contrast, the iterative approach allows for some reworking as part of the process.

Build One Slice at a Time

Assuming that you are taking an iterative prototyping approach, you should build a single slice of functionality at a time. Imagine that your order-taking system must accomplish three tasks:

- Accept an order.
- Bill the customer's credit card.
- Contact the inventory system to issue a shipping order.

Rather than attempting a shallow implementation of all three function points, a better approach is to pick a chunk of functionality and implement it in its entirety.

The exception to this rule involves user interface development. The program's user interface is the only component that users will see on a day-to-day basis, so they should be able to see a full-scale mockup of it as early as possible. It's not necessary that all functions be fully implemented; perhaps you just load the list boxes with static text, and not all buttons may work. Nevertheless, the user should experience the basic look-and-feel and navigation of the program. The user interface typically elicits the largest number of requirements changes, so it's helpful to begin its development early. One note of caution: Make sure, when demonstrating a user-interface mockup, to emphasize that it is actually a mockup and that significant development work remains to provide a fully implemented system.

Build the Difficult Components First

The temptation in any endeavor is to deal with the easiest things first and defer the more difficult items until later. This approach is not a good idea in building systems; instead, the best strategy is to attack the most challenging problems as early as possible. Even during requirements gathering, you might build small proof-of-concept programs to test elements of the design about which you have feasibility concerns.

Talk to Your Users

It's the easiest thing in the world for members of a development team to isolate themselves and crank out a system that's clean, efficient, and doesn't do what the users need. If you're building a replacement for an existing system, the users can be your best ally. They're experts on the system—they know what it does, what problems exist with it, and what the new system should do. In an MIS context, a helpful exercise is for members of the development team to sit with users and watch them work. If you're building a system for a Web-based enterprise, this step becomes more difficult. Note, however, that users are rarely shy about indicating what they don't like about a system. This information is absolutely precious; use it wisely.

Keep It Simple

Always strive for simplicity. If you find yourself handling a lot of special cases, take a step back and attempt to consolidate the cases. Some problems require complex solutions, but sometimes complexity simply grows over time. Question basic assumptions. If enormous complexity exists, ask why it's there. Maybe you can eliminate it.

Conduct Walkthroughs

Hold **walkthroughs,** both for designs and for implementation code. A walkthrough is a meeting in which the developer of a particular module presents it to a relatively small group of peers. Typically, the group walks through the code line by line in great detail. At any point, the reviewers can interrupt with questions or comments. Walkthroughs have several purposes:

- Knowledge dissemination. Because the code is analyzed by several people, the reviewers gain an understanding of how the code works. This step prevents situations where a programmer gets a new job and no one knows how to maintain the code.
- Error detection. Having several pairs of eyes look at a piece of code often turns up errors missed by the original developer. It's best to head off errors as early as possible.
- Improvement. Often, a reviewer may suggest a better approach to some problem than the one used by the developer.
- Education. Walkthroughs can be helpful in educating new staff members about the coding standards and practices of your shop, allowing them to see parts of the system to which they might not otherwise be exposed.

Some general tips on walkthroughs follow:

- Walkthroughs should be performed relatively early in the development process. The rule of thumb at one shop where the author worked was that a walkthrough should be conducted when the implementation was complete and compiled cleanly, but before significant testing was done.

The idea here is to keep the process moving, rather than having developers strive for perfection before the walkthrough takes place.

- Give the reviewers adequate time to examine and become familiar with the code.
- Do not accept silence as assent; a walkthrough where no one makes any comments is relatively useless.
- Generally, managers should not be included in a walkthrough; their presence can intimidate people into silence. It's only natural that employees don't want to make one another "look bad" in front of management.
- All comments made at a walkthrough should be logged, and later checked to ensure that the requested changes have been made.
- There is no shame in having someone find an error in your code. We all make mistakes. Even the author has never had a piece of code undergo a walkthrough without receiving any comments. The only shame is in having an error get into production.

Use Version Control

Find a version-control package you like, and use it religiously. When the chips are down and your code starts breaking, it's wonderful to be able to revert to an earlier version while you find the problems.

Use a Code Profiler

Profiling tools track the execution of your code and report how much time the program spent executing each line. The results of code profiling are often surprising—the rule of thumb is that 90 percent of a program's execution time is devoted to 10 percent of its code. Finding that 10 percent and optimizing it can help speed things up dramatically.

Establish Your Interfaces Early

Before building anything serious, you should establish a firm concept of the interfaces that the various modules will use to communicate with one another. You might want to provide skeletal implementations as part of the design. If the interfaces between modules are fixed, developers can work relatively independently, because they know which arguments are expected and which values will be returned. Also, fixing the interfaces allows developers to create dummy modules that can be used to emulate the functionality of not-yet-developed modules. If the interfaces are being continually modified, developers must spend more time coordinating changes among themselves. In EJB terms, this recommendation means that, before development of a bean's implementation class begins, its home and remote interfaces should be created and should not be changed.

Build Early and Often

Do not defer integration of your system components until the end of the development phase. During the development process, you should integrate code as it is developed. Integrate all of the completed code, build it, and then test it. Take this step often. Frequent building can help find integration problems early in the process.

Having an integrated system against which to test is helpful in the development process. It provides checks to ensure that the components work together smoothly.

You may decide to integrate pre-walkthrough code on a daily basis. Arguments can be made both for and against this approach. On the positive side, including all code in the daily build can highlight compatibility problems early, minimizing wasted time in development. On the negative side, integrating "raw" code can lead to spurious errors in testing, if an already-tested piece of code depends on a "raw" piece of code that contains errors.

For small projects, the team leader can take responsibility for performing the daily build. For larger projects, one or more people may be dedicated to full-time version control and build maintenance. During one of the author's projects, we handled this issue as follows:

- At the end of the day, developers would e-mail me the current version of their code. The code should compile with no errors.
- The next day, I would immediately do a build on the system.
- After the build, I'd run a set of test cases.
- If any problems arose during the build or test phases, I'd notify the developer whose code was affected, and he or she would incorporate any necessary changes into the next day's work.

Perform Regression Testing

Along with daily builds, daily regression testing can facilitate early detection of potential problems. One approach to this stage is to require that developers provide a set of test cases as part of their deliverable. Test cases for various modules can then be consolidated into one large program, which is run after a new build and logs information on the successful or unsuccessful completion of the various test cases. Again, the team leader typically takes the responsibility for running the regression tests and notifying the developers when tests fail.

Choose Appropriate Test Cases

At a minimum, your test cases should ensure that all of your code executes at some point during the course of the test. Several tools for Java are currently available to ensure that you use an appropriate coverage test.

A canon of testing states that you cannot test all paths through a system. Nevertheless, you can ensure that all paths through a given module are executed. The problem with testing all paths through a system is that a combinatorial explosion of numbers of paths occurs when the application includes several deeply nested modules. For example, if there are 5 paths through method 1 and 5 paths through method 2, then there are 25 potential paths through the pair. For a large and complex system, it quickly becomes unfeasible to test all paths through the system. Good code coverage testing is still better than no testing at all.

In addition to ensuring adequate coverage, test cases should include some completely flawed data, to see how a program behaves when it receives bad data. Practicing defensive programming throughout your entire system can unnecessarily increase the size and complexity of the system, but, the portions of your system that deal with user input or other data from outside your system should nevertheless validate the data carefully before passing it on to the internal workings of your system.

Generate Test Cases While Implementing the Application

I like to test each method as I develop it. After writing a method, I consider putting together a set of test cases that exercise the code, and then run it. This approach may keep me from going too far down a wrong track. It's helpful to know that, if you encounter unexpected behavior when implementing a method, the methods on which your method depends have already been tested.

Automate Everything

When I'm developing an application, two scripts are essential to my work:

- A "make," or "deploy," script that recompiles my code, packages it, and deploys it.
- A "go," or "run," script runs the code through a series of test cases.

The EJB deployment process is a fairly intricate one. You must

- Compile your code.
- Generate your deployment descriptor.
- Bundle everything up into a .jar file.
- Deploy the .jar file in your container.

Automating the build and run processes may result in fewer cases where you must spend an hour looking for a bug that turns out to be the result of an incompletely executed build or deployment. For a large project, a makefile can ensure that all of your code is correctly compiled. If you're not familiar with the make utility, I highly recommend that you use it.

Understand the Role of Testing

It is a canon of Total Quality Management (a fundamentally sound approach, even if implementations of it have been flawed) that you can't test quality into a product. No amount of testing can guarantee a perfect product. Despite this caveat, testing can go a long way toward ensuring that a product functions well and has no obvious errors.

CHAPTER 9

A Nontrivial Example

In this chapter, we will build a slightly more complex system than those created in earlier chapters. A fairly detailed walkthrough of the steps that it took to arrive at the final code is provided. Because so much code exists, however, we won't do a line-by-line explanation unless there's something particularly interesting about a given piece of code.

Requirements

The requirements for this example in terms of this book can be stated as follows:

- Show a real-world system.
- Make sure it's not overly complex in terms of requirements.
- Exercise many of the features of EJB.

This example involves a time-tracking system—a system that would allow employees to log their hours electronically instead of handing in paper time-sheets that are then keyed in. It's easy to see the value of such a system (and it should make a good demonstration system to implement if you're trying to prove the business efficacy of EJB to your boss), and it is relatively straight-forward to construct. With that in mind, let's examine the following set of project requirements:

- The project should use a graphical user interface.
- The front end should be generic enough that it could be used in a servlet if desired.
- The project should allow employees to enter their times.
- Employees should be able to charge time to more than one contract.

- Employees should be able to query the database to see their time records for any arbitrary range of dates.
- Managers should be able to obtain aggregate reports for all of their employees.
- Employees should not be able to examine the time records of other employees.

Because the main goal of this project is to demonstrate EJB functionality, the following EJB-oriented requirements were also created:

- The project should use an access control list to determine whether the user is an employee or a manager.
- The project should use a Session bean as its interface to the client and use Entity beans to interact with the underlying database.

Design

Now that our requirements are complete, we can proceed to design. After considering several different design approaches, we settle on our desired design. Before describing this design and explaining why it was selected, let's address a few issues that came up during the course of design

Relationships in EJB

Some of our initial designs contained many more beans than the final design does. Two questions occurred that led us to simplify our hierarchy:

- Should we develop reference trees at create time, or should we defer them until they are actually needed? You may prefer to do most of the setup early in the process, so that response time once the user is in the application is quicker. Instantiating a tree of references at initialization time seemed a bit wasteful, however. Remember, remote references are not free; establishing them takes time, and maintaining them requires some overhead on the server's part. Assuming 1 manager with 10 employees, each of whom works on 4 contracts, for a 52-week period you would need to generate $52 * 4 * 10 = 2080$ remote references to represent one year's worth of data.
- Once the relationships are set up, what good will they do? For example, imagine that a manager wants to query for all hours worked by his employees between two dates. The steps involved would be as follows:
  1. Iterate through all entries in the list of employee references. For each employee reference:
     2. Iterate through the list of all time entry references. For each time entry reference:

      3. Invoke a method to get the date of the entry.
      4. Check whether the date falls within the given boundaries.
      5. If it does, add it to the set of data to return.
   end ForEach
      6. Return the data to the Employee object.
 end ForEach
      7. Aggregate the data and return them to the caller.

We could potentially optimize this procedure by retrieving the data stored in the time entry object in advance and storing the information in a local array together with its remote reference. This tactic might result in a "stale data" problem, though; if the underlying data for a particular time entry were updated, the array must be updated as well. Also, the net result is that the contents of the time entry database table must be mirrored in memory on the EJB server, which seems a particularly wasteful use of resources. Also, traversing this tree of references would almost certainly be slower than issuing a query against the underlying relational database.

At this point, it becomes apparent that the best way to manage relationships for this example is to leave the relationships in the database and use queries to build the appropriate aggregate datasets at runtime.

Relationships in General

Despite our design for this example, in many situations it is helpful to express relationships among objects as part of the object model. Martin Fowler's book *Analysis Patterns* illustrates some cases where this concept applies. You may also wish to avail yourself of a full-blown object-relational mapping tool, such as JavaBlend, if complex relationships must be mirrored in your object mode. Alternatively, you could use an EJB implementation that supports complex relationship maps.

Detailed Design

At this point, we have put together a good object model as depicted in Figure 9.1. Now let's move to a more detailed level and begin specifying the methods performed by each object. To this point, we haven't been particularly careful in specifying where each of the methods falls, but have simply maintained a list of methods for objects scribbled on scraps of paper. Now it's time to formalize the process.

Some utility objects not included in Figure 9.1 also found their way into the design. They include the following items:

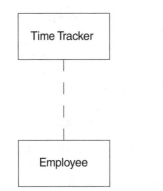

Figure 9.1.   The final object diagram. Lines represent containment relationships.

- The MyIdentity class used in the example in Chapter 7 will allow the TimeTracker bean to query the container to see whether the client has an identity of "manager."
- The TimeSheetLine class is used to pass the data that would be contained in a TimeEntry object (employee ID, date, hours worked, and contract) back to the client. Before eliminating the TimeEntry object from the system, we had thought to use this class to pass TimeEntry data to remote clients. In general, it's preferable to pass a plain old class containing the data to a client, rather than passing a remote reference and allowing the client to query it for data. Remember, we want to keep remote invocations to a minimum for performance reasons.

For the TimeTracker, the following methods are necessary:

- boolean isManager()—Because the system provides different levels of functionality depending on whether the user is an employee or a manager it should include a method that the client program can query at runtime to decide whether the user is a manager. The client can then gray out menu choices or disable buttons that should be used only if the user is a manager. Remember, we'll be using access control lists to guarantee that employees do not have access to methods that are reserved for managers only, but it's not polite not to force the client to handle SecurityExceptions if you can avoid it.
- TimeSheetLine[] getHours(Date start, Date end)—This method retrieves the hours worked on all contracts for the currently logged-in employee between "start" and "end."
- void setHours(TimeSheetLine tsl)—This method sets the hours for the currently logged-in employee according to the values in the argument TimeSheetLine object. This call is passed to an underlying Employee object.

- `TimeSheetLine[] getEmployeeHours(int employeeID, Date start, Date end)`—This function, which is restricted to managers, fetches the hours for a particular employee between "start" and "end." This method throws a NotYourEmployeeException if the employee does not work directly for the manager.
- `TimeSheetLine[] getAggregateHours(Date start, Date end)`—Another "for-managers-only" function, it retrieves the hours worked by all of the manager's employees between "start" and "end."

For the `Employee` object, the following methods are necessary:

- `TimeSheetLine getHours(TimeSheetLine tsl)`—This method queries the database for values in timesheet line; it returns the value if found or "null" if the value doesn't exist. This function is mainly used internally in `setHours(TimeSheetLine)`. Its inclusion became important when we designed the implementation of `setHours()`, which should either update an existing row or insert a new row depending on whether the row currently exists. A cleaner approach is to allow the method to call a `getHours()` method to check for existence than to simply implement another SQL query, because the method can later be reused in other places if necessary and can be independently tested. Because this method will be used only internally, it is not included as part of the remote interface for the `Employee` class.
- `void setHours(TimeSheetLine tsl)`—This method uses getHours to see whether the row currently exists in the database. If it does, the method updates the existing row with the new arguments. If it doesn't, the method inserts the argument values.
- `TimeSheetLine[] getHours(Date start, Date end)`—This method retrieves the hours worked by this employee between "start" and "end."

We now have a good core set of functionality. There are other sorts of queries that a manager might wish to perform; if you're feeling inspired, you can add them after the example is working. For instance, it might be useful for the `Employee` and `Manager` classes to be able to query for hours by contract number.

NOTE: For a real system, the simple manager/employee relationship used in `getEmployeeHours` would be a potential source of problems. For instance, imagine that a president has 10 vice-presidents as her direct employees, and each of the vice-presidents has 10 division directors as his or her direct employees. The arrangement used in this sample system would prevent the president from querying to obtain the hours of a division director. Some possible solutions for this problem follows:

- Eliminate the exception mechanism. This tactic would allow anyone with manager status to query the timesheet records of anyone else in the company, which is probably not what you want.
- Directly represent the transitive manager/employee relationship in the underlying database. In this example, you could create a table representing employer/employee relationships and insert rows to indicate that the division director is an employee of both the vice-president and the president.
- Use Fowler's analysis patterns to implement the organizational hierarchy as an object model in itself.

Database Design

The database design was undertaken quite early in this project and has remained relatively static ever since. Basically, the database includes the following tables:

- TIME_ENTRIES, which contains the individual timesheet entries
- EMPLOYEES, which contains records for each employee

For the EMPLOYEES table, the table structure is as follows:

```
create table EMPLOYEES
(EMPLOYEE_ID int,
MANAGER_ID int,
FNAME  varchar(32),
LNAME varchar(32))
```

The primary key for this table is EMPLOYEE_ID. There should be only one row per EMPLOYEE_ID value. MANAGER_ID, a foreign key to the EMPLOYEES table, points to the EMPLOYEE_ID of the manager to whom this employee reports. FNAME and LNAME are simply placeholders for whatever non–time-tracking information is related to the Employee.

At this point, we reevaluate the Employee object's home and remote interfaces and decide several things:

- For this simple time-tracking system, which is not a full-blown human resources management system, there should be no way to create a new Employee object. On the other hand, presumably the time-tracking system could later be incorporated into a full-blown human resources management system, so we should provide a create() method on the Employee home interface. As a compromise, we will include a create() method, but omit any mechanism for creating a new Employee from the TimeTracker interface. To ensure that some disgruntled employee doesn't simply write his or her own client to maliciously create hordes of new employees, we create another access control list called `hrmanager` (for "human resources manager") and permit only members of this group to access the `create()` method.

- The user interface would be a bit friendlier if it displayed the person's name on the screen, so we provide a `getEmployeeInfo()` method to retrieve various elements of interest for the client to display. We use a class to send all of the data at the same time, rather than creating a set of atomic "getter" methods, so as to improve the network efficiency of querying for information. In the real world, some portions of the `EMPLOYEES` table probably should not be returned.
- Because the class may be used in broader circumstances one day, we include a `setEmployeeInfo()` method that accepts an `EmployeeInfo` class as its argument and updates the underlying database accordingly. This method is also restricted for use by only members of the hrmanagers group.

The `TIME_ENTRIES` table has the following structure:

```
create table TIME_ENTRIES(
EMPLOYEE_ID int,
MYDATE date,
HOURS double,
CONTRACT int)
```

This table has a composite primary key, made up of `EMPLOYEE_ID`, `MYDATE`, and `CONTRACT`.

Detailed Design of the `TimeTracker` Class

Now that the classes and interfaces have been set, it's time to embark on detailed design. First, let's look at the `TimeTracker` class. For each method to be implemented, we'll give pseudocode describing its functionality. In addition, any global properties and assumptions regarding the class will be specified.

`isManager()`

This method will be implemented using EJB's `EJBContext.isCaller-InRole()` method. `isManager()` will return true if the caller has the role "manager" and false otherwise.

`TimeSheetLine[] getHours(Date start, Date end)`

This method will simply call the underlying `Employee` object's `setHours()` method. After the employee has logged in, the TimeTracker bean keeps a reference to the Employee bean that corresponds to the user. This reference is used to perform inserts and queries for the user's timesheet.

```
void setHours(TimeSheetLine tsl)
```

Similarly to the getHours() method, this method invokes the underlying Employee object's setHours() method with the specified argument.

```
TimeSheetLine[] getEmployeeHours(int employeeID, Date start,
Date end)
```

Use of this method will be restricted to managers. It will use an SQL query such as

```
select EMPLOYEE_ID, MYDATE, HOURS, CONTRACT
from TIME_ENTRIES
where MYDATE >= start
and MYDATE <= end
and EMPLOYEE_ID = employeeID
```

to place the results into an array of TimeSheetLine objects and return the results. To make the process more efficient and eliminate the need for a query to count the objects before performing the actual query, TimeSheetLine objects will be created on the fly and stored in a hash table, and a counter will keep track of the number of rows returned. After all data are retrieved, the method will create an array of the appropriate length and insert the TimeSheetLine objects from the hash table into this array. Finally, it will return the array. If no values were found matching the query criteria, "null" will be returned.

```
TimeSheetLine[] getHours(Date start, Date end)
```

This method is another managers-only method. It uses the manager's employeeID (which, as you'll recall, is stored at login time) to query the database for all data on all employees who work for the manager. The SQL code will look roughly like this:

```
select EMPLOYEE_ID, MYDATE, HOURS, CONTRACT
from TIME_ENTRIES
where MYDATE >= start
and MYDATE <= end
and EMPLOYEE_ID in ( select EMPLOYEE_ID
        from EMPLOYEES
        where MANAGER_ID = employeeID)
```

Remember, in this case, the lowercase employeeID refers to the employee ID of the manager who is currently logged in.

This method will use a temporary hash table to store results, consolidate the results into an array of TimeSheetLine objects, and then return this array.

TimeTracker will use the CALLER_IDENTITY specifier for its "run-as" mode. Thus requests made to the Employee bean through the TimeTracker interface will carry the identity of the caller, rather than the identity of the bean.

Detailed Design of the Employee *Class*

```
TimeSheetLine[] getHours(Date start, Date end)
```

This method will use an SQL query such as the following:

```
select EMPLOYEE_ID, MYDATE, HOURS, CONTRACT
from TIME_ENTRIES
where MYDATE >= start
and MYDATE <= end
```

We use ">=" and "<=" to ensure that this query can be used to retrieve the data for a single date as well as for a range of dates. From a database standpoint, it would be more efficient to implement a second method to retrieve data only from a single date, but this approach would require more work on the developer's part. For now, this strategy will suffice; we can always extend it later if necessary. The temporary hash table approach used earlier will also be employed in this routine, to obviate the need for creating a second entry. In fact, because this mechanism will be used repeatedly, it makes sense to create a class to encapsulate the functionality.

```
TimeSheetLine getHours(TimeSheetLine tsl)
```

This method is intended for internal use as a convenience method by the Employee class; it is not included in the remote interface. It will perform a query based on the argument TimeSheetLine class. The query will look something like this:

```
select EMPLOYEE_ID, MYDATE, HOURS, CONTRACT
from TIME_ENTRIES
where EMPLOYEE_ID = tsl.employeeID
and MYDATE = tsl.date
and CONTRACT = tsl.contract
```

If a row is found, the method will construct a new TimeSheetLine object and return it. If no row is found, it will return "null."

```
void setHours(TimeSheetLine tsl)
```

This method first calls the getHours() method with the argument TimeSheetLine class to see whether a row with this primary key already exists. If a row already exists, its hours field is updated with an SQL statement like the following:

```
update TIME_ENTRIES
set HOURS = tsl.hours
where EMPLOYEE_ID = tsl.employeeID
and MYDATE = tsl.date
and CONTRACT = tsl.contract
```

If no row exists, a new row is inserted, using the following SQL:

```
insert into TIME_ENTRIES ( EMPLOYEE_ID, MYDATE, HOURS,
CONTRACT)
values(tsl.employeeID, tsl.date, tsl.hours, tsl.contract)
```

At this point, it would be nice to include a way to delete existing entries, in case an employee makes a mistake when entering his or her data. Let's add a deleteHours() method to the remote interface and implementation class.

```
deleteHours(TimeSheetLine tsl)
```

This method deletes a row from the TimeEntry object using the following SQL:

```
delete from TIME_ENTRIES
where EMPLOYEE_ID = tsl.employeeID
and MYDATE = tsl.date
and CONTRACT = tsl.contract
```

```
public EmployeeInfo getEmployeeInfo()
```

This method takes the information currently held in the bean's managed fields, puts it into an EmployeeInfo object, and returns it to the caller. This method is accessible by only members of the hrmanager group.

```
public void setEmployeeInfo(EmployeeInfo ei)
```

This method takes the argument EmployeeInfo class and inserts its values into the Employee's managed fields. This method is accessible by only members of the hrmanager group.

```
public EmployeePK ejbFindByPrimaryKey(EmployeePK pk)
```

This method queries the Employee database and either returns the appropriate primary key or throws a FinderException if the key is not found. It performs a database query such as the following:

```
select EMPLOYEE_ID
from EMPLOYEES
where EMPLOYEE_ID = pk.employeeID
```

```
public EmployeePK ejbCreate(EmployeeInfo ei)
```

This method is restricted to the hrmanager group. It sets the managed values of this bean according to the arguments in the EmployeeInfo object.

Designing the TimeSheetHash Class

This class is relatively straightforward, so we won't linger over its design. Basically it must satisfy the following requirements:

- The class should inherit from `java.util.Hashtable`.
- It should include a `getTimeSheetLines()` method that returns the values currently contained in an array of `TimeSheetLine` objects.

Designing the Client

Here's some pseudocode for the client:

1. Log in. For Session EJBs, this login takes place when the client invokes the `create()` method. At this time, the user ID and password are validated against the bean's access control lists. Additionally, the employee ID is passed in at this time, allowing the underlying Session bean to be created.

2. Decide whether the user is an employee or a manager, and display the appropriate user interface.

3. Retrieve the employee's information, and display it in the client.

Once the client has been created, it should provide user interface functions that allow the user to perform the following tasks:

- Review his or her timesheet entries
- Insert or update a particular entry
- Delete a particular entry

Additionally, if the user is a manager, the bean should provide a panel to perform the manager-level queries. This task would best be handled on a separate pop-up form.

Implementation

Now that the design is fully specified, implementation should be a breeze. We have made the following implementation choices:

- To use bean-managed persistence for the Employee bean
- To establish a database connection as early as possible in the Employee bean's life, and use it throughout the life

For this example, let's begin from the bottom and work upward, first implementing the Employee bean, then the TimeTracker bean, and finally the client. At each stage, we will implement a simple test client to exercise the functionality of the bean and ensure that it works before attempting to use it in a higher-level object. In a larger project, it is generally helpful to implement a skeletal version of the entire system relatively early in the process, and then use this skeleton as a framework for testing new functionality as it is implemented.

Building the Database

The data definition language (DDL) to create the tables used in this example follows:

```
drop table EMPLOYEES;
create table EMPLOYEES
(EMPLOYEE_ID int,
MANAGER_ID int,
FNAME  varchar(32),
LNAME varchar(32));
```

drop table TIME_ENTRIES;

```
create table TIME_ENTRIES(
EMPLOYEE_ID int,
MYDATE DATE,
HOURS double precision,
CONTRACT int);
```

For initial creation, don't include the `drop table` statements. It's convenient to leave them in for later operations in case you decide to change the table schema (assuming, of course, that the table doesn't hold anything of importance. In real life, database schemas change very rarely, and usually the ALTER TABLE command is preferred over dropping and recreating the table.

Setting Up the Access Control Lists

The access control lists for this example have the following format:

```
weblogic.password.hrmgr1=hrpassword1
weblogic.security.group.hrmanagers=hrmgr1
weblogic.password.emp1=emppassword1
weblogic.password.emp2=emppassword2
weblogic.password.emp3=emppassword3
weblogic.security.group.employees=emp1,emp2,emp3
weblogic.password.mgr1=mgrpassword1
weblogic.password.mgr2=mgrpassword2
weblogic.password.mgr3=mgrpassword3
weblogic.security.group.managers=mgr1,mgr2,mgr3
weblogic.security.group.empsandmanagers=emp1,emp2,emp3,mgr1,
mgr2,mgr3,hrmgr1
```

We have four groups:

- employees, who have normal permissions
- managers, who can review the time records of their employees
- hrmanagers, who have the ability to create new instances of Employee objects

- empsandmanagers, a convenience grouping that contains everyone except hrmanagers

Because the current implementation provides only a time-tracking system, it would probably be a good idea to leave the hrmanagers group with no entries. Nevertheless, we will use it to test the functionality of the Employee bean, so we'll include it here.

Implementing the Employee Bean

Writing the Skeleton Methods

This step is relatively straightforward—just implement the methods in the home and remote interfaces with empty implementations. At this point, we simply want to check the access control lists to ensure that everything works.

Writing the Test Client

The test client used here closely resembles the clients used in previous chapters. It will execute the various methods of the Employee.

Filling in the Skeletons

You may prefer to carry out testing on a per-method basis. That is, after completing implementation of a particular method, you can run some tests on the method before moving on. Before we get rolling too fast, let's figure out how to handle our database connections. For this bean, we would like to reuse the same database connection over the life of the bean. In particular, the connection should be available in the finder method. In looking at the state transition diagram for the Entity bean (see Figure 9.1), notice that setEntityContext() is called. First, let's insert code to establish and drop the database connection into setEntityContext() and unsetEntityContext().

NOTE: When implementing a class, you may find it helpful to use a comment line as an "it-works" line. This comment indicates that everything above the line has been tested, and everything below it has not. Start the line at the top of the class and move it downward, method by method, as you implement and test things. When you reach the end of the class, you can be sure that you haven't missed anything.

Note that a relatively large number of SQL commands in this class don't return anything. To clean up the code and provide for uniform exception handling, we create a method called `executeUpdate()` that takes an argument SQL statement, executes it, and catches any exceptions that may occur.

During the course of testing, it becomes apparent that the system was ignoring our attempts to attach access control lists to the `create()` and `remove()` methods. As that functionality is required, we decide to implement a method in the bean to check whether the caller is of the appropriate class and to throw an exception if the caller is not.

NOTE: WebLogic comes with an evaluation version of a database management system called Cloudscape. You can interact with Cloudscape programmatically (through JDBC), via a graphical interface, or via the command line. For hardcore development, a command-line SQL interface is generally preferable because it allows you to batch frequently performed operations (such as the creation of test data or database cleanup after a test has been run). You can use the following command in your batch file to run Cloudscape's command-line tool:

```
java -Djdbc.drivers=COM.cloudscape.core.JDBCDriver -
Dcloudscape.system.home=c:\weblogic\eval\cloudscape\data
COM.cloudscape.tools.ij.Main %1
```

To test your programs, try inserting a set of data into the database consisting of rows that almost match your query conditions. For example, imagine that you have the following query:

```
update foo
set value = 1
where condition1 = 1
and condition2 = 2
and condition3 = 3
```

You would insert four rows of data into your database:

- A row that matches all the conditions—it should be updated
- A row that matches all conditions except condition1—it should not be affected
- A row that matches all conditions except condition2—it should not be affected
- A row that matches all conditions except condition3—it should not be affected

After you've inserted your test data, run a select statement on the table via the command line, and save its output to a file. Next, run your program, and run the select statement again. Finally, examine your data to ensure that only the row that should have changed was affected.

Another useful check is to put the SQL queries used in your program into a file that can be run through the command-line interpreter. This strategy cross-checks that your program produces the appropriate results.

Also, keep an eye on the dates when developing test data. The `java.sql.Date` constructor takes the following arguments in the following formats:

- Year (integer)—given in terms of "year-1900"; that is, 1998 would be "98" and "2000" would be "100"
- Month (integer)—given from 0 to 11, where 0 is January and 11 is December
- Day (integer)—from 1 to 31

JDBC can convert from the `java.sql.Date` type to the type used by your database. It's easy to make mistakes in your test data, however, because the database itself will generally use a different format:

- Year will be four digits
- Month will range from 1 to 12
- The date will be in a yyyy-mm-dd format

If your queries produce strange results, perhaps a mismatch has occurred between your `java.sql.Date` values and the values in the underlying database format.

Following are some sample test data to test the condition:

```
Date start = new Date(98, 0, 1);       //Jan. 1, 1998
Date end = new Date(98, 11, 11);       //December 11, 1998
TimeSheetLine[] tslArray = cust.getHours(start, end);
connect 'jdbc:cloudscape:ejbdemo';
delete from employees;
insert into employees(employee_id, manager_id, fname, lname)
values( 1, 2, 'buckle', 'mashoe');
delete from time_entries;
insert into time_entries(employee_id, mydate, hours, contract)
values (1, DATE'1998-05-05', 3.0, 1);
insert into time_entries(employee_id, mydate, hours, contract)
values (1, DATE'1998-05-05', 3.0, 2);
```

(Should be in)

```
insert into time_entries(employee_id, mydate, hours, contract)
values (1, DATE'1998-01-01', 3.0, 3);
```

(Should be out—too early)

```
insert into time_entries(employee_id, mydate, hours, contract)
values (1, DATE'1997-12-31', 3.0, 3);
```

(Should be in)

```
insert into time_entries(employee_id, mydate, hours, contract)
values (1, DATE'1998-12-11', 3.0, 3);
```

(Should be out—too late)

```
insert into time_entries(employee_id, mydate, hours, contract)
values (1, DATE'1998-12-12', 3.0, 3);
```

Because we have two getHours() methods, one more general than the other, we chose to implement the general method first and call it from the specific method. That is, the actual functionality of the getHours() method is implemented in the method

```
getHours(int employeeID, Date start, Date end)
```

The getHours(Date start, Date end) method simply invokes the more general method with the instance's employeeID as the first argument and returns the results. The more general method is protected by an access control list, so it can't be invoked by anyone who is not a member of the hrmanagers list through that user's remote interface. A perfectly acceptable approach is to invoke it within a less-privileged method within the bean implementation class; method calls within a bean do not go through the access control list mechanism. You should be cautious about calling privileged methods from nonprivileged ones, because errors in your implementation could potentially introduce a back-door way to circumvent your access control lists. This method is a read-only method, and the user cannot modify the value of employeeID before calling it, so calling this method from a nonprivileged method is relatively safe. This approach offers two major advantages:

- You reuse code, so you work less.
- You must test the core function only once; other tests are relatively trivial.

The Final Product

Here, in all its glory, is the final implementation of the Employee class.

Employee *Home Interface*

Listing 9.1 gives our home interface.

Listing 9.1   Employee Home Interface

```
1   package book.chap09.timetracker;
2   import javax.ejb.EJBHome;
3   import java.rmi.RemoteException;
4   import javax.ejb.CreateException;
5   import javax.ejb.FinderException;
6
7   public interface EmployeeHome extends EJBHome
8   {
9
10      public Employee create(int employeeID, int managerID,
        String fname, String lname) throws RemoteException,
        CreateException;
11      public Employee findByPrimaryKey(EmployeePK pk) throws
        RemoteException, FinderException;
12  }
```

Employee *Remote Interface*

Listing 9.2 gives our remote interface.

Listing 9.2   Employee Remote Interface

```
1   package book.chap09.timetracker;
2   import javax.ejb.EJBObject;
3   import java.rmi.RemoteException;
4   import java.security.Identity;
5   import java.sql.Date;
6
7   import book.chap09.timetracker.TimeSheetLine;
8
9   public interface Employee extends EJBObject
10  {
11
12      public TimeSheetLine[] getHours(Date start, Date end)
        throws RemoteException;
13
14      public void setHours(TimeSheetLine tsl) throws
        RemoteException;
15
16      public TimeSheetLine getHours(TimeSheetLine tsl) throws
        RemoteException;
17
18      public void deleteHours(TimeSheetLine tsl) throws
        RemoteException;
19
20      public EmployeeInfo getEmployeeInfo() throws
        RemoteException;
21
22      public void setEmployeeInfo(EmployeeInfo ei) throws
        RemoteException;
23
24  }
```

Employee *Implementation*

Appendix C provides the full implementation of the `Employee` class. Some things of note about this class:

- The method called `isDirty` allows us to avoid reading and writing the database unless the data have actually been modified. (Tengah allows you to specify the name of a method for the container to interrogate before it attempts to invoke the `ejbLoad()` and `ejbStore()` methods.)
- Lines 80–95 implement a method called `executeUpdate()`; this convenience method takes any insert, update, or delete command and executes it. Because this method is present, the only time we need to implement special-case JDBC code is during selects.
- Similarly, `executeCountQuery()` (lines 145–176) executes an arbitrary SQL select string that returns a count.
- On line 264, the `ejbRemove()` method invokes a method called `isHRManager()`. As noted during the requirements, only managers from human resources are permitted to add or remove an employee—hence the exception.
- The `TimeSheetHash` class appears in lines 307–327. A fairly large number of methods must query the database for the same sets of data and then return arrays. The trick with arrays is that you must know the size of the array before allocating it. On the other hand, JDBC does not necessarily indicate how many rows appear in the result set. As a compromise, the `TimeSheetHash` acts as a thin wrapper around a `java.util.Hashtable`; the source code for this class appears later in this chapter.
- The `setHours()` method (starting on line 420) first queries to see whether a row exists that matches the keys of the incoming data. If a row exists, the method updates it. If no row exists, a new one is inserted.

Employee *Primary Key Class*

Listing 9.3 provides the code for our primary key class.

Listing 9.3   Employee Primary Key Class

```
1    package book.chap09.timetracker;
2    public class EmployeePK implements java.io.Serializable
3    {
4       public int employeeID;
5
6       public EmployeePK()
7       {
```

```
8
9     }
10    public EmployeePK(int employeeID)
11    {
12        this.employeeID = employeeID;
13    }
14  }
```

EmployeeInfo *Class*

Listing 9.4 gives the code for the EmployeeInfo class.

Listing 9.4 EmployeeInfo Class

```
1   package book.chap09.timetracker;
2
3   public class EmployeeInfo implements java.io.Serializable
4   {
5     public int employeeID;
6     public int managerID;
7     public String fname;
8     public String lname;
9
10    public EmployeeInfo(int employeeID, int managerID, String
      fname, String lname)
11    {
12        this.employeeID = employeeID;
13        this.managerID = managerID;
14        this.fname = fname;
15        this.lname = lname;
16    }
17  }
```

The Employee bean uses this simple class to pass employee information back to the client. Only four fields appear in this employee record, but there could potentially be many more fields.

MyIdentity *Class*

Listing 9.5 gives the code for the MyIdentity class.

Listing 9.5 MyIdentity Class

```
1   package book.chap09.timetracker;
2   import java.security.Identity;
3
4   public class MyIdentity extends Identity
5   {
6     public MyIdentity(String id)
7     {
8         super(id);
9     }
10  }
```

This class is simply a wrapper around the `Identity` class that allows it to be instantiated and subsequently used in `isCallerInRole()`.

TimeSheetLine *Class*

Listing 9.6 gives the code for the `TimeSheetLine` class.

Listing 9.6   TimeSheetLine Class

```
1    package book.chap09.timetracker;
2    import java.sql.Date;
3
4    public class TimeSheetLine implements java.io.Serializable
5    {
6      public int employeeID;
7      public int contract;
8      public Date date;
9      public double hours;
10     public TimeSheetLine(int employeeID, Date date, double
         hours, int contract)
11     {
12        this.employeeID = employeeID;
13        this.date = date;
14        this.hours = hours;
15        this.contract = contract;
16
17     }
18   }
```

This class is used to convey timesheet data between the client, the TimeTracker bean, and the Employee bean.

TimeSheetHash *Class*

Listing 9.7 gives the code for the `TimeSheetHash` class.

Listing 9.7   TimeSheetHash Class

```
1    package book.chap09.timetracker;
2    import java.sql.Date;
3    import java.util.Enumeration;
4
5    public class TimeSheetHash extends java.util.Hashtable
6    {
7      TimeSheetLine[] getTimeSheetLines()
8      {
9
10
11         int size = size();
12         TimeSheetLine[] contents = new TimeSheetLine[size];
13         //get list of keys in hash table
14         Enumeration mykeys = keys();
```

```
15
16          //for each key, retrieve the contents
17          for (int i = 0; i < size; i++)
18          {
19              contents[i] = (TimeSheetLine)get
                (mykeys.nextElement());
20
21          }
22          return contents;
23
24      }
25
26      public void add(int employeeID, Date date, double hours,
        int contract)
27      {
28          TimeSheetLine tsl = new TimeSheetLine(employeeID,
            date, hours, contract);
29          put(tsl, tsl);
30
31      }
32
33  }
```

As you can see, the `TimeSheetHash` object is quite simple. It saves quite a bit of repetitive coding.

The Deployment Descriptor

The deployment descriptor is presented in its entirety in Appendix C. The textual information in the deployment descriptor is generated through Tengah's sample deployment descriptor. You can see some background information about the various fields in the descriptor, and note some of the fields that are not included in the core deployment descriptor.

Implementing the TimeTracker Bean

We have now implemented and tested the Employee bean. Let's move on to the TimeTracker bean. We'll start by creating the home and remote interfaces, and then creating skeletal implementations for each home and remote method. We will analyze the skeletal methods one by one, implementing each one and testing it as we go.

Implementation of the `getHours` method is very simple. We merely use the `Employee` reference stored within the TimeTracker bean, call the Employee bean's `getHours()` method, and return the result. Of course, we must encase this operation in a `try` block, because a RemoteException may occur during the course of the method's execution. Alternatively, we could simply allow the RemoteException to propagate upward to the client. In this case, it makes sense to allow the exception to propagate, because the client must handle the RemoteException anyway.

During the implementation of the `getEmployeeHours` method, we noticed that it threw a NotYourEmployeeException (an exception declared so as to indicate that this employee does not report to the manager who is performing the query). The Employee bean's method does not throw this exception. At this point, we have three options:

- We can revisit the Employee bean and modify its method so that it checks whether the caller is the manager of the employee. This idea is not necessarily bad, but would require us to revisit already tested code. Also, this functionality is not necessarily part of the set of requirements for the Employee bean.
- We can use the Employee bean's method, but first query to ensure that this particular manager is the manager of the employee. This tactic is not a bad approach, but would require two queries.
- We can write a new SQL query that selects rows only if the employee works for the manager who is performing the query.

We decide to go with the third option. In general, it's best not to use two queries if one can accomplish the job.

NOTE: An interesting caveat applies to identities. The client must log in and present credentials. Once the login has taken place, however, beans can communicate with one another without reauthenticating, as long as you specify the `runAsMode` as `CLIENT_IDENTITY`.

ASIDE: In preparing test data, try to develop a set of data that you can run before each invocation of your test client, rather than letting the test client itself generate the test data. With this approach, you start from the same set of initial conditions every time.

In testing the `setHours()` method, we notice that the `Employee` method allows `setHours()` to be called for an employee other than the employee who is currently logged in. Again, we have options for fixing this problem:

- We can modify the `Employee` class to allow only the logged-in user to insert rows for himself or herself. We could even ensure that the

Employee bean ignores the employee number in the argument
`TimeSheetLine` object.
* We can add a check in the `TimeTracker` method to ensure that the
  employee is not trying to modify someone else's time, and throw an
  exception if so.

We choose the second option. Perhaps there is a valid reason for someone
to be able to change another employee's time record, so we decide to leave the
general functionality in the Employee bean and protect it in the TimeTracker
bean. We also create a new exception, NotYourIDException, that is thrown if
the client tries to modify someone else's time records.

The Home Interface

Listing 9.8 gives the code for our home interface.

Listing 9.8   Home Interface

```
1    package book.chap09.timetracker;
2    import javax.ejb.EJBHome;
3    import java.rmi.RemoteException;
4    import javax.ejb.CreateException;
5
6
7    public interface TimeTrackerHome extends EJBHome
8    {
9
10      public TimeTracker create(int employeeID) throws
         RemoteException, CreateException;
11   }
```

The Remote Interface

Listing 9.9 gives the code for our remote interface.

Listing 9.9   Remote Interface

```
1    package book.chap09.timetracker;
2    import javax.ejb.EJBObject;
3    import java.rmi.RemoteException;
4    import java.security.Identity;
5    import java.sql.Date;
6
7    import book.chap09.timetracker.TimeSheetLine;
8
9    public interface TimeTracker extends EJBObject
10   {
11      public EmployeeInfo getEmployeeInfo() throws
         RemoteException;
12
```

```
13    public boolean isManager() throws RemoteException;
14
15    public TimeSheetLine[] getHours(Date start, Date end)
      throws RemoteException;
16
17    public TimeSheetLine[] getEmployeeHours(int employeeID,
      Date start, Date end) throws RemoteException,
      NotYourEmployeeException;
18
19    public TimeSheetLine[] getAggregateHours(Date start, Date
      end) throws RemoteException;
20
21    public void setHours(TimeSheetLine tsl) throws
      RemoteException, NotYourIDException;
22
23    public void deleteHours(TimeSheetLine tsl) throws
      RemoteException, NotYourIDException;
24
25  }
```

Exceptions

Listing 9.10 Exception: Attempting to Modify Another Employee's Time Entry

```
1   package book.chap09.timetracker;
2
3   public class NotYourIDException extends Exception
4   {
5     public NotYourIDException(String s)
6     {
7         super(s);
8     }
9   }
```

The exception in Listing 9.10 is thrown when a user attempts to modify a time entry that is not his or her own.

Listing 9.11   Exception: Attempting to Look at the Timesheet of Another Manager's Employee

```
1   package book.chap09.timetracker;
2
3   public class NotYourEmployeeException extends Exception
4   {
5     public NotYourEmployeeException(String s)
6     {
7         super(s);
8     }
9   }
```

The exception in Listing 9.11 is thrown when a manager attempts to look at the timesheet data of an employee who does not work for that manager.

Notes About the Implementation Class

The `isManager()` method is included in the remote interface so that the client can figure out whether to display the portions of the form that allow managers to perform queries against other employees.

The code to create and free database connections and bean references has been encapsulated into four methods: `establishEJBReference()`, `establish-DBConnection()`, `closeEJBReference()`, and `closeDBConnection()`. There is no method call that is analogous to `close()` for EJB references; `remove()` differs in that it deletes the underlying object. To leave the object in peace but eliminate its reference, our best option is to assign the reference the value of "null."

The EJB specification (Section 6.4.1) mandates that the container should manage the saving and restoring of EJB references during passivation and activation, but not all containers correctly implement this. Note that we close the database connection in `ejbPassivate()` and restore it again in `ejb-Activate()`. You should not maintain references such as this one when your bean is passivated.

Many of the methods from lines 138–175 simply pass on the incoming arguments to methods on the underlying entity bean.

On line 175 and elsewhere, we use prepared statements so that JDBC will convert the `Date` objects to whatever underlying representation the database expects to see.

Line 175 uses a subquery to ensure that all elements in the result set will have the caller as a manager.

The Deployment Descriptor

Appendix C gives the code for the deployment descriptor for the TimeTracker bean.

Implementing the Real Client

For the client, we use an old front-end once used for an RMI example. Although it includes a few deprecated bits here and there, it's basically sound.

First, we rip out the RMI bits and insert EJB bits. This task is fairly straightforward. We add an extra panel on the bottom of the frame that appears if the user is a manager and allows the user to perform queries either for a particular employee or for all of that manager's employees.

Because our original code dated from JDK 1.0.2, we decide to delete the old-style APIs. We run javac with the -deprecation flag to warn about deprecated methods. The biggest jump from JDK 1.0.2 to JDK 1.1 involved the revamped event model, which went from an inheritance-based model to a registered-listener model. Here are some steps to make a relatively easy conversion:

- Implement the ActionListener interface in your class.
- Change your event-handling function to this format: `public void actionPerformed (ActionEvent evt)`.
- Search for references to `event.target` and replace them with `event.getSource()`.
- Change all returns in this function to return nothing.
- Implement the WindowListener interface in your class.

The Client Implementation Class

A few things of note about this class:

- It started as a JDK 1.0.2 class and was later ported to JDK 1.1.x.
- The class implements ActionListener. It would be cleaner to have a separate class implement ActionListener, but a more straightforward approach is to port an old piece of code that uses the JDK 1.0.2 event model if we will simply implement it in the class.
- Lines 46–116 perform most of the user interface setup. Another small routine on lines 283–299 sets up a special panel that managers can use to perform queries. The `ResultFrame` class (lines 302–327) is used as a pop-up box to display the results of these queries.
- Lines 104–112 create an anonymous inner class to handle window-closing events. Note the strange syntax used on line 108 to refer to an object variable of the class `TimeTrackerFrame`. The inner class is actually a separate class and therefore doesn't carry the normal "this" pointer associated with the `TimeTrackerFrame` class. It can, however, access the this pointer by saying `TimeTrackerFrame.this.<variable-name>`.
- Lines 141–144 add the managers-only panel after the login and validation tasks have been performed.
- In lines 167–168 and 241–242, we have hard-coded some date ranges. This step was purely a matter of expediency.

An Applet to Run the Client

Listing 9.12 provides an applet to run our client.

Listing 9.12   Applet for the Timesheet Application

```
1    //TimeTrackerApplet -- this class creates an instance of
     TimeTrackerFrame
```

```
 2    import java.applet.*;
 3    public class TimeTrackerApplet extends Applet
 4    {
 5      TimeTrackerFrame ttf = null;
 6      String host;
 7      public void start()
 8      {
 9          //get name of remote host
10      host = getCodeBase().getHost();
11
12      System.out.println("connecting to" + host);
13          //create new instance of TimeTrackerFrame,
14          //passing the hostname, and "true" to
15          //indicate applet mode.
16      ttf = new TimeTrackerFrame(true);
17      ttf.show();
18      }
19      //called when browser leaves page
20      public void stop()
21      {
22          //dispose of frame
23      ttf.dispose();
24      ttf = null; //set reference to null
25      }
26    }
```

Here's a handy way to turn an application into an applet. Simply write the application as a frame, and then write a simple wrapper applet that pops up the frame.

Deployment Issues

The only really strange thing happening with our deployment is that two beans appear in the same Jar file. This approach doesn't present a problem, as long as you declare the beans in your manifest file, as in Listing 9.13.

Listing 9.13   The Manifest File

```
1    Name: book/chap09/timetracker/EmployeeBeanDD.ser
2    Enterprise-Bean: True
3
4    Name: book/chap09/timetracker/TimeTrackerBeanDD.ser
5    Enterprise-Bean: True
```

Conclusion

This example required quite a chunk of coding. Indeed, this chapter's example represents a thorough workout for EJB. Of course, this application is relatively trivial compared with full-blown MIS systems, but it should give you a sense of how larger EJB systems will work together.

CHAPTER 10

Implementations and Future Directions

This chapter discusses implementations of EJB that are or will be available from various vendors. It also looks at the future of the Enterprise JavaBeans specification itself, with the author peering into his crystal ball to discuss some potential future directions that EJB may take.

EJB Implementations

The only implementations of EJB commercially available at the time of this book's publication were WebLogic and EJBHome. Naturally, the chapter will discuss them at greater length than other products. Don't construe this emphasis as favoritism; EJB offerings from some of the other vendors could be just as good or even better.

WebLogic

WebLogic was the first EJB 1.0-compliant server to become available. WebLogic implementations have been created for every EJB specification revision since well before the first released in December 1997. During the course of this book, we have noted a few of WebLogic's non-EJB features. This server also offers a considerable number of other features:

- JDBC drivers
- RMI server
- HTTP server

- Servlets
- JNDI services
- Integration with Microsoft's Component Object Model (COM)
- Integration with CORBA (though the EJB-to-CORBA mapping is not yet supported)
- A language called JHTML that can be used for server-side HTML scripting
- A graphical tool to aid in the creation of deployment descriptors

WebLogic supports both bean-managed and container-managed Entity beans. It is available for Win32 platforms (Windows 95, Windows 98, and Windows NT), for a variety of UNIX flavors, and for the AS/400 platform as well.

WebLogic doesn't provide Rapid Application Development (RAD) tools for the creation of EJB beans. The company anticipates that these RAD tools will rapidly be incorporated into Java development environments.

Support for WebLogic is in a class by itself. Support personnel are invariably skilled and knowledgeable, and problems are fixed quickly.

EJBHome

The EJBHome implementation is a freeware EJB implementation available for download from the Web site http://www.ejbhome.com. The software was created by developers, for developers, in the interests of furthering interest in EJB.

The product has now gone through a few releases and is becoming a relatively full-featured environment. Full-blown EJB servers tend to be expensive. It's good to have a small, lightweight, free server that people can use to get their feet wet in EJB.

The EJBHome implementation supports Entity beans.

Other EJB Vendors

Vendor: Bluestone
URL: www.bluestone.com
Product Name: SapphireWeb
Entity Support: Yes
Platforms: Windows NT, Windows 95, Sun OS, Sun Solaris, SGI, IBM
    RS/6000, Hewlett-Packard Series 9000, DEC Alpha (NT and UNIX),
    Siemens Nixdorf, Pyramid, MIPS-ABI
Other Protocols Supported: COM, CORBA
Special Features: Unified application server/development environment

Graphical Deployment Tools: Yes
Graphical Development Tools: Yes
Bluestone is one of the original application server vendors. It has added
   EJB support to its SapphireWeb system, starting with version 5.

Vendor: BEA

URL: www.beasys.com
Product Name: M3
Platforms: Windows NT (Intel), Windows NT (Alpha), Sun Solaris
   (SPARC), IBM AIX, Digital UNIX, HP/UX
Other Protocols Supported: IIOP, COM/ActiveX
Special Features: Connectivity with CICS, IMS, and other systems
BEA is an old-line transaction processor vendor. The M3 product will be
   based on its experiences with the Tuxedo TP monitor. Though BEA has
   purchased WebLogic, it will continue with its M3 product as well.

Vendor: Gemstone

URL: www.gemstone.com
Product Name: Gemstone/J 2.0
Other Protocols Supported: IIOP
Gemstone is a long-time player in the high-end Java virtual machine
   world. Its Gemstone/J 2.0 product will use IIOP as the underlying
   protocol, but allow developers to use plain RMI syntax in developing
   clients.

Vendor: IBM

URL: www.software.ibm.com/ts/cics
Product Name: CICS Transaction Server
Platforms: VSE/ESA, MVS/ESA, OS/390, OS/2, Windows NT, Solaris,
   AIX
Special features: Integration with existing CICS software
CICS is the world's most oft-used transaction processor; support for EJB
   within CICS has been announced for mid-1999.

Vendor: IBM

URL: www.software.ibm.com/ad/cb
Product Name: Component Broker
Platforms: Windows NT, AIX, OS/390
Other Protocols Supported: ActiveX, IIOP
Graphical Deployment Tools: Yes
Graphical Development Tools: Yes
ComponentBroker is IBM's middleware component management
   software.

Vendor: IBM
URL: www.software.ibm.com/websphere
Product Name: WebSphere application server, Advanced Edition
Platforms: AIX, Solaris, AS/400, OS/390
Other Protocols Supported: HTTP, JSP, JNDI, IIOP
Graphical Development Tools: Integrated with Visual Age for Java
WebSphere is IBM's unified application server/Web server.

Vendor: Information Builders
URL: www.ibi.com/ejbshow
Product Name: EDA Enterprise Component Broker
Platforms: Pure Java; should run anywhere
Other Protocols Supported: HTTP, IIOP, JDBC, JNDI
Special Features: Connectivity with CICS, EDA
Graphical Deployment Tools: Yes
Graphical Development Tools: Comes with Symantec Visual Cafe; will
    also work with other IDEs

Vendor: Inprise
URL: www.inprise.com
Product Name: Inprise Application Server
Platforms: Windows NT, Solaris, HP-UX, AIX
Other Protocols Supported: IIOP, HTTP, COM
Special Features: Integration with VisiBroker CORBA ORB
Graphical Deployment Tools: Yes
Graphical Development Tools: Inprise JBuilder included
Inprise is a new name for Borland, chosen after Borland purchased
    Visigenic, a leading CORBA ORB vendor.

Vendor: Novera
URL: www.novera.com
Product Name: JBusiness 4
Entity Support: No
Platforms: Sun Solaris 2.5.1 and 2.6, HP-UX 10.2, Windows NT 4.0,
    Windows 95 and 98 for clients
Other Protocols Supported: IIOP, SSL
Graphical Deployment Tools: Yes

Vendor: Oracle
URL: www.oracle.com
Product Name: Oracle Application Server 4.0
In addition, Oracle 8i will support EJB.

Vendor: Persistence Software
URL: www.persistence.com
Product Name: PowerTier for EJB
Entity Support: Yes
Platforms: Windows NT, AIX, Solaris, HP-UX
Special Features: Includes RAD tools for application development

Vendor: Secant
URL: www.secant.com
Product Name: Extreme Enterprise Server for Enterprise JavaBeans
Entity Support: Yes
Platforms: Windows95/98 (client only), Windows NT 4.x, Solaris 2.6 (in
    beta), HP-UX 10.2 (first quarter 1999), AIX (second quarter 1999),
    and AS/400 (planned)
Other Protocols Supported: IIOP

Vendor: SilverStream
URL: www.silverstream.com
Product Name: SilverStream Application Server 3.0
Platforms: Windows NT 4 with Service Pack 3 and the Microsoft Virtual
    Machine for Java (ships with the product), Windows 95/98 with the
    Microsoft Virtual Machine for Java, Sun Solaris 2.6
Other Protocols Supported: HTTP, IIOP
Special Features: Integration with ERP systems (SAP, Peoplesoft)
Graphical Deployment Tools: Yes
Graphical Development Tools: Yes

Vendor: Sun Microsystems
URL: www.netdynamics.com
Product Name: NetDynamics Application Server
Other Protocols Supported: IIOP
Special Features: Integration with ERP systems (SAP, Peoplesoft)
Graphical Deployment Tools: Yes
Graphical Development Tools: Yes

Vendor: Sybase
URL: www.sybase.com/products/eastudio
Product Name: Sybase Enterprise Application Server
Other Protocols Supported: COM/ActiveX, IIOP, HTTP, XML
Graphical Deployment Tools: Yes

Vendor: Valto Systems
URL: www.valto.com

Product Name: Ejipt
Entity Support: Yes
Platforms: Windows, Solaris, Linux
Other Protocols Supported: SSL
Special Features: Designed specifically to be embedded in other application servers

Vendor: Visient
URL: www.visient.com
Product Name: Arabica
Entity Support: Yes
Other Protocols Supported: IIOP
Graphical Deployment Tools: Yes

Because the EJB world is moving so fast, this list will likely include a few more entries by the time you read this book. For late-breaking news, check JavaSoft's EJB Development Tools Web page at http://java.sun.com/products/ejb/tools1.html.

Future Directions for EJB

Predicting the future is always a tricky business. Sun, however, has mentioned several things about future versions of the EJB specification. First, an interim release of the specification is coming very soon. This release is mainly a "bug fix" that addresses some weaknesses in the initial EJB 1.0 specification. In particular, it will include the following additions:

- A standard approach for authenticating clients
- A standard approach for specifying the behavior of finder methods for container-managed Entity beans

These two additions will make life much easier for the developer who wants to write portable, write-once-run-everywhere beans.

Beyond that, the picture becomes a bit cloudier. No definite timetable has been set for the release of the EJB 2.0 specification. (The EJB roadmap released by Sun—and discussed later in this chapter—doesn't mention any version numbers, so it's anyone's guess as to which of the phases is EJB 2.0.) The only certainty at this point is that EJB 2.0 will require containers to support Entity EJBs (which most implementations do anyway). A likely bet is that EJB 2.0 will include hooks for interoperating with the Java Messaging Service (JMS). The following features have been mentioned in the specification for future releases of EJB:

- Allowing Java 2 collections in addition to the `java.util.Enumeration` type as the return type for finder methods that return more than one primary key (section 9.9.1).
- Allowing EJB beans to act as OTS recoverable objects (section 11.1).
- Supporting nested transactions (section 11.1).
- Allowing beans to manage their Identity at runtime (Appendix A).
- Allowing beans themselves to be serialized (Appendix A).
- Providing the capability for clients to retrieve a URL reference that represents an EJB object (Appendix A).
- Creating a standard protocol between EJB containers and EJB servers, which would allow containers written by one vendor to be deployed on servers written by another vendor (Appendix A).

Additionally, since the java.security.Identity object has been deprecated in Java 2, future versions of the EJB specification will support Java 2-compliant representations of an identity.

Sun's EJB Roadmap

On December 8, 1998, Sun released a "roadmap" describing the future of the EJB specification. This document describes three major phased releases of EJB specification revisions. The first release, code-named Moscone, will mainly focus on tightening up some of the overly vague areas of the 1.0 specification. In particular, the Moscone release will include an Extensible Markup Language (XML)-based specification for describing container-managed finder methods for Entity EJB beans in a uniform way. This revision is scheduled for public review in the first quarter of 1999, and will be finalized in the second quarter of 1999.

The second phase of the EJB specification revisions, code-named Javitz, is described as focusing on the integration of EJB with existing systems. One can only speculate as to what this integration will entail. This specification will become available for public review six to nine months after Moscone is released.

The third phase of the EJB specification revisions, code-named Milano, will focus on further defining Entity beans. This specification will become available for public review six to nine months after Javitz is released.

Additionally, Sun has announced that it will provide a reference implementation of Enterprise JavaBeans, as well as a set of compliance tests designed to ensure compatibility across different EJB containers. The reference implementation will be available as a technology preview in the second quarter of 1999, with a beta becoming available in the third quarter of 1999 and a full release in the fourth quarter of 1999.

> **NOTE:** A "reference implementation" is not intended to be a full-blown commercial product. It mainly ensures that commercial implementers can refer to a model when implementing their own EJB containers. It's also useful as a portability checker; if your beans run in the reference implementation, you can be more confident that they will run in other servers as well.

A Bit of Stargazing

Fortune-telling has always been a dangerous occupation—but an irresistible impulse. Here is the author's vision of the future of EJB.

The first generation of EJB products will likely experience quite a few problems with interoperability. They will work well when acting as standalone application servers or when communicating with other machines running software from the same vendor, but will balk at talking to other machines running software from other vendors. This difficulty is par for the course in distributed systems.

The interoperability problems will decrease over time, as vendors test one another's implementations. A vendor working group has already formed with the idea of testing EJB servers to ensure compatibility. Sun will release a conformance testing suite and a reference implementation, which will further the cause of interoperability.

Initially, EJB will start small. It will be used mainly in proof-of-concept systems and small departmental systems. As it proves itself capable, however, it will quickly be used to develop larger and more powerful systems.

At some point, vertical-market vendors will introduce EJB versions of their products to expand their markets.

Eventually, EJB servers will become as ubiquitous as database servers are now.

The process of developing EJBs will become much easier as graphical tools that automate much of the scutwork of developing beans are released.

The **Object Management Group (OMG)** will embrace Enterprise Java-Beans and use it as a server-side component model.

Conclusion

You should now have a solid understanding of the EJB technology. I encourage you to start working with it as soon as you possibly can; in programming, you learn at least as much from implementing as you do from reading.

I hope that reading this book has left you excited about EJB and eager to start working with it. When I first heard about EJB, the idea of write-once-run-anywhere server-side components, I was highly skeptical. Upon reading the specification, however, I was amazed that, yes, they'd pulled it off. I remember the feeling that I had upon reading the original Java whitepaper way back in 1995; reading the EJB specifications gave me much the same feeling.

EJB appears to be relatively easy to work with (the fairly large examples used in the book would have been far larger if we had to build our own concurrency, persistence, and transaction support from scratch). EJB will likely age well, eventually emerging as everyone's first choice when designing distributed transactional systems.

APPENDIX A

Source Code for Chapter 4

Home Interface for the Bag Example

```
1    package book.chap04.bag;
2    import javax.ejb.EJBHome;
3    import java.rmi.RemoteException;
4    import javax.ejb.CreateException;

5    public interface BagHome extends EJBHome
6    {

7       public Bag create(int custID) throws RemoteException,
         CreateException;
8       public Bag create(String custname, String custaddr)
         throws RemoteException, CreateException;
9    }
```

Remote Interface for the Bag Example

```
1    package book.chap04.bag;
2    import javax.ejb.EJBObject;
3    import java.rmi.RemoteException;

4    public interface Bag extends EJBObject
5    {
6       //get list of inventory
7       public InventoryItem[] getInventory() throws
         RemoteException;
8       //add an item to the bag
9       public void addItem(String itemcode, int quantity)
         throws RemoteException, ItemNotFoundException;
10      //remove an item from the bag
11      public void removeItem(String itemcode, int quantity)
         throws RemoteException, ItemNotFoundException;
12      //list the contents of the bag
```

```
13    public InventoryItem[] getBagContents() throws
      RemoteException;
14    //execute the order
15    public void finalizeOrder() throws RemoteException;
16    //get customer ID
17    public int getCustID() throws RemoteException;

18  }
```

InventoryItem *Class*

```
1    package book.chap04.bag;

2    public class InventoryItem implements java.io.Serializable,
     Cloneable
3    {
4      //package visibility by default
5      public String itemCode;
6      public String itemDesc;
7      public int quantity;
8      public double price;

9      public Object clone()
10     {
11       try
12       {
13         return super.clone();

14       }
15       catch (CloneNotSupportedException e)
16       {
17         return null;
18       }
19     }
20   }
```

ItemNotFoundException *Exception*

```
1    package book.chap04.bag;
2    public class ItemNotFoundException extends Exception
3    {
4    }
```

BagBean *Implementation Class*

```
1    package book.chap04.bag;
2    import javax.ejb.SessionBean;
3    import javax.ejb.SessionContext;
4    import javax.ejb.CreateException;
5    import java.util.Hashtable;
```

```
6    import java.sql.Connection;
7    import java.sql.PreparedStatement;
8    import java.sql.Statement;
9    import java.sql.DriverManager;
10   import java.sql.SQLException;
11   import java.sql.ResultSet;
12   import java.util.Enumeration;
13   import java.util.Properties;

14   //import weblogic.common.*;

15   public class BagBean implements SessionBean
16   {
17   //T3Client t3c;
18   public  int custID;
19   transient private  SessionContext ctx;
20   public  InventoryItem inventory[];
21   public  Hashtable bag = new Hashtable();
22   public  String databaseURL;
23   public  String JDBCDriverName;
24   transient private Connection c;

25     public void setSessionContext(SessionContext ctx)
26     {
27       this.ctx = ctx;
28     }


29     public void ejbCreate(String custname, String custaddr)
       throws CreateException
30     {

31       //WebLogic-specific connection to logging facilities
32   //    try
33   //    {
34   //    String URL = "t3://localhost:7001";
35   //    t3c = new T3Client(URL);
36   //    t3c.connect();
37   //    }catch(Exception e) {}

38     init();
39     try
40     {
41     c = DriverManager.getConnection(getDBURL());
42     }
43     catch (SQLException e)
44     {
45       throw new CreateException("Can't create connection to
       database");
46     }
47     initInventory();
48     this.custID = createCustomer(custname, custaddr);
49
```

```
50      }

51      public void ejbCreate(int custID) throws CreateException
52      {
53        //WebLogic-specific connection to logging facilities
54  //      try
55  //      {
56  //      String URL = "t3://localhost:7001";
57  //      t3c = new T3Client(URL);
58  //      t3c.connect();
59  //      }catch(Exception e) {}

60        init();
61        //set up connection
62        //this connection will be managed in passivate,
          activate, and remove
63        try
64        {
65        c = DriverManager.getConnection(getDBURL());
66        }
67        catch (SQLException e)
68        {
69          throw new CreateException("Can't establish database
            connection");
70        }
71        initInventory();
72        this.custID = custID;

73      public void init() throws CreateException
74      {
75        Properties props = ctx.getEnvironment();
76        databaseURL = (String)
          props.get("bagBean.databaseURL");
77        JDBCDriverName = (String) props.get
          ("bagBean.JDBCDriverName");
78        //load the JDBC driver
79        try
80        {
81        Class.forName(JDBCDriverName).newInstance();
82        }
83        catch(Exception e)
84        {
85          throw new CreateException("Could not load JDBC
            driver");
86        }
87      }

88      public InventoryItem findItem(String itemcode) throws
        ItemNotFoundException
89      {
90        for (int i = 0; i < inventory.length; i++)
91        {
92          if (inventory[i].itemCode.equals(itemcode))
```

```
93              {
94                  return inventory[i];
95              }
96          }
97          throw new ItemNotFoundException();
98      }

99      public void initInventory()
100     {
101         //query database to get count of inventory objects
102         String query = "select count(*) from inventory";
103         try
104         {

105         Statement stmt = c.createStatement();
106         ResultSet rs = stmt.executeQuery(query);
107         rs.next();
108         int count = rs.getInt(1);
109         //System.out.println("count is " + count);

110         //query database to load inventory table

111         inventory = new InventoryItem[count];
112         query = "select itemcode, itemdesc, quantity, price
                from inventory";
113         rs = stmt.executeQuery(query);
114         rs.next();
115         for (int i = 0; i < count; i++)
116         {
117             inventory[i] = new InventoryItem();
118             inventory[i].itemCode = rs.getString(1);
119             inventory[i].itemDesc = rs.getString(2);
120             inventory[i].quantity = rs.getInt(3);
121             inventory[i].price = rs.getDouble(4);
122             rs.next();


123         }
124         }//end try block
125         catch (SQLException e)
126         {
127         log("initInventory:SQL Exception: " + e);
128         }
129     }

130     public int getCustID()
131     {
132         return custID;
133     }


134
135     //returns the database URL to use
136     public String getDBURL()
```

```
137    {
138
139      return databaseURL;
140    }

141    public void ejbActivate()
142    {
143      try
144      {
145      c = DriverManager.getConnection(databaseURL);
146      }
147      catch (SQLException e)
148      {
149      log("ejbActivate: SQL Exception: " + e);

150      }

151    }

152    public void ejbPassivate()
153    {
154      try
155      {
156      c.close();
157      }
158      catch (SQLException e)
159      {
160      log("ejbPassivate: SQL Exception: " + e);
161      }
162    }

163    public void ejbRemove()
164    {
165      try
166      {
167      c.close();
168      }
169      catch (SQLException e)
170      {
171      log("ejbRemove: SQL Exception: " + e);
172      }
173    }

174    public void addItem(String itemcode, int quantity)
       throws ItemNotFoundException
175    {
176      //add itemcode and quantity to local order
177
178      if (bag.containsKey(itemcode))
179      {
180        InventoryItem i = (InventoryItem)bag.get(itemcode);
181        i.quantity += quantity;
182      }
```

```
183      else
184      {
185      InventoryItem i = findItem(itemcode);
186      InventoryItem ii = (InventoryItem) i.clone();
187      ii.quantity = quantity;
188      bag.put (itemcode, ii);
189      }
190    }


191    public void removeItem(String itemcode, int quantity)
       throws ItemNotFoundException
192    {
193      //remove the argument item and quantity from the in-
         ventory
194      itemcode = itemcode;
195      if (bag.containsKey(itemcode))
196      {
197        InventoryItem ii = (InventoryItem)bag.get(itemcode);
198        //remove all of it
199        if (ii.quantity <= quantity)
200          {
201          bag.remove(itemcode);
202          }
203        else
204          //only remove the requested quantity
205          {
206          ii.quantity -= quantity;
207          }
208      }
209      else
210      {
211        throw new ItemNotFoundException();
212      }
213    }

214    public InventoryItem[] getBagContents()
215    {
216      //return the contents of the inventory
217      int size = bag.size();
218      InventoryItem[] contents = new InventoryItem[size];
219      //get list of keys in hashtable
220      Enumeration keys = bag.keys();
221      //for each key, retrieve the contents
222      for (int i = 0; i < size; i++)
223      {
224        contents[i] = (InventoryItem)bag.get
           (keys.nextElement());
225      }
226      return contents;
227    }

228    public int createCustomer(String name, String address)
```

```
229     {
230       //given a name and address, create a customer
231       //in the database, and return the customer identifier
232       try
233       {
234       String query = "insert into customers (cust_id,
          cust_name, cust_addr) values ((select max(cust_id) from
          customers) + 1, '" +name + "', '" + address + "')";
235       Statement stmt = c.createStatement();
236       int count = stmt.executeUpdate(query);
237       stmt.close();
238       stmt = c.createStatement();
239       query = "select max(cust_id) from customers";
240       ResultSet rs = stmt.executeQuery(query);
241       rs.next();
242       int custid = rs.getInt(1);
243       rs.close();
244       stmt.close();
245       return custid;
246       }
247       catch (SQLException e)
248       {
249         log("SQLException in createCustomer: " + e);
250         return 0;
251       }
252     }

253     public void log(String message)
254     {
255     //WebLogic-specific logging routine
256 //    try
257 //    {
258 //    t3c.services.log().log(message);
259 //    }catch(Exception ex) {}
260     }

261     public void finalizeOrder()
262     {
263       try{
264       //insert rows into table
265       InventoryItem ii[] = new InventoryItem[bag.size()];
266       ii = getBagContents();
267       String query = "insert into orders(cust_id, itemcode,
          quantity) values( ? , ? , ?)";
268       PreparedStatement ps = c.prepareStatement(query);
269       for (int i = 0; i < ii.length; i++)
270       {
271         ps.setInt(1, this.custID);
272         ps.setString(2, ii[i].itemCode);
273         ps.setInt(3, ii[i].quantity);
274         ps.executeUpdate();
275       }
276       }catch(SQLException e){
```

```
277          log("SQL exception in finalizeOrder: " + e);
278        }
279    }

280    public InventoryItem[] getInventory()
281    {
282      return inventory;
283    }

284 }
```

BagBean Client

```
1    import book.chap04.bag.Bag;
2    import book.chap04.bag.BagHome;
3    import book.chap04.bag.ItemNotFoundException;
4    import book.chap04.bag.InventoryItem;

5    import javax.naming.InitialContext;
6    import javax.naming.NamingException;
7    import java.rmi.RemoteException;
8    import javax.ejb.RemoveException;
9    import javax.ejb.CreateException;

10   public class BagClient
11   {
12     public static void printInventory(InventoryItem[] bag)
13     {
14       for (int i = 0; i < bag.length; i++)
15       {
16         System.err.println("bag.[" + i + "].itemCode = " +
             bag[i].itemCode);
17         System.err.println("bag.[" + i + "].itemDesc = " +
             bag[i].itemDesc);
18         System.err.println("bag.[" + i + "].quantity = " +
             bag[i].quantity);
19         System.err.println("bag.[" + i + "].price = " +
             bag[i].price);
20       }
21     }
22     public static void main(String[] argv)
23     {
24
25       System.err.println("client is running");
26       try
27       {
28       InitialContext ic = new InitialContext();
29       System.err.println("looked up initial context");
30       BagHome bh = (BagHome) ic.lookup("BagHome");
31       System.err.println("looked up home interface");
32       Bag b = bh.create("Tom Valesky", "His house");
33       System.err.println("created remote interface");
```

```
34        int ID = b.getCustID();
35        System.err.println("Your customer ID is " + ID);
36        InventoryItem[] inventory = b.getInventory();
37        System.err.println("got inventory");
38        System.err.println("----------available
          inventory----------");
39        printInventory(inventory);
40        b.addItem(inventory[0].itemCode, 1);
41        b.addItem(inventory[0].itemCode, 1);
42        b.addItem(inventory[1].itemCode, 2);
43        System.err.println("----------contents of bag before
          remove----------");
44        InventoryItem[] bag = b.getBagContents();
45        printInventory(bag);
46        b.removeItem(inventory[1].itemCode, 1);
47        bag = b.getBagContents();
48        System.err.println("----------contents of bag after
          remove----------");
49        printInventory(bag);
50        b.removeItem(inventory[1].itemCode, 1);
51        bag = b.getBagContents();
52        System.err.println("----------contents of bag after
          another remove----------");
53        printInventory(bag);
54        b.finalizeOrder();

55        b.remove();

56        System.err.println("this next thing will throw an
          exception");
57        b.finalizeOrder();

58        System.err.println("done with BagClient");

59        }
60        catch (NamingException e)
61        {
62          System.err.println("NamingException caught");
63          e.printStackTrace();
64        }
65        catch (RemoteException e)
66        {
67          System.err.println("RemoteException caught");
68          e.printStackTrace();
69        }
70        catch (RemoveException e)
71        {
72          System.err.println("RemoveException caught");
73          e.printStackTrace();
74        }
75        catch (CreateException e)
76        {
77          System.err.println("CreateException caught");
78          e.printStackTrace();
```

```
79        }
80        catch (ItemNotFoundException e)
81        {
82          System.err.println("ItemNotFoundException caught");
83          e.printStackTrace();
84        }

85    }
86  }
```

Bag2 Home Interface

```
1    package book.chap04.bag2;
2    import javax.ejb.EJBHome;
3    import java.rmi.RemoteException;
4    import javax.ejb.CreateException;

5    public interface Bag2Home extends EJBHome
6    {
7       public Bag2 create() throws RemoteException,
         CreateException;
8    }
```

Bag2 Remote Interface

```
1    package book.chap04.bag2;
2    import javax.ejb.EJBObject;
3    import java.rmi.RemoteException;

4    public interface Bag2 extends EJBObject
5    {
6       //get list of inventory
7       public InventoryItem[] getInventory() throws
         RemoteException;
8       //add an item to the bag
9       public void addItem(int custid, String itemcode, int
         quantity) throws RemoteException;
10      //remove an item from the bag
11      public void removeItem(int custid, String itemcode, int
         quantity) throws RemoteException, ItemNotFoundException;
12      //list the contents of the bag
13      public InventoryItem[] getBagContents(int custid) throws
         RemoteException;
14      //execute the order
15      public void finalizeOrder(int custid) throws
         RemoteException;
16      //get customer ID
17      public int newCustomer(String name, String addr) throws
         RemoteException;
18  }
```

Bag2 Bean Implementation

```
1    package book.chap04.bag2;
2    import javax.ejb.SessionBean;
3    import javax.ejb.SessionContext;
4    import javax.ejb.CreateException;
5    import java.util.Hashtable;
6    import java.sql.Connection;
7    import java.sql.PreparedStatement;
8    import java.sql.Statement;
9    import java.sql.DriverManager;
10   import java.sql.SQLException;
11   import java.sql.ResultSet;
12   import java.util.Enumeration;
13   import java.util.Properties;

14   //import weblogic.common.*;

15   public class Bag2Bean implements SessionBean
16   {
17   //T3Client t3c;
18   transient private SessionContext ctx;

19     public void init() throws CreateException
20     {
21       Properties props = ctx.getEnvironment();
22       String JDBCDriverName = (String) props.get
         ("bag2Bean.JDBCDriverName");
23       //load the JDBC driver
24       try
25       {
26       Class.forName(JDBCDriverName).newInstance();
27       }
28       catch(Exception e)
29       {
30         throw new CreateException("Could not load JDBC
           driver");
31       }
32     }

33     public void setSessionContext(SessionContext ctx)
34     {
35       this.ctx = ctx;
36     }

37     public void ejbCreate() throws CreateException
38     {
39   //    try
40   //    {
41   //    String URL = "t3://localhost:7001";
42   //    t3c = new T3Client(URL);
43   //    t3c.connect();
44   //    }catch(Exception e) {}
```

```
45      init();
46    }

47    //returns the database URL to use
48    public String getDBURL()
49    {
50      //read this from a property
51      Properties props = ctx.getEnvironment();
52      return (String) props.get("bag2Bean.databaseURL");
53
54    }

55    public void ejbActivate()
56    {

57    }

58    public void ejbPassivate()
59    {

60    }

61    public void ejbRemove()
62    {

63    }

64    public void addItem(int custid, String itemcode, int
      quantity)
65    {
66      try{
67      Connection c = DriverManager.getConnection(getDBURL());
68      int quantityOrdered = getItemCount(custid, itemcode,
        c);
69      if (quantityOrdered > 0)
70      {
71        //update
72        String query = "update orders set quantity = " +
          (quantityOrdered + quantity )+ " where cust_id = " +
          custid + " and itemcode = '" + itemcode + "'";
73
74        Statement s = c.createStatement();
75        s.executeUpdate(query);
76        s.close();
77      }
78      else
79      {
80        //insert
81        String query = "insert into orders(cust_id,
          itemcode, quantity) values( ? , ? , ?)";
82        PreparedStatement ps = c.prepareStatement(query);
83        ps.setInt(1, custid);
84        ps.setString(2, itemcode);
```

```
85          ps.setInt(3, quantity);
86          ps.executeUpdate();
87          ps.close();
88        }
89      //insert rows into table
90      c.close();
91      }catch(SQLException e){
92        log("SQL exception in addItem: " + e);
93      }
94    }

95    public int getItemCount(int custid, String itemcode,
      Connection c) throws SQLException
96    {
97      //Note: For our example, the business rule is that, if
98      //there are no items ordered, the row is deleted. In
99      //other cases, you may want to throw an exception
100     //rather than simply returning 0, to differentiate
101     //between cases where a row exists with a field
        containing 0, and a case where no row exists.
102     String query = "select quantity from orders where
        cust_id = "+ custid +" and itemcode = '"+itemcode+"'";
103     Statement s = c.createStatement();
104     ResultSet rs = s.executeQuery(query);
105     boolean more = rs.next();
106     int quantity;
107     if (!more)
108     {
109       quantity = 0;
110     }
111     else //more rows
112     {
113       quantity = rs.getInt(1);
114     }
115     rs.close();
116     s.close();
117     return quantity;
118   }


119   public void deleteRow(int custid, String itemcode,
      Connection c) throws SQLException
120   {
121     String query = "delete from orders where cust_id = "+
        custid +" and itemcode = '"+itemcode+"'";
122     Statement s = c.createStatement();
123     int count = s.executeUpdate(query);
124     s.close();
125   }

126   public void updateRow(int custid, String itemcode,
      Connection c, int oldQuantity, int itemsToRemove) throws
      SQLException
```

```
127    {
128       Statement s = c.createStatement();
129       String query = "update orders set quantity = " +
          (oldQuantity - itemsToRemove) + "where cust_id = "+
          custid +" and itemcode = '"+itemcode+"'";
130       int count = s.executeUpdate(query);
131       s.close();
132    }

133    public void removeItem(int custid, String itemcode, int
       quantity) throws ItemNotFoundException
134    {
135      try{
136      Connection c = DriverManager.getConnection(getDBURL());
137      int numOrdered = getItemCount(custid, itemcode, c);
138      if (numOrdered == 0)
139         {
140         c.close();
141         throw new ItemNotFoundException();
142         }
143      log ("numOrdered = " + numOrdered);
144      if (numOrdered <= quantity)
145      {
146      // remove table entry
147      deleteRow(custid, itemcode, c);
148      }
149      else
150      {
151      // update table with reduced amount
152      updateRow(custid, itemcode, c, numOrdered, quantity);
153      }
154      c.close();
155      }catch(SQLException e){
156         log("SQL exception in removeItem: " + e);
157      }
158    }

159    public InventoryItem[] getBagContents(int custid)
160    {
161      InventoryItem[] inventory;
162      //query database to get count of inventory objects
163      String query = "select count(*) from orders where
         cust_id = " + custid;
164      try
165      {
166      Connection c = DriverManager.getConnection(getDBURL());
167      Statement stmt = c.createStatement();
168      ResultSet rs = stmt.executeQuery(query);
169      rs.next();
170      int count = rs.getInt(1);
171      //query database to load inventory table
172      inventory = new InventoryItem[count];
```

```
173     query = "select itemcode, quantity from orders where
        cust_id = " + custid + "";
174     rs = stmt.executeQuery(query);
175     rs.next();
176     for (int i = 0; i < count; i++)
177     {
178       inventory[i] = new InventoryItem();
179       inventory[i].itemCode = rs.getString(1);
180       inventory[i].quantity = rs.getInt(2);
181       rs.next();
182     }
183     rs.close();
184     stmt.close();
185     c.close();
186     return inventory;
187     }//end try block
188     catch (SQLException e)
189     {
190     log("initInventory:SQL Exception: " + e);
191     return null;
192     }
193   }

194   public int newCustomer(String name, String address)
195   {
196     //given a name and address, create a customer
197     //in the database, and return the customer identifier
198     try
199     {
200     String query = "insert into customers (cust_id,
        cust_name, cust_addr) values ((select max(cust_id) from
        customers) + 1, '" +name + "', '" + address + "')";
201     Connection c = DriverManager.getConnection(getDBURL());
202     Statement stmt = c.createStatement();
203     int count = stmt.executeUpdate(query);
204     stmt.close();
205     stmt = c.createStatement();
206     query = "select max(cust_id) from customers";
207     ResultSet rs = stmt.executeQuery(query);
208     rs.next();
209     int custid = rs.getInt(1);
210     rs.close();
211     stmt.close();
212     c.close();
213     return custid;
214     }
215     catch (SQLException e)
216     {
217       log("SQLException in createCustomer: " + e);
218       return 0;
219     }
220   }
```

```
221    public void log(String message)
222    {
223 //     try
224 //     {
225 //     t3c.services.log().log(message);
226 //     }catch(Exception ex) {}
227    }

228    public void finalizeOrder(int custid)
229    {
230      //update another table from the orders table for the
         custid
231      try{
232      //insert rows into table
233      Connection c = DriverManager.getConnection(getDBURL());
234      String query = "insert into final_orders (cust_id,
         itemcode, quantity) select cust_id, itemcode, quantity
         from orders where cust_id = " + custid + "";
235
236      Statement stmt = c.createStatement();
237      stmt.executeUpdate(query);
238      stmt.close();
239      //get rid of info in the orders table
240      query = "delete from orders where cust_id = " + custid
         + "";
241      stmt = c.createStatement();
242      stmt.executeUpdate(query);
243      stmt.close();
244      c.close();
245      }catch(SQLException e){
246        log("SQL exception in finalizeOrder: " + e);
247      }
248    }

249    public InventoryItem[] getInventory()
250    {
251      //query database to get count of inventory objects
252      String query = "select count(*) from inventory";
253      try
254      {
255      Connection c = DriverManager.getConnection(getDBURL());
256      Statement stmt = c.createStatement();
257      ResultSet rs = stmt.executeQuery(query);
258      rs.next();
259      int count = rs.getInt(1);
260      System.out.println("count is " + count);
261      rs.close();
262      //query database to load inventory table
263      InventoryItem []inventory = new InventoryItem[count];
264      query = "select itemcode, itemdesc, quantity, price
         from inventory";
265      rs = stmt.executeQuery(query);
```

```
266        rs.next();
267        for (int i = 0; i < count; i++)
268        {
269          inventory[i] = new InventoryItem();
270          inventory[i].itemCode = rs.getString(1);
271          inventory[i].itemDesc = rs.getString(2);
272          inventory[i].quantity = rs.getInt(3);
273          inventory[i].price = rs.getDouble(4);
274          rs.next();
275        }
276        rs.close();
277        stmt.close();
278        c.close();
279        return inventory;
280        }//end try block
281        catch (SQLException e)
282        {
283        log("initInventory:SQL Exception: " + e);
284        return null;
285        }
286      }
287  }
```

Bag2 Client

```
1    import book.chap04.bag2.Bag2;
2    import book.chap04.bag2.Bag2Home;
3    import book.chap04.bag2.ItemNotFoundException;
4    import book.chap04.bag2.InventoryItem;

5    import javax.naming.InitialContext;
6    import javax.naming.NamingException;
7    import java.rmi.RemoteException;
8    import javax.ejb.RemoveException;
9    import javax.ejb.CreateException;

10   public class Bag2Client
11   {
12     public static void printInventory(InventoryItem[] bag)
13     {
14       for (int i = 0; i < bag.length; i++)
15       {
16         System.out.println("bag.[" + i + "].itemCode = " +
                bag[i].itemCode);
17         System.out.println("bag.[" + i + "].itemDesc = " +
                bag[i].itemDesc);
18         System.out.println("bag.[" + i + "].quantity = " +
                bag[i].quantity);
19         System.out.println("bag.[" + i + "].price = " +
                bag[i].price);
20       }
21     }
```

```
22    public static void main(String[] argv)
23    {
24      double tab;
25      System.out.println("client is running");
26      try
27      {
28      InitialContext ic = new InitialContext();
29      System.out.println("looked up initial context");
30      Bag2Home bh = (Bag2Home) ic.lookup("Bag2Home");
31      System.out.println("looked up home interface");
32      Bag2 b = bh.create();
33      System.out.println("created remote interface");
34      int custID = b.newCustomer("Bob Smith", "some address
        info");
35      System.out.println("Your customer ID is " + custID);
36      InventoryItem[] inventory = b.getInventory();
37      System.out.println("got inventory");
38      System.out.println("----------available
        inventory----------");
39      printInventory(inventory);
40      b.addItem(custID, inventory[0].itemCode, 1);
41      b.addItem(custID, inventory[1].itemCode, 1);
42      b.addItem(custID, inventory[1].itemCode, 1);
43      System.out.println("----------contents of bag before
        remove----------");
44      InventoryItem[] bag = b.getBagContents(custID);
45      printInventory(bag);
46      System.out.println("should be 2 of itemcode " +
        inventory[1].itemCode + " and 1 of itemcode " +
        inventory[0].itemCode);
47      b.removeItem(custID, inventory[1].itemCode, 1);
48      bag = b.getBagContents(custID);
49      System.out.println("----------contents of bag after
        remove----------");
50      printInventory(bag);
51      System.out.println("should be 1 of itemcode " +
        inventory[1].itemCode + " and 1 of itemcode " +
        inventory[0].itemCode);
52      b.removeItem(custID, inventory[1].itemCode, 1);
53      bag = b.getBagContents(custID);
54      System.out.println("----------contents of bag after
        another remove----------");
55      printInventory(bag);
56      System.out.println("should be 0 of itemcode " +
        inventory[1].itemCode + " and 1 of itemcode " +
        inventory[0].itemCode);
57      b.finalizeOrder(custID);
58      b.remove();
59      System.out.println("this next thing will throw an
        exception");
60      b.finalizeOrder(custID);
61      System.out.println("done with Bag2Client");
62      }
```

```
63        catch (NamingException e)
64        {
65          System.out.println("NamingException caught");
66          e.printStackTrace();
67        }
68        catch (RemoteException e)
69        {
70          System.out.println("RemoteException caught");
71          e.printStackTrace();
72        }
73        catch (RemoveException e)
74        {
75          System.out.println("RemoveException caught");
76          e.printStackTrace();
77        }
78        catch (CreateException e)
79        {
80          System.out.println("CreateException caught");
81          e.printStackTrace();
82        }
83            catch (ItemNotFoundException e)
84    {
85          System.out.println("ItemNotFoundException caught");
86          e.printStackTrace();
87        }
88      }
89    }
```

APPENDIX B

Source Code for Chapter 5

Implementation of OrderBean (Container-Managed Persistence)

```
1    package book.chap05.order;
2    import javax.ejb.EntityBean;
3    import javax.ejb.EntityContext;
4    import javax.ejb.CreateException;

5    public class OrderBean implements EntityBean
6    {

7        transient private EntityContext ctx;
8        public int custid;
9      public String itemcode;
10     public int quantity;

11       public void setEntityContext(EntityContext ctx)
12       {
13         this.ctx = ctx;
14       }
15         public void unsetEntityContext()
16         {
17         this.ctx = null;
18         }


19       public void ejbCreate(int custid, String itemcode, int
         quantity) throws CreateException
20       {

21         this.custid = custid;
22         this.itemcode = itemcode;
23         this.quantity = quantity;

24
25       }
```

```
26      public void ejbPostCreate(int custid, String itemcode,
        int quantity) throws CreateException
27      {
28      }


29      public void ejbActivate()
30      {


31      }

32      public void ejbPassivate()
33      {


34      }

35      public void ejbRemove()
36      {


37      }

38      public void ejbLoad()
39      {

40      }

41      public void ejbStore()
42      {

43      }


44      public void setQuantity(int quantity)
45      {
46        this.quantity = quantity;
47      }
48      public int getCustID()
49      {
50        return this.custid;
51      }
52      public String getItemCode()
53      {
54        return this.itemcode;
55      }
56      public int getQuantity()
57      {
58        return this.quantity;
59      }
60   }
```

Client for Container-Managed Entity Bean

```
1    import book.chap05.order.Order;
2    import book.chap05.order.OrderHome;
3
4    import javax.naming.InitialContext;
5    import javax.naming.NamingException;
6    import java.rmi.RemoteException;
7    import javax.ejb.RemoveException;
8    import javax.ejb.CreateException;
9    import javax.ejb.FinderException;
10   import java.util.Enumeration;
11
12   public class OrderClient
13   {
14     public static void main(String[] argv)
15     {
16
17       System.out.println("client is running");
18       try
19       {
20       InitialContext ic = new InitialContext();
21       System.out.println("looked up initial context");
22       OrderHome oh = (OrderHome) ic.lookup("OrderHome");
23       System.out.println("looked up home interface");
24       Order o1 = oh.create(1, "1", 1);
25       Order o2 = oh.create(1, "2", 2);
26       System.out.println("created remote interface");
27       Enumeration e = oh.findByCustID(1);
28       Order o;
29       while (e.hasMoreElements())
30       {
31         System.out.println("found another");
32         o = (Order) e.nextElement();
33         System.out.println("custID: " + o.getCustID());
34         System.out.println("itemcode: " + o.getItemCode());
35         System.out.println("quantity: " + o.getQuantity());
36         System.out.println("removing...");
37         o.remove();
38         System.out.println("removed");
39       }
40
41       System.out.println("done with OrderClient");
42
43       }
44       catch (FinderException e)
45       {
46         System.out.println("FinderException caught");
47         e.printStackTrace();
48
49       }
50       catch (NamingException e)
51       {
```

```
52        System.out.println("NamingException caught");
53        e.printStackTrace();
54      }
55    catch (RemoveException e)
56
57        System.out.println("RemoveException caught");
58        e.printStackTrace();
59      }
60    catch (CreateException e)
61    {
62        System.out.println("CreateException caught");
63        e.printStackTrace();
64      }
65
66    catch (RemoteException e)
67    {
68        System.out.println("RemoteException caught");
69        e.printStackTrace();
70      }
71    }
72  }
```

Implementation Bean for Bean-Managed Persistence

```
1     package book.chap05.customer;
2     import javax.ejb.EntityBean;
3     import javax.ejb.EntityContext;
4     import javax.ejb.CreateException;
5     import javax.ejb.FinderException;
6     import java.sql.Connection;
7     import java.sql.ResultSet;
8     import java.sql.DriverManager;
9     import java.sql.Statement;
10    import java.sql.SQLException;
11    import java.sql.ResultSet;
12    import java.util.Properties;
13    import java.util.Vector;
14    import java.util.Enumeration;


15    public class CustomerBean implements EntityBean
16    {
17        transient private EntityContext ctx;
18      private int custid;
19      private String name;
20      private String addr;


21      public String getName()
22      {
23        return name;
24      }
```

```
25     public void setName(String name)
26     {
27       this.name = name;
28     }
29     public String getAddress()
30     {
31       return addr;
32     }
33     public void setAddress(String addr)
34     {
35       this.addr = addr;
36     }
37     public int getCustID()
38     {
39       return custid;
40     }

41     public void setEntityContext(EntityContext ctx)
42     {
43       this.ctx = ctx;
44       Properties props = ctx.getEnvironment();
45       String JDBCDriverName = (String) props.get
         ("customerBean.JDBCDriverName");
46       //load the JDBC driver

47       try
48       {

49       Class.forName(JDBCDriverName).newInstance();
50       }
51       catch (Exception e)
52       {

53       }

54     }
55       public void unsetEntityContext()
56       {
57       this.ctx = null;
58       }

59     public CustomerPK ejbCreate(String custname, String
       custaddr) throws CreateException
60     {
61       //create customer as in session bean

62       try
63       {
```

```
64      //given a name and address, create a customer
65      //in the database, and return the customer identifier
66      String query = "insert into customers (cust_id,
        cust_name, cust_addr) values ((select max(cust_id) from
        customers) + 1,"' + custname + '", "'+ custaddr + '")";
67      Connection c = DriverManager.getConnection(getDBURL());
68      Statement stmt = c.createStatement();
69      int count = stmt.executeUpdate(query);
70      stmt.close();
71      stmt = c.createStatement();
72      query = "select max(cust_id) from customers";
73      ResultSet rs = stmt.executeQuery(query);
74      rs.next();
75      int custid = rs.getInt(1);
76      rs.close();
77      stmt.close();
78      c.close();
79      this.custid = custid;
80        this.name = custname;
81        this.addr = custaddr;
82        CustomerPK custPK = new CustomerPK();
83        custPK.custid = custid;
84      return custPK;
85      }
86      catch (Exception e)
87      {
88         throw new CreateException();
89      }


90
91      }


92      public void ejbPostCreate(String custname, String
        custaddr) throws CreateException
93      {
94      }


95      public void ejbActivate()
96      {

97      }

98      public void ejbPassivate()
99      {

100     }

101     public void ejbRemove()
102     {
103         //delete row by custid
```

```
104    try
105    {

106    String query = "delete from customers where cust_id =
       " + this.custid;
107    executeUpdate(query);

108    }
109    catch (Exception e)
110    {
111    }
112    }

113    public void ejbLoad()
114    {

115        //read in values from database

116    try
117    {
118    CustomerPK pk = (CustomerPK)ctx.getPrimaryKey();
119    this.custid = pk.custid;

120    Connection c = DriverManager.getConnection(getDBURL());
121    //update
122    String query = "select cust_name, cust_addr from
       customers where cust_id = " + this.custid;
123    Statement s = c.createStatement();
124    ResultSet rs = s.executeQuery(query);
125    boolean more = rs.next();
126    if (more)
127      {
128      this.name = rs.getString(1);
129      this.addr = rs.getString(2);
130      }
131    rs.close();
132    s.close();
133    c.close();
134    }
135    catch (SQLException e)
136    {
137    }
138    }

139    public void ejbStore()
140    {

141        //write out values to database
142    try
143    {
```

```
144    String.query = "update customers set cust_name = '"+
       this.name +"', cust_addr = '" + this.addr + "' where
       cust_id = " + this.custid;
145      executeUpdate(query);

146    }
147    catch (Exception e)
148    {
149    }

150  }

151    public void executeUpdate(String SQLCommand) throws
       SQLException
152    {

153    Connection c = DriverManager.getConnection(getDBURL());
154    //update
155    String query = SQLCommand;

156    Statement s = c.createStatement();
157    s.executeUpdate(query);
158    s.close();
159    c.close();
160    }
161  public String getDBURL()
162  {
163    //read this from a property
164    Properties props = ctx.getEnvironment();
165    return (String) props.get("customerBean.databaseURL");
166
167  }

168    public CustomerPK ejbFindByPrimaryKey(CustomerPK pk)
       throws FinderException
169    {

170    //query database for primary key
171    int count = executeCountQuery("select count(*) from
       customers where custid = " + pk.custid);
172    if (count == 1)
173    {
174      return pk;
175    }
176    else if (count < 1)
177    {
178      throw new FinderException("row not found for custid
       " + pk.custid + ";count was " + count);
179    }
180    else // (count > 1)
181    {
182      throw new FinderException("more than one row found
       for custid " + pk.custid + ";count was " + count);
```

```
183
184      }

185      //throw finder exception if not found


186   }
187   public Enumeration ejbFindByName(String name)
188   {

189      //do query for pks
190      try
191      {


192      Connection c = DriverManager.getConnection(getDBURL());
193      //update
194      String query = "select cust_id from customers where
         cust_name like '%" + name + "%'";




195      Statement s = c.createStatement();
196      ResultSet rs = s.executeQuery(query);



197      //create enumeration object
198      Vector v = new Vector();
199      CustomerPK pk;
200      //populate with pks

201      boolean more = rs.next();
202      while (more)
203      {

204        pk = new CustomerPK();
205        pk.custid = rs.getInt(1);
206        v.addElement(pk);
207        more = rs.next();
208      }
209      rs.close();
210      s.close();
211      c.close();


212      return v.elements(); //vector returns an enumeration
         of all values in the table

213      }//end try
214      catch (SQLException e)
```

```
215        {
216            return null;
217        }
218     }

219     public int executeCountQuery(String SQLCommand)
220        {

221          try
222          {
223          Connection c = DriverManager.getConnection(getDBURL());
224          String query = SQLCommand;

225          Statement s = c.createStatement();
226          ResultSet rs = s.executeQuery(query);
227          f (!rs.next())
228          {
229          System.out.println("executeCountQuery retrieved no
                 rows for query "+ query);
230          rs.close();
231          s.close();
232          return 0;
233          }
234          int retval = rs.getInt(1);
235          rs.close();
236          s.close();
237          return retval;
238          }
239          catch (SQLException e)
240          {
241
242          return 0;
243          }
244        }

245   }
```

Client for the Bean-Managed Persistence Example

```
1     import book.chap05.customer.Customer;
2     import book.chap05.customer.CustomerPK;
3     import book.chap05.customer.CustomerHome;

4     import javax.naming.InitialContext;
5     import javax.naming.NamingException;
6     import java.rmi.RemoteException;
7     import javax.ejb.RemoveException;
8     import javax.ejb.CreateException;
9     import javax.ejb.FinderException;
10    import java.util.Enumeration;

11    public class CustomerClient
```

```
12  {
13      public static void main(String[] argv)
14      {
15
16          System.out.println("client is running");
17          try
18          {
19          InitialContext ic = new InitialContext();
20          System.out.println("looked up initial context");
21          CustomerHome ch = (CustomerHome) ic.lookup
            ("CustomerHome");
22          System.out.println("looked up home interface");
23          Customer cust = ch.create("Jake Terwilliger", "His
            house");
24          System.out.println("created remote interface");
25          System.out.println (" custid = " + cust.getCustID());
26          System.out.println (" name = " + cust.getName());
27          System.out.println (" address = " +
            cust.getAddress());
28          CustomerPK pk = (CustomerPK) cust.getPrimaryKey();

29          //imagine that time passes here, or this program is
30          //finished, and a later program wants to use the
31          //primary key

32          cust = null;
33          cust = ch.findByPrimaryKey(pk);
34          System.out.println("Found by primary key lookup");
35          System.out.println (" custid = " + cust.getCustID());
36          System.out.println (" name = " + cust.getName());
37          System.out.println (" address = " +
            cust.getAddress());
38          cust.remove();
39          System.out.println("removed bean");

40          //still more time passes


41          cust = null;
42          Enumeration e = ch.findByName("Terwilliger");
43          int i = 0;
44          while (e.hasMoreElements())
45          {
46              System.out.println("found " + ++i);
47              cust = (Customer) e.nextElement();
48              System.out.println (" custid = " +
                cust.getCustID());
49              System.out.println (" name = " + cust.getName());
50              System.out.println (" address = " +
                cust.getAddress());
51          }

52          System.out.println("done with CustomerClient");
```

```
53          }
54      catch (NamingException e)
55      {
56          System.out.println("NamingException caught:" + e);
57          e.printStackTrace();
58      }
59      catch (RemoveException e)
60      {
61          System.out.println("RemoveException caught:" + e);
62          e.printStackTrace();
63      }
64      catch (FinderException e)
65      {
66          System.out.println("FinderException caught:" + e);
67          e.printStackTrace();
68      }

69      catch (CreateException e)
70      {
71          System.out.println("CreateException caught:" + e);
72          e.printStackTrace();
73      }

74      catch (RemoteException e)
75      {
76          System.out.println("RemoteException caught:" + e);
77          e.printStackTrace();
78      }
79  }
80  }
```

APPENDIX C

Source Code for Chapter 9

Implementation of the Employee Entity Bean

```
1    package book.chap09.timetracker;
2    import javax.ejb.EntityBean;
3    import javax.ejb.EntityContext;
4    import javax.ejb.CreateException;
5    import javax.ejb.RemoveException;
6    import javax.ejb.FinderException;
7    import java.security.Identity;
8    import java.sql.Date;
9    import java.sql.Connection;
10   import java.sql.ResultSet;
11   import java.sql.SQLException;
12   import java.sql.PreparedStatement;
13   import java.sql.Statement;
14   import java.sql.DriverManager;
15   import java.util.Properties;
16
17   import book.chap09.timetracker.MyIdentity;
18   import book.chap09.timetracker.TimeSheetLine;
19
20
21   public class EmployeeBean implements EntityBean
22   {
23   transient private     EntityContext ctx;
24   transient private Connection c;
25   transient private boolean isDirty; //boolean thingie used
     by weblogic
26
27
28   //properties stored in database
29   public int employeeID;
30   public int managerID;
31   public String fname;
32   public String lname;
33
```

```
34
35      public void setEntityContext(EntityContext ctx)
36      {
37        this.ctx = ctx;
38        establishDBConnection();
39        isDirty = true;
40      }
41      public void unsetEntityContext()
42      {
43        System.out.println("unsetEntityContext called");
44        closeDBConnection();
45        this.ctx = null;
46      }
47
48
49
50      public EmployeePK ejbCreate(int employeeID, int
        managerID, String fname, String lname) throws
        CreateException
51      {
52        if (!isHRManager())
53        {
54          throw new CreateException("User is unauthorized to
          create new employee objects");
55        }
56
57        this.employeeID = employeeID;
58        this.managerID = managerID;
59        this.fname = fname;
60        this.lname = lname;
61
62      //insert new row into database table
63      String query = "insert into EMPLOYEES( EMPLOYEE_ID,
        MANAGER_ID, FNAME, LNAME) values (" + employeeID + ",
        " + managerID + ", '" + fname + "', '" + lname + "')";
64      executeUpdate(query);
65        isDirty = false; //we just synchronized with the
        database
66      return new EmployeePK(employeeID);
67
68
69      }
70
71      public void ejbPostCreate(int employeeID, int managerID,
        String fname, String lname)
72      {
73
74      }
75
76
77
78
79    //executes a DML statement that returns no data
```

```
80      public void executeUpdate(String SQLCommand)
81      {
82        try
83        {
84      //update
85      String query = SQLCommand;
86
87      Statement s = c.createStatement();
88      s.executeUpdate(query);
89      s.close();
90        }
91        catch (SQLException e)
92        {
93        log("SQLException in executeUpdate: query was: " +
            SQLCommand + "\nException was " + e);
94        }
95      }
96
97      public void log(String message)
98      {
99        System.out.println(message);
100       }
101   public boolean isModified()
102   {
103      return isDirty;
104   }
105
106     public void establishDBConnection()
107     {
108     Properties props = ctx.getEnvironment();
109     String databaseURL = (String)
        props.get("employeeBean.databaseURL");
110     String JDBCDriverName = (String)
        props.get("employeeBean.JDBCDriverName");
111     //load the JDBC driver
112     try
113     {
114     Class.forName(JDBCDriverName).newInstance();
115     c = DriverManager.getConnection(databaseURL);
116     }
117     catch(Exception e)
118     {
119     log("Could not establish database connection");
120     }
121     }
122     public void closeDBConnection()
123     {
124     try
125     {
126     System.out.println("closing database connection");
127     c.close();
128     }
129       catch(Exception e)
```

```
130      {
131      log("Could not close database connection");
132      }
133
134      }
135
136    public boolean isHRManager()
137    {
138      MyIdentity mgr_role = new MyIdentity("hrmanagers");
139      return ctx.isCallerInRole(mgr_role);
140
141    }
142
143
144  //executes a query that returns only a count
145    public int executeCountQuery(String SQLCommand)
146      {
147
148        try
149        {
150      //update
151      String query = SQLCommand;
152
153      Statement s = c.createStatement();
154      ResultSet rs = s.executeQuery(query);
155      if (!rs.next())
156        {
157        System.out.println("executeCountQuery retrieved no
               rows for query "+ query);
158        rs.close();
159        s.close();
160        return 0;
161        }
162      int retval = rs.getInt(1);
163      rs.close();
164      s.close();
165      return retval;
166        }
167        catch (SQLException e)
168        {
169          log("SQLException in executeUpdate: query was: " +
               SQLCommand);
170        return 0;
171        }
172      }
173
174
175    public EmployeePK ejbFindByPrimaryKey(EmployeePK pk)
       throws FinderException
176    {
177      //query database for primary key
178      int count = executeCountQuery("select count(*) from
             employees where employee_id = " + pk.employeeID);
```

```
179        if (count == 1)
180        {
181          return pk;
182        }
183        else if (count < 1)
184        {
185          throw new FinderException("row not found for
             employeeID " + pk.employeeID + ";count was " +
             count);
186        }
187        else // (count > 1)
188        {
189          throw new FinderException("more than one row found
             for employeeID " + pk.employeeID + ";count was " +
             count);
190
191        }
192
193        //throw finder exception if not found
194      }
195
196
197
198      public void ejbLoad()
199      {
200
201        if (!isDirty)
202          {
203          return;
204          }
205          EmployeePK pk = (EmployeePK)ctx.getPrimaryKey();
206          this.employeeID = pk.employeeID;
207        String query = "select manager_id, fname, lname from
             employees where employee_id = " + employeeID;
208
209          try
210          {
211        //update
212
213
214
215        Statement s = c.createStatement();
216        ResultSet rs = s.executeQuery(query);
217        if (!rs.next())
218        {
219          log("ejbLoad retrieved no row for query " + query);
220          return;
221        }
222        managerID = rs.getInt(1);
223        fname = rs.getString(2);
224        lname = rs.getString(3);
225        rs.close();
226        s.close();
```

```
227        }
228        catch (SQLException e)
229        {
230        log("SQLException in ejbLoad: query was: " + query);
231        }
232      isDirty = false;
233
234    }
235
236    public void ejbStore()
237    {
238      if (!isDirty)
239        {
240        return;
241        }
242      executeUpdate("update employees set manager_id = " +
             managerID + ", fname = '" + fname + "', lname = '" +
             lname + "' where employee_id = " + employeeID);
243        isDirty = false;
244
245
246
247    }
248
249
250
251    public void ejbActivate()
252    {
253    }
254    public void ejbPassivate()
255    {
256
257    }
258
259
260    public void ejbRemove() throws RemoveException
261    {
262      //delete from employees where employeeID = employeeID
263
264      if (!isHRManager())
265      {
266        throw new RemoveException("User is unauthorized to
             remove employee objects");
267      }
268      //comment this removal out for now; for some reason,
             doesn't seem to work
269      executeUpdate("delete from employees where employee_id
             = " + employeeID);
270
271    }
272
273
274    public TimeSheetLine[] getHours(Date start, Date end)
```

```
275    {
276      //reuse more general form
277      //this should be OK because it's not called through
         remote interface
278      return getEmployeeHours(this.employeeID, start, end);
279
280    }
281
282
283
284
285    public TimeSheetLine[] getEmployeeHours(int emplID, Date
       start, Date end)
286    {
287      System.out.println("Called getEmployeeHours");
288
289      String query = "select employee_id, mydate, hours,
         contract from time_entries where employee_id = ? and
         mydate >= ? and mydate <= ? order by 2, 4"; // 2 and 4
         are column positions
290
291        try
292        {
293      //the only reason I'm using a prepared statement here
         is to get JDBC to convert the date formats
294      PreparedStatement ps = c.prepareStatement(query);
295      ps.setInt(1, emplID);
296      ps.setDate(2, start);
297      ps.setDate(3, end);
298      ps.executeQuery();
299      ResultSet rs = ps.getResultSet();
300      boolean more = rs.next();
301      if (!more)
302      {
303        log("getHours retrieved no row for query " + query);
304        return null;
305      }
306      //simplifies the handling of ResultSets
307      TimeSheetHash tsh = new TimeSheetHash();
308      int empID;
309      java.sql.Date dt;
310      double hrs;
311      int cont;
312
313      while (more)
314      {
315        empID = rs.getInt(1);
316        dt = rs.getDate(2);
317        hrs = rs.getDouble(3);
318        cont = rs.getInt(4);
319        tsh.add(empID, dt, hrs, cont);
320
321
```

```
322      more = rs.next();
323    }
324    rs.close();
325    ps.close();
326
327    return tsh.getTimeSheetLines();
328
329      }
330      catch (SQLException e)
331      {
332      log("SQLException in getHours: query was: " + query
         + "\nException was " + e);
333      }
334
335
336    return null;
337
338  }
339
340  public TimeSheetLine getHours(TimeSheetLine tsl)
341  {
342    //generate dynamic SQL based on data in argument
343    //do query against database
344    //if row found, populate new TimeSheetLine struct and
         return
345    //if not, return "null"
346
347
348    String query = "select employee_id, mydate, hours,
         contract from time_entries where employee_id = ? and
         mydate = ? and contract = ?";
349
350      try
351      {
352  //the only reason I'm using a prepared statement here is
       to get JDBC to convert the date formats
353  PreparedStatement ps = c.prepareStatement(query);
354  ps.setInt(1, tsl.employeeID);
355  ps.setDate(2, tsl.date);
356  ps.setInt(3, tsl.contract);
357  ps.executeQuery();
358  ResultSet rs = ps.getResultSet();
359  boolean more = rs.next();
360  if (!more)
361  {
362    log("getHours retrieved no row for query " + query);
363    return null;
364  }
365  //simplifies the handling of ResultSets
366  TimeSheetLine tsl2 = new TimeSheetLine(rs.getInt(1),
       rs.getDate(2), rs.getDouble(3), rs.getInt(4));
367  rs.close();
368  ps.close();
```

```
369
370     return ts12;
371
372         }
373       catch (SQLException e)
374       {
375       log("SQLException in getHours: query was: " + query
          + "\nException was " + e);
376       }
377
378     return null;
379
380   }
381
382
383   public EmployeeInfo getEmployeeInfo()
384   {
385
386     return new EmployeeInfo(employeeID, managerID, fname,
          lname);
387
388   }
389
390   public void setEmployeeInfo(EmployeeInfo ei)
391   {
392     if (ei.employeeID == 0)
393       {
394       log("invalid employee ID");
395       return;
396       }
397     if ((ei.managerID == 0) && (ei.fname == null) &&
          (ei.lname == null))
398       {
399         log("nothing to do");
400         return;
401       }
402     if (ei.managerID > 0)
403       {
404         managerID = ei.managerID;
405       }
406     if (fname != null)
407       {
408         fname = ei.fname;
409       }
410     if (lname != null)
411       {
412         lname = ei.lname;
413       }
414
415     isDirty = true;
416   }
417
418
```

```
419
420    public void setHours(TimeSheetLine tsl)
421    {
422      //find out if there's a row to get
423      TimeSheetLine tsl2 = getHours(tsl);
424      String query;
425      if (tsl2 == null) //no row in database
426      {
427        //note the order of args; I did this so I could
           reuse the same prepared statement for both queries
428        query = "insert into time_entries (hours,
           employee_id, contract, mydate)  values (?, ?, ?,
           ?)";
429
430      }
431      else
432      {
433        query = "update time_entries set hours = ? where
           employee_id = ? and contract = ? and mydate = ?";
434        //update
435      }
436
437        try
438        {
439      //the only reason I'm using a prepared statement here
         is to get JDBC to convert the date formats
440      PreparedStatement ps = c.prepareStatement(query);
441      ps.setDouble(1, tsl.hours);
442      ps.setInt(2, tsl.employeeID);
443      ps.setInt(3, tsl.contract);
444      ps.setDate(4, tsl.date);
445      ps.executeUpdate();
446
447      ps.close();
448
449
450        }
451      catch (SQLException e)
452      {
453      log("SQLException in getHours: query was: " + query
         + "\nException was " + e);
454      }
455
456
457    }
458
459
460
461
462    public void deleteHours(TimeSheetLine tsl)
463    {
464      //delete from time_entries where PK = tsl.pk
465
```

```
466        String query;
467        query = "delete from time_entries  where employee_id =
           ? and contract = ? and mydate = ?";
468
469          try
470          {
471        //the only reason I'm using a prepared statement here
           is to get JDBC to convert the date formats
472        PreparedStatement ps = c.prepareStatement(query);
473        ps.setInt(1, tsl.employeeID);
474        ps.setInt(2, tsl.contract);
475        ps.setDate(3, tsl.date);
476        ps.executeUpdate();
477
478        ps.close();
479
480
481          }
482        catch (SQLException e)
483        {
484        log("SQLException in getHours: query was: " + query
           + "\nException was " + e);
485          }
486
487    }
488
489  }
```

Deployment Descriptor for the Employee Entity Bean

```
1   (EntityDescriptor
2   ; For entity EJBeans, this file must start with
    "(EntityDescriptor"
3   ; For session EJBeans, this file must start with "(Session
    Descriptor"
4
5   beanHomeName   EmployeeHome
6   ; JNDI name of EJBean
7
8   enterpriseBeanClassName  book.chap09.timetracker.
    EmployeeBean
9   ; The EJBean class
10
11  homeInterfaceClassName  book.chap09.timetracker.
    EmployeeHome
12  ; The home interface implemented by a class generated by
13  ; the EJB compiler (ejbc).
14  ; See "homeClassName" below to plug in your own home
    class.
15
16  remoteInterfaceClassName  book.chap09.timetracker.Employee
17
```

```
18   primaryKeyClassName  book.chap09.timetracker.EmployeePK
19   ; This interface is implemented by an "EJBObject," a
     wrapper
20   ; class that is generated by the EJB compiler (ejbc). This
     wrapper
21   ; interposes between a caller and the EJB bean, and deals
     with
22   ; concurrency, transactions, and security. See
     "ejbObjectClassName"
23   ; below to plug in your own EJBObject class.
24
25   isReentrant  false
26   ; Either "true" or "false."
27   ; If true, the same transaction is allowed to revisit an
     EJB bean.
28   ; If the EJB bean does not support transactions or if a
     transaction
29   ; is not active, a lock is taken out on behalf of the
     EJBObject.
30   ; Session EJB beans cannot be reentrant; this property
     must be "false."
31
32   (accessControlEntries
33   ; DEFAULT    [employees managers]
34    DEFAULT    [empsandmanagers]
35    setEmployeeInfo    [hrmanager]
36    getEmployeeInfo    [hrmanager]
37   ; Specifies security access control for the EJB bean as a
     whole (under
38   ; the DEFAULT entry) and/or provides method-specific
     access control
39   ; entries.
40   ;
41
42
43
44   ;
45   ; Names in the entries represent user names or role names.
     Roles
46   ; map to groups, and it is up to the associated realm to
     judge
47   ; which string is a user name and which is a role.
48   ; The realm can be specified by setting the "realmClass"
     property below.
49   ; Methods with the same name but with different signatures
     can be
50   ; distinguished by supplying the complete method
     signature.
51   ;
52   ; Example:
53   ; DEFAULT            [admin guest paul]
54   ; deposit            [everyone]
55   ; "withdraw(double)"       [paul john]
```

```
56    ; "withdraw(int)"              [amadeus admin]
57    ;
58    ; Note:
59    ; The method name is that of the corresponding home or re-
      mote interface,
60    ; not that of the EJB bean itself. (After all, you are
      controlling access from
61    ; outside.) Method names that are not single words must be
      enclosed in
62    ; double quotes(").
63    ); end accessControlEntries
64
65    (controlDescriptors
66    ; This section decides the runtime properties when a
      method is called.
67    ; The DEFAULT subsection applies to all methods, but can
      be overridden
68    ; on a per-method basis, similar to the
      "accessControlEntries" above.
69    (DEFAULT
70    isolationLevel   TRANSACTION_SERIALIZABLE
71    ; Sets the JDBC transaction isolation level
72    ;
73    ; TRANSACTION_READ_UNCOMMITTED
74    ; Dirty reads, nonrepeatable reads, and phantom reads can
      occur.
75    ;
76    ; TRANSACTION_READ_COMMITTED
77    ; Dirty reads prevented; nonrepeatable and phantom reads
      possible.
78    ;
79    ; TRANSACTION_REPEATABLE_READ
80    ; Dirty and nonrepeatable reads prevented; phantom reads
      possible.
81    ;
82    ; TRANSACTION_SERIALIZABLE
83    ; The strictest isolation level; all of the above problems
      avoided.
84
85    transactionAttribute   TX_REQUIRED
86    ; TX_BEAN_MANAGED  EJB bean starts and ends transaction.
87    ; TX_MANDATORY  Caller must start transaction.
88    ; TX_REQUIRED  EJB bean requires a transaction; Tengah
      will
89    ;      start one if caller hasn't already done so.
90    ; TX_NOT_SUPPORTED Tengah suspends caller's transaction
91    ;      before calling EJB bean.
92    ; TX_REQUIRES_NEW  Tengah starts a new transaction for
      every call.
93    ; TX_SUPPORTS  Tengah simply passes the caller's
      transaction along.
94
95    runAsMode   CLIENT_IDENTITY
```

```
 96   ; This option sets the effective user identity; options
      are:
 97   ; CLIENT_IDENTITY  The caller's identity is passed to the
      EJB bean.
 98   ; SPECIFIED_IDENTITY  See "runAsIdentity" below.
 99   ; SYSTEM_IDENTITY  "system" in the WebLogic realm.
100
101   ; runAsIdentity  paul
102   ; If "runAsMode" is set to SPECIFIED_IDENTITY, assume the
      identity
103   ; given by "runAsIdentity" before passing the call to the
      EJB bean.
104   ); end DEFAULT
105   ); end controlDescriptors
106
107   (environmentProperties
108   ; realmName  "my.realm"
109   employeeBean.databaseURL  "jdbc:weblogic:jts:ejbPool"
110   employeeBean.JDBCDriverName  "weblogic.jdbc.jts.Driver"
111
112   ; The entity responsible for authenticating users with
113   ; their passwords or other credentials.
114   ; Defaults to the "weblogic" realm.
115
116   ; homeClassName
117   ; For a home interface called "Foo," the EJB compiler
      generates
118   ; an implementation called "FooHomeImpl." You can inherit
      from
119   ; it and override or provide new methods in a custom class
      by
120   ; specifying that class's name for this property.
121
122   ; ejbObjectClassName
123   ; For a remote interface called "Foo," the EJB compiler
      generates
124   ; an implementation called "FooEOImpl." You can inherit
      from
125   ; it and override or provide new methods in a custom class
      by
126   ; specifying that class's name for this property.
127
128   maxBeansInFreePool  20
129   ; Tengah EJB maintains a free pool of beans for every bean
      class.
130   ; This property decides the size of the pool.
131
132   maxBeansInCache   100
133   ; Maximum number of objects of this class that are allowed
      in memory.
134   ; Objects are kept in an LRU chain, and the ones dropped
      from the
135   ; end of the chain are passivated.
```

```
136
137    idleTimeoutSeconds  10
138    ; The LRU chain (see "maxBeansInCache" above) is scrubbed
       of
139    ; inactive objects after at least this many seconds
140
141    ; isModifiedMethodName  isModified
142    ; Applicable only to entity EJB beans.
143    ; The name of the EJB method called when the EJB bean is
       stored.
144    ; If a method is not specified, Tengah always assumes that
       the EJB bean
145    ; has been modified and always saves it. Providing a
       method and setting
146    ; it as appropriate will improve performance.
147
148
149    ); end environmentProperties
150
151
152
153    ); end EntityDescriptor or SessionDescriptor
154
```

Implementation Class for the TimeTracker Session Bean

```
1     package book.chap09.timetracker;
2     import java.rmi.RemoteException;
3     import java.security.Identity;
4     import java.sql.Date;
5     import java.sql.PreparedStatement;
6     import java.sql.SQLException;
7     import java.sql.ResultSet;
8     import java.sql.Connection;
9     import java.sql.DriverManager;
10    import java.util.Properties;
11    import javax.ejb.SessionBean;
12    import javax.ejb.SessionContext;
13    import javax.ejb.CreateException;
14    import javax.ejb.FinderException;
15    import javax.naming.InitialContext;
16    import javax.naming.Context;
17
18    import book.chap09.timetracker.MyIdentity;
19    import book.chap09.timetracker.TimeSheetLine;
20    import book.chap09.timetracker.EmployeeBean;
21    import book.chap09.timetracker.EmployeePK;
22
23    public class TimeTrackerBean implements SessionBean
24    {
25
26    transient private    SessionContext ctx;
```

```
27    transient private Connection c;
28    public int employeeID;
29    transient private Employee user;
30
31
32       public boolean isManager()
33       {
34         System.out.println("Called isManager");
35         MyIdentity mgr_role = new MyIdentity("managers");
36         return ctx.isCallerInRole(mgr_role);
37
38       }
39
40       public void setSessionContext(SessionContext ctx)
41       {
42         this.ctx = ctx;
43       }
44
45       public void log(String message)
46       {
47         System.out.println(message);
48       }
49
50
51       public void ejbCreate(int employeeID) throws
      CreateException
52       {
53         this.employeeID = employeeID;
54         establishEJBReference();
55         establishDBConnection();
56
57
58
59       }
60
61       public void ejbPassivate()
62       {
63         log("ejbPassivate called");
64         closeEJBReference();
65         closeDBConnection();
66       }
67
68       public void ejbRemove()
69       {
70         log("ejbRemove called");
71         closeEJBReference();
72         closeDBConnection();
73       }
74
75
76          public void establishDBConnection()
77          {
78          Properties props = ctx.getEnvironment();
```

```
79        String databaseURL = (String) props.get
          ("timetrackerBean.databaseURL");
80        String JDBCDriverName = (String) props.get
          ("timetrackerBean.JDBCDriverName");
81        //load the JDBC driver
82        try
83        {
84        Class.forName(JDBCDriverName).newInstance();
85        c = DriverManager.getConnection(databaseURL);
86        }
87        catch(Exception e)
88        {
89          log("Could not establish database connection");
90        }
91        }
92        public void closeDBConnection()
93        {
94        try
95        {
96        System.out.println("closing database connection");
97        c.close();
98        c = null;
99        }
100       catch(Exception e)
101       {
102         log("Could not close database connection");
103       }
104
105       }
106
107
108     public void closeEJBReference()
109     {
110       log("Called closeEJBReference");
111       user = null;
112     }
113
114
115
116     public void establishEJBReference()
117     {
118
119       try
120       {
121
122       InitialContext ic = new InitialContext();
123       log("looked up initial context");
124       EmployeeHome ch = (EmployeeHome) ic.lookup
          ("EmployeeHome");
125       EmployeePK pk = new EmployeePK(employeeID);
126       user = ch.findByPrimaryKey(pk);
127       log("found the bean");
128       ic.close();
```

```
129
130      }
131      catch(Exception e)
132      {
133        log ("Exception occurred while establishing
           connection to Employee bean: " + e);
134      }
135
136    }
137
138    public EmployeeInfo getEmployeeInfo() throws
       RemoteException
139    {
140      return user.getEmployeeInfo();
141    }
142
143    public TimeSheetLine[] getHours(Date start, Date end)
       throws RemoteException
144    {
145
146
147      return user.getHours(start, end);
148
149    }
150
151    public void setHours(TimeSheetLine tsl) throws
       RemoteException, NotYourIDException
152    {
153      log("Called setHours");
154      if (tsl.employeeID != this.employeeID)
155        {
156        throw new NotYourIDException("You are attempting to
           modify someone else's time record");
157        }
158      user.setHours(tsl);
159    }
160
161
162    public void deleteHours(TimeSheetLine tsl) throws
       RemoteException, NotYourIDException
163    {
164      log("Called deleteHours");
165      if (tsl.employeeID != this.employeeID)
166        {
167        throw new NotYourIDException("You are attempting to
           modify someone else's time record");
168        }
169      user.deleteHours(tsl);
170    }
171
172    public TimeSheetLine[] getEmployeeHours(int employeeID,
       Date start, Date end) throws  NotYourEmployeeException
173    {
```

```
174        log("getEmployeeHours called");
175        String query = "select employee_id, mydate, hours,
           contract from time_entries where employee_id = ? and
           mydate >= ? and mydate <= ? and employee_id in (select
           employee_id from employees where manager_id = ?) ";
176
177          try
178          {
179        //the only reason I'm using a prepared statement here
           is to get JDBC to convert the date formats
180        PreparedStatement ps = c.prepareStatement(query);
181        ps.setInt(1, employeeID);
182        ps.setDate(2, start);
183        ps.setDate(3, end);
184        ps.setInt(4, this.employeeID);
185        ps.executeQuery();
186        ResultSet rs = ps.getResultSet();
187        boolean more = rs.next();
188        if (!more)
189        {
190          throw new NotYourEmployeeException("Employee does not
             work for you");
191        }
192        //simplifies the handling of ResultSets a bit.
193        TimeSheetHash tsh = new TimeSheetHash();
194        int empID;
195        java.sql.Date dt;
196        double hrs;
197        int cont;
198
199
200        while (more)
201        {
202          empID = rs.getInt(1);
203          dt = rs.getDate(2);
204          hrs = rs.getDouble(3);
205          cont = rs.getInt(4);
206          tsh.add(empID, dt, hrs, cont);
207          more = rs.next();
208        }
209        rs.close();
210        ps.close();
211        return tsh.getTimeSheetLines();
212
213        }
214        catch(SQLException e)
215        {
216          log("Exception caught in getEmployeeHours: " + e +
             "\n Query was: " + query);
217          return null;
218        }
219
220
```

```
221
222     }
223
224
225
226     public TimeSheetLine[] getAggregateHours(Date start, Date
        end)
227     {
228       log("getAggregateHours called");
229       String query = "select employee_id, mydate, hours,
          contract from time_entries where mydate >= ? and
          mydate <= ? and employee_id in (select employee_id
          from employees where manager_id = ?) ";
230
231         try
232         {
233       //the only reason I'm using a prepared statement here
          is to get JDBC to convert the date formats
234       PreparedStatement ps = c.prepareStatement(query);
235       ps.setDate(1, start);
236       ps.setDate(2, end);
237       ps.setInt(3, this.employeeID);
238       ps.executeQuery();
239       ResultSet rs = ps.getResultSet();
240       boolean more = rs.next();
241       if (!more)
242       {
243         log("No rows found for employees of employee " +
            employeeID);
244         return null;
245       }
246       //simplifies the handling of ResultSets
247       TimeSheetHash tsh = new TimeSheetHash();
248       int empID;
249       java.sql.Date dt;
250       double hrs;
251       int cont;
252
253
254       while (more)
255       {
256         empID = rs.getInt(1);
257         dt = rs.getDate(2);
258         hrs = rs.getDouble(3);
259         cont = rs.getInt(4);
260         tsh.add(empID, dt, hrs, cont);
261
262
263         more = rs.next();
264       }
265       rs.close();
266       ps.close();
267       return tsh.getTimeSheetLines();
```

```
268
269        }
270      catch(SQLException e)
271      {
272        log("Exception caught in getAggregateHours: " + e +
           "\n Query was: " + query);
273        return null;
274      }
275    }
276
277
278
279
280    public void ejbActivate()
281    {
282      log("ejbActivate called");
283
284      establishDBConnection();
285      log("got DB connection");
286      establishEJBReference();
287      log("got reference");
288
289    }
290
291
292
293  }
294
295
```

Deployment Descriptor for the TimeTracker Session Bean

```
1    (SessionDescriptor
2    ; For entity EJBeans, this file must start with
     "(EntityDescriptor"
3    ; For session EJBeans, this file must start with "(Session
     Descriptor"
4
5    beanHomeName  TimeTrackerHome
6    ; JNDI name of EJBean
7
8    enterpriseBeanClassName  book.chap09.timetracker.
     TimeTrackerBean
9    ; The EJBean class
10
11   homeInterfaceClassName  book.chap09.timetracker.
     TimeTrackerHome
12   ; The home interface implemented by a class generated by
13   ; the EJB compiler (ejbc).
14   ; See "homeClassName" below to plug in your own home
       class.
15
```

```
16    remoteInterfaceClassName   book.chap09.timetracker.
      TimeTracker
17    ; This interface is implemented by an "EJBObject," a
      wrapper
18    ; class that is generated by the EJB compiler (ejbc). This
      wrapper
19    ; interposes between a caller and the EJB bean, and deals
      with
20    ; concurrency, transactions, and security. See
      "ejbObjectClassName"
21    ; below to plug in your own EJBObject class.
22
23    isReentrant  false
24    ; Either "true" or "false."
25    ; If true, the same transaction is allowed to revisit an
      EJB bean.
26    ; If the EJB bean does not support transactions or if a
      transaction
27    ; is not active, a lock is taken out on behalf of the
      EJBObject.
28    ; Session EJB beans cannot be reentrant; this property
      must be "false."
29
30    (accessControlEntries
31    ; DEFAULT          [admin guest paul]
32    DEFAULT            [empsandmanagers]
33    "getAggregateHours" [managers]
34    "getEmployeeHours" [managers]
35    ; Specifies security access control for the EJB bean as a
      whole (under
36    ; the DEFAULT entry) and/or provides method-specific
      access control
37    ; entries.
38    ;
39
40
41
42    ;
43    ; Names in the entries represent user names or role names.
      Roles
44    ; map to groups, and it is up to the associated realm to
      judge
45    ; which string is a user name and which is a role.
46    ; The realm can be specified by setting the "realmClass"
      property below.
47    ; Methods with the same name but with different signatures
      can be
48    ; distinguished by supplying the complete method
      signature.
49    ;
50    ; Example:
51    ; DEFAULT    [admin guest paul]
52    ; deposit    [everyone]
```

```
53   ; "withdraw(double)"      [paul john]
54   ; "withdraw(int)"         [amadeus admin]
55   ;
56   ; Note:
57   ; The method name is that of the corresponding home or
     remote interface,
58   ; not of the EJB bean itself. (After all, you are
     controlling access from
59   ; outside.) Method names that are not single words must be
     enclosed in
60   ; double quotes(").
61   ); end accessControlEntries
62
63   (controlDescriptors
64   ; This section decides the runtime properties when a
     method is called.
65   ; The DEFAULT subsection applies to all methods, but can
     be overridden
66   ; on a per-method basis, similar to the
     "accessControlEntries" above.
67   (DEFAULT
68   isolationLevel   TRANSACTION_SERIALIZABLE
69   ; Sets the JDBC transaction isolation level
70   ;
71   ; TRANSACTION_READ_UNCOMMITTED
72   ; Dirty reads, nonrepeatable reads, and phantom reads can
     occur.
73   ;
74   ; TRANSACTION_READ_COMMITTED
75   ; Dirty reads prevented; nonrepeatable and phantom reads
     possible.
76   ;
77   ; TRANSACTION_REPEATABLE_READ
78   ; Dirty and nonrepeatable reads prevented; phantom reads
     possible.
79   ;
80   ; TRANSACTION_SERIALIZABLE
81   ; The strictest isolation level; all of the above problems
     avoided.
82
83   transactionAttribute   TX_NOT_SUPPORTED
84   ; TX_BEAN_MANAGED  EJB bean starts and ends transaction.
85   ; TX_MANDATORY  Caller must start transaction.
86   ; TX_REQUIRED  EJB bean requires a transaction, Tengah
     will
87   ;     start one if caller hasn't already done so.
88   ; TX_NOT_SUPPORTED Tengah suspends caller's transaction
89   ;     before calling EJB bean.
90   ; TX_REQUIRES_NEW  Tengah starts a new transaction for
     every call.
91   ; TX_SUPPORTS  Tengah simply passes the caller's
     transaction along.
92
```

```
 93   runAsMode CLIENT_IDENTITY
 94   ; This option sets the effective user identity; options
      are:
 95   ; CLIENT_IDENTITY  The caller's identity is passed to the
      EJB bean.
 96   ; SPECIFIED_IDENTITY  See "runAsIdentity" below.
 97   ; SYSTEM_IDENTITY  "system" in the WebLogic realm.
 98
 99   ; runAsIdentity  paul
100   ; If "runAsMode" is set to SPECIFIED_IDENTITY, assume the
      identity
101   ; given by "runAsIdentity" before passing the call to the
      EJB bean.
102   ); end DEFAULT
103   ); end controlDescriptors
104
105   (environmentProperties
106   ; realmName "my.realm"
107   timetrackerBean.databaseURL  "jdbc:weblogic:jts:ejbPool"
108   timetrackerBean.JDBCDriverName  "weblogic.jdbc.jts.Driver"
109
110   ; The entity responsible for authenticating users with
111   ; their passwords or other credentials.
112   ; Defaults to the "weblogic" realm.
113
114   ; homeClassName
115   ; For a home interface called "Foo," the EJB compiler
      generates
116   ; an implementation called "FooHomeImpl." You can inherit
      from
117   ; it and override or provide new methods in a custom class
      by
118   ; specifying that class's name for this property.
119
120   ; ejbObjectClassName
121   ; For a remote interface called "Foo," the EJB compiler
      generates
122   ; an implementation called "FooEOImpl." You can inherit
      from
123   ; it and override or provide new methods in a custom class
      by
124   ; specifying that class's name for this property.
125
126   maxBeansInFreePool  20
127   ; Tengah EJB maintains a free pool of beans for every bean
      class.
128   ; This property decides the size of the pool.
129
130   maxBeansInCache  100
131   ; Maximum number of objects of this class that are allowed
      in memory.
132   ; Objects are kept in an LRU chain, and the ones dropped
      from the
```

```
133  ; end of the chain are passivated.
134
135  idleTimeoutSeconds  10
136  ; The LRU chain (see "maxBeansInCache" above) is scrubbed
     of
137  ; inactive objects after at least this many seconds
138
139
140
141  (persistentStoreProperties
142  ; This section specifies the persistent store properties
     for
143  ; Entity EJB beans with container-managed persistence and
144  ; stateful Session EJB beans.
145  ; For Entity EJB beans with EJB bean-managed persistence
     and
146  ; stateless Session EJB beans, this section is not
     required.
147
148  persistentStoreType file
149  ; Either "file," "jdbc," or a custom type.
150  ; The type is used to identify the specific section below
151  ; that provides additional information for setting up
152  ; the appropriate persistent storage.
153
154
155
156  (file
157  persistentDirectoryRoot  c:\mystore
158  ; If specified, all instances of an EJB bean
159  ; (example: "examples.ejb.AccountBean")
160  ; are stored under the "persistentDirectoryRoot"
161  ; (example: "c:\mystore\examples_ejb_AccountBean\
     <primaryKey>.db")
162  ; with the name of the EJB bean converted to a directory
     name.
163  ; Defaults to a directory "mystore" in the directory
164  ; where Tengah was started.
165
166  ); end file
167
168  ); end persistentStoreProperties
169  ); end environmentProperties
170
171
172
173  ; Session EJB bean-specific properties:
174  ; For session EJB beans you must specify the state
     management type
175  ; and the session timeout in seconds.
176
177  stateManagementType  STATEFUL_SESSION
178  ; Either STATELESS_SESSION or STATEFUL_SESSION.
```

```
179  ; The type of Session EJB bean.
180
181  sessionTimeout  60; seconds
182
183  ; end Session EJB bean-specific properties
184
185  ); end EntityDescriptor or SessionDescriptor
186
```

TimeTracker Client Implementation

```
1    //TimeTrackerFrame -- this is the user interface portion
     of the code.
2    import book.chap09.timetracker.TimeTracker;
3    import book.chap09.timetracker.TimeTrackerHome;
4    import book.chap09.timetracker.TimeSheetLine;
5    import book.chap09.timetracker.NotYourIDException;
6
7    import java.sql.Date;
8    import javax.naming.InitialContext;
9    import javax.naming.Context;
10   import java.util.Properties;
11   import java.text.DateFormat;
12   import java.awt.*;
13   import java.awt.event.*;
14   import java.rmi.RemoteException;
15
16
17   public class TimeTrackerFrame extends Frame implements
     ActionListener
18   {
19     //Instance variables
20
21     boolean appletMode;
22     int empno;
23     TextArea reportWindow;  //window to display time reports
24     boolean loggedIn = false;  //login status
25     Button loginButton = new Button("Login");  //triggers
       login() call
26     TextField loginName;  //username for login
27     TextField loginPassword;  //password for login
28     TextField loginEmpno;  //employee number
29     TimeTracker tt;  //reference to server object
30     TextField contract;  //input field: contract
31     TextField hours;  //input field: hours
32     TextField date;  //input field: date
33     Button modifyButton = new Button("Modify"); //triggers
       setHours() call
34     Button deleteButton = new Button("Delete"); //triggers
       setHours() call
35     String user;  //userid -- saved because
36     //loginName is blanked
```

```
37       //after login
38       Button mgrQuery = new Button("Query");
39       TextField mgrEmpno = new TextField();
40       TextField mgrStartDate = new TextField();
41       TextField mgrEndDate = new TextField();
42
43       WindowAdapter wa;
44
45
46       public TimeTrackerFrame(boolean appletMode)
47       {
48
49           //check to see if it's an applet
50           this.appletMode = appletMode;
51
52           setLayout(new BorderLayout());
53
54           //set up login panel
55           Panel lp = new Panel();
56           //Grid layout - 4 rows, 2 columns
57           lp.setLayout(new GridLayout(4, 2));
58           lp.add(new Label("User Name"));
59           loginName = new TextField();
60           lp.add(loginName);
61           lp.add(new Label("Password"));
62           loginPassword = new TextField();
63           //set echo char to '*' so password
64           //isn't echoed
65           loginPassword.setEchoChar('*');
66           //add objects to panel layout manager
67           lp.add(loginPassword);
68           lp.add(new Label("Employee Number"));
69           loginEmpno = new TextField();
70           lp.add(loginEmpno);
71
72           //setup actionlisteners for buttons
73           loginButton.addActionListener(this);
74           modifyButton.addActionListener(this);
75           deleteButton.addActionListener(this);
76           mgrQuery.addActionListener(this);
77
78           lp.add(loginButton);
79           //add panel to parent layout manager
80           add(lp, "North");
81
82           //set up modification panel
83           Panel mp = new Panel();
84           //Grid layout - 8 rows, 1 column
85           mp.setLayout(new GridLayout(8, 1));
86           mp.add(new Label("Date"));
87           date = new TextField();
88           mp.add(date);
89           mp.add(new Label("Contract"));
```

```
90          contract=new TextField();
91          mp.add(contract);
92          mp.add(new Label("Hours Worked"));
93          hours = new TextField();
94          mp.add(hours);
95          mp.add(modifyButton);
96          mp.add(deleteButton);
97            //add panel to parent layout manager
98          add(mp, "East");
99            //add report window to parent layout manager
100         reportWindow = new TextArea();
101         add(reportWindow, "Center");
102
103         //an inner class!
104         wa = new WindowAdapter () {
105         public void windowClosing(WindowEvent we)
106           {
107           System.out.println("window event: " + we);
108           if (!TimeTrackerFrame.this.appletMode)
109             {
110             System.exit(0); //leave
111             }
112         } };
113
114       addWindowListener(wa);
115       pack();
116     }
117
118     public void actionPerformed (ActionEvent evt)
119     {
120       if (evt.getSource() == loginButton)
121       {
122         System.out.println("Attempting to login");
123       loggedIn = false;
124         //clear report window
125       reportWindow.setText("");
126       try
127       {
128
129       Properties p = new Properties();
130       p.put(Context.INITIAL_CONTEXT_FACTORY,
131         "weblogic.jndi.T3InitialContextFactory");
132       p.put(Context.PROVIDER_URL, "t3://localhost:7001");
133       p.put(Context.SECURITY_PRINCIPAL,
            loginName.getText());
134       p.put(Context.SECURITY_CREDENTIALS,
            loginPassword.getText());
135
136       InitialContext ic = new InitialContext(p);
137
138       TimeTrackerHome tth = (TimeTrackerHome)ic.lookup
            ("TimeTrackerHome");
139       empno = Integer.parseInt(loginEmpno.getText());
```

```
140        tt = tth.create(empno); //set at class level
141        if (tt.isManager())
142        {
143          setupManagerPanel();
144        }
145        loggedIn = true;
146        ic.close();
147        }
148        catch(Exception e)
149        {
150        loggedIn = false;
151        System.out.println("Exception occurred during login:
           " + e);
152
153        }
154        if (loggedIn)
155        {
156        user = loginName.getText(); //save login name
157        loginName.setText("");        //clear loginName box
158        loginPassword.setText("");  //clear password box
159        loginEmpno.setText("");       //clear password box
160
161          //if logged in successfully,
162          //display report
163        try
164        {
165        //query for data about this person
166        //convert to string
167        Date start = new Date(98, 0, 1);
168        Date end = new Date(98, 11, 31);
169        TimeSheetLine tslArray[] = tt.getHours(start, end);
170        String s = tslToText(tslArray);
171        reportWindow.setText(s);
172        }
173        catch(RemoteException e)
174        {
175        System.out.println("Exception occurred: " + e);
176        }
177
178        } //end if logged in
179
180        }//end if loginButton
181
182      else if (evt.getSource() == mgrQuery)
183        {
184        try
185        {
186        TimeSheetLine[] tslArray;
187
188        Date start = Date.valueOf(mgrStartDate.getText());
189        Date end = Date.valueOf(mgrEndDate.getText());
190
191        if (mgrEmpno.getText().length() == 0)
```

```
192          {
193            tslArray = tt.getAggregateHours(start, end);
194
195
196          }
197          else
198          {
199            int en = Integer.parseInt(mgrEmpno.getText());
200            tslArray = tt.getEmployeeHours(en, start, end);
201
202          }
203
204          new ResultFrame(tslToText(tslArray));
205          }
206          catch(Exception e) //could be one of 2 remote
             exceptions, etc
207          {
208          System.out.println("Exception caught in mgrQuery
             handler : " + e);
209          }
210          } //end mgrQuery
211        else if ((evt.getSource() == modifyButton) ||
           (evt.getSource() == deleteButton))
212          {
213            //make sure we're logged in first
214          if (!loggedIn)
215          {
216          return;
217          }
218          try
219          {
220            //modify data
221            //display new report
222            //send update
223          String tdt = date.getText();
224          Date dt = Date.valueOf(tdt);
225          int ctrct = Integer.parseInt(contract.getText());
226
227          if (evt.getSource() == deleteButton)
228          {
229            double hrs = 0;
230            TimeSheetLine tsl = new TimeSheetLine(empno, dt,
             hrs, ctrct);
231            tt.deleteHours(tsl);
232          }
233          else
234          {
235            double hrs = Double.valueOf(hours.getText()).
             doubleValue();
236            TimeSheetLine tsl = new TimeSheetLine(empno, dt,
             hrs, ctrct);
237            tt.setHours(tsl);
238          }
```

```
239        //query database for new data
240        //convert to text format
241        Date start = new Date(98, 0, 1);
242        Date end = new Date(98, 11, 31);
243        TimeSheetLine tslArray[] = tt.getHours(start, end);
244        String s = tslToText(tslArray);
245
246        reportWindow.setText(s);
247        }
248        catch(RemoteException e)
249        {
250        System.out.println("Remote exception occurred: " + e);
251        }
252        catch(NotYourIDException e)
253        {
254        System.out.println("You are attempting to set someone
           else's time values");
255        }
256
257
258     } //end modified
259
260    } //end of method
261
262    public static void main(String[] argv)
263    {
264      TimeTrackerFrame t = new TimeTrackerFrame (false);
265      t.show();
266    }
267
268    public String tslToText(TimeSheetLine[] tsl)
269    {
270      String s = "";
271
272      for (int i = 0; i < tsl.length; i++)
273      {
274      s += tsl[i].employeeID + "\t";
275      s += tsl[i].date + "\t";
276      s += tsl[i].contract + "\t";
277      s += tsl[i].hours + "\t\n";
278
279      }
280      return s;
281
282    }
283    void setupManagerPanel()
284    {
285      System.out.println("called setupManagerPanel");
286      Panel p = new Panel();
287      p.setLayout(new GridLayout(4, 2)); //3rows 2cols
288      p.add(new Label("Employee ID"));
289      p.add(mgrEmpno);
```

```
290      p.add(new Label("Start Date"));
291      p.add(mgrStartDate);
292      p.add(new Label("End Date"));
293      p.add(mgrEndDate);
294      p.add(mgrQuery);
295      add(p, "South");
296      pack();
297    }
298
299  }
300
301
302  class ResultFrame extends Frame implements ActionListener
303  {
304    Button close = new Button("Close");
305    public ResultFrame(String results)
306    {
307      System.out.println("new resultFrame: " + results);
308      TextArea reportWindow = new TextArea();
309      this.setLayout(new BorderLayout());
310      reportWindow.setText(results);
311      add(reportWindow, "Center");
312      close.addActionListener(this);
313      add(close, "South");
314      pack();
315      show();
316    }
317    public void actionPerformed (ActionEvent evt)
318    {
319      if (evt.getSource() instanceof Button)
320      {
321      setVisible(false);
322      dispose();
323    }
324
325    }
326
327  }
```

GLOSSARY

Access control list (ACL) A list of which entities are allowed to invoke which objects and methods.

Accessor method A method that retrieves the value of a particular property of a class. For example, the method `getSessionTimeout()` of the `SessionDescriptor` class is an accessor method. The general pattern for naming accessor methods is to start with "get" and then provide the name of the property in question; for example, `getSessionTimeout()` is an accessor method that retrieves the value of the `sessionTimeout` property. For Boolean properties, a second accessor method with the prefix "is" is normally provided—for example, the `isReentrant()` method of the `DeploymentDescriptor` class. (If you use the "is" prefix, you should still include a method with the "get" prefix).

Activation Term used for the operation where a container reloads the state of a bean from persistent storage and makes it available again.

ACID properties Atomicity, consistency, isolation, and durability.

Atomicity The property of transactions that states that all actions that are part of a transaction will be executed as a logical unit; either all will complete successfully, or the transaction will be undone.

Bean-managed persistence For Entity beans, using handwritten SQL (or some other handwritten persistence mechanism) within the bean to manage the storage and retrieval of its state information.

Begin In transaction processing, a notification to the transaction processor that the following statements should be executed as a transaction. The transaction continues until either "commit" or "rollback" is encountered.

Business rules The logic that governs how data are processed.

Callback   A method that is intended to be called by an external entity. Typically, callbacks are used to notify a class that an event has occurred.

CICS   Customer Information Control System; a transaction processor produced by IBM. Typically, it runs on mainframes, but is available for other platforms as well.

Commit   In transaction processing, a notification to the transaction processor that the transaction is completed, and that any changes should be written to permanent storage in the database.

Consistency   The property of transactions that states that the underlying database will always be in a reasonable state. It guarantees that, if a transaction fails in midoperation, the database will not be left in a partially modified state; any changes to the database must be undone.

Container-managed persistence   For Entity beans, allowing the container to take care of managing the state information of your Entity beans.

CORBA   Common Object Request Brokering Architecture; a specification for communicating among object-oriented programs in a platform-neutral way.

COS   Common Object Services; a set of services specified by the OMG.

Declarative transaction management   An approach to transaction management where a component specifies what type of transaction support it requires, rather than actively managing the start and end points of its transactions.

Deployment descriptor   A serialized Java object that contains information on how to deploy a given EJB bean.

Design pattern   A description of a design that is known to work well for a given problem.

DNS   Domain Name Service; the naming service that translates symbolic host names to numeric IP addresses.

DSS   Decision support system; a system that accesses data mainly in a read-only mode.

Durability   The property of transactions that states that, once the transaction has been completed, the changes are stored in such a fashion that they will not be removed.

EIS   Enterprise information system; a system that accesses data mainly in a read-only mode.

EJB   Enterprise JavaBeans.

EJB container   An execution environment for Enterprise JavaBeans components. The container provides the beans with services such as transaction management and persistence and insulates them from direct contact with the outside world.

EJBObject   A proxy object on the server side that implements a bean's remote interface. The EJBObject receives calls from the skeleton and forwards them to the EJB bean implementation.

EJB server   An execution environment for EJB containers. The EJB server provides the container with access to network services and any other services it needs to perform its tasks. The EJB 1.0 specification does not define the interface between the server and the container, but the basic relationship is that an EJB server contains one or more EJB containers, and each container can contain one or more beans.

Entity bean   A long-lived bean that represents data in an underlying data store and can be shared by multiple clients.

Facade   A design pattern for providing access to legacy systems. Basically, the idea of this pattern is to create a "wrapper" class that provides a friendly interface to the rest of your system and handles legacy-specific issues internally.

Finder method   For entity EJBs, a method used to look up existing Entity EJB objects. The findByPrimaryKey() method takes a primary key as its argument and returns a single reference to an Entity EJB. Other finder methods can take arbitrary arguments and return either a single reference or a set of references. If a set of references is returned, the finder method will return a set of primary keys in a data structure that implements the java.util.Enumeration interface.

Flat transaction   In transaction processing, a program that cannot execute a transaction inside another transaction.

Getter method   An accessor method. See *accessor method*.

Handle   A serializable reference to a bean. A handle can be stored to a file or other persistent store and used later to reobtain a reference to a remote bean.

Home interface   An EJB component interface that allows clients to look up and/or create EJB objects.

HTTP tunneling   Translating a conversation into a series of HyperText Transfer Protocol (HTTP) requests and responses; often desirable when communication through a firewall is required.

IDL Interface definition language; a language used to specify the arguments and return types of remote procedures in a language-neutral way.

Indexed property A method that takes an array index as its argument and returns a single object that represents the object at the position in the array specified by the index. For example, invoking the `DeploymentDescriptor` accessor method

```
public AccessControlEntry getAccessControlEntries(int index);
```

with an argument of 4 would return the fourth element in the array of access control entries.

Isolation The property of transactions that states that, until a transaction has been committed, its state is not visible from outside itself.

JavaBean A reusable software component that can be manipulated visually in a builder tool.

JDK Java Development Kit.

JMS Java Message Service; a specification for interfacing Java programs with message queuing software.

JNDI Java Naming and Directory Interface; a set of objects that provide a uniform API for accessing naming and directory services from Java programs. In the EJB world, JNDI is used by clients to locate EJB objects.

JVM Java Virtual Machine.

Marshalling In distributed computing, the transformation of data from a local type into a type suitable for transmission over the network.

Message queuing An e-mail-like approach to distributed communication in which requests are sent asynchronously into a holding area called a "message queue," from which they can be retrieved and executed at leisure by the server.

Metadata Data about data; descriptive information about a particular object. In the EJB world, metadata are most often encountered in the EJBMetaData interface and in the JDBC DatabaseMetaData and ResultSetMetaData interfaces.

Method A function or procedure provided by an object.

Method signature The combination of a method's name, arguments, return type, and exceptions.

Mutator method A method that modifies the value of a particular property of a class. For example, the method `setSessionTimeout()` of the `SessionDescriptor` class is a mutator method. The general pattern for naming mutator methods is to start with "set" and then provide the name of the property in question; for example, `setSessionTimeout()` is a mutator method that modifies the value of the `sessionTimeout` property.

Name collision   A situation where two classes in the same namespace have the same name. Name collisions can be avoided in Java through the use of packages.

Naming service   A service that associates a symbolic name with an object.

Nested transaction   In transaction processing, a nested transaction is one that runs from begin to completion within the scope of another transaction.

No-argument constructor   A constructor that takes no arguments.

OLAP   Online analytical processing; a system that accesses data mainly in a read-only mode.

OLE   Object Linking and Embedding; Microsoft's model for object communication.

OLTP   Online transaction processing; an OLTP system typically must handle a large volume of updates to a database.

OMG   Object Management Group; the group that is responsible for promulgating the CORBA standards.

ORB   Object request broker; an ORB provides the mechanism for remote communication.

Passivation   A term used to describe the operation where an EJB container saves the state of a given bean to persistent storage and swaps it out. Passivation is similar to the virtual-memory concept of swapping out a memory page to disk.

Port number   In socket programming, an unsigned integer used to represent a particular application or service.

Presentation logic   That portion of a system responsible for displaying data to the user; a system's user interface.

Primary key   A value or combination of values that allows you to uniquely specify an entity. If two entity EJBs reside in the same home interface and have the same primary key, they are considered to be identical.

Query plan   The actual set of operations that a database performs for a given SQL query. If a query is performing poorly, examining its query plan can be quite helpful.

Remote interface   The interface that the client uses to interact with an EJB object on a server.

RMI Remote Method Invocation; a Java-specific API for accessing remote objects.

rmic The RMI compiler; it generates stubs and skeletons from Java .class files.

Rollback Undoing any intermediate processing that a transaction may have performed; after rollback, it is as if the transaction had never begun.

RPC Remote procedure call; an API for invoking a procedure on a remote computer.

Serializable In Java, able to be converted automatically to a persistent representation suitable for storage in a file or network transmission.

Servlet A Java replacement for CGI. Servlets are Java classes that are invoked by a Web server in response to HTTP requests and generate Hypertext Markup Language (HTML) as their output.

Session bean A relatively short-lived bean used by a single client.

Setter method A mutator method. See *mutator method*.

Skeleton In CORBA, a server-side proxy object that is responsible for retrieving arguments from the network and passing them to the program.

Sockets An approach to communication among distributed applications.

SSL Secure Sockets Layer; an encryption protocol for sockets.

Stateful Session bean A bean that preserves information about the state of its conversation with the client. This conversation may consist of several calls that modify the conversation state, followed by a final call that writes the result to a database.

Stateless Session bean A bean that does not save information about the state of its conversation with a client.

Stub A client-side proxy for a remote routine. The stub takes the arguments that are passed to it by the client, passes them over the network to the server, retrieves any return value, and passes the return value back to the client.

Walkthrough A meeting in which the creator of a module or specification presents it to the member of a group, who review it for correctness.

INDEX